Becoming Mother

Becoming Mother
a journey of identity

Sharon Tjaden-Glass

Lucky Frog Press

Becoming Mother: A Journey of Identity © 2015, Sharon Tjaden-Glass

ISBN: 978-0-9963328-0-4
Library of Congress Control Number: 2015911015

I have tried to recreate events, locales and conversations from my memories of them. In order to maintain their anonymity in some instances I have changed the names of individuals and places, I may have changed some identifying characteristics and details such as physical properties, occupations, and places of residence.

Poem on pp. 85-86, by Dee Dee Mccall, "These Last Few Hours"
Poem on pp. 29-30, by Kahlil Gibran, "On Children," from *The Prophet*, 1923.
Fearless Formula Feeder.com is referenced with the permission of owner, Suzanne Barston

Cover design and layout by Suzanne Richardt, http://www.suzyrichardt.com
Cover text set in Italianno © 2011 by TypeSETit, http://www.typesetit.com
Cover photograph taken by Doug Glass
Lucky Frog Press logo created by Cate Schoenharl

Lucky Frog Press
Dayton, OH

For you, first-time mother

The Journey

Preface

T his is a book for mothers, those who love mothers, and those who are thinking of becoming mothers.

But most of all, this book is for you, first-time expecting mother. Especially if you've had years of freedom before embarking on this journey. Especially if you wonder what motherhood might do to your relationships. Or your career. Or your personality.

Maybe you found this book while searching for a book on pregnancy. There are a lot of them out there. But most of them focus on the physical changes—and their knowledge and advice ends soon after birth. They don't typically explore the mental and emotional wreckage left behind after you are hit by the tidal wave of new motherhood.

I've chosen to write this book as a memoir for this very reason. Through a narrative, I can take you into my mind and emotions to help you see how every experience is magnified, obscured, distorted, or colored by new motherhood.

Or maybe you found this book by searching for a memoir about motherhood. There are a lot of those out there, too. They will tell you extraordinary, harrowing stories of remarkable pregnancies, high-drama births, infant loss, mothering a child with special needs, or what it's like to be a non-traditional parent.

But these are also probably not what you're looking for. They are exciting because they are exceptional. We marvel at these amazing feats accomplished on high wires, but the truth is that most of us live down here in the crowded masses.

And what if I told you that a typical story of becoming a mother is also pretty extraordinary?

That is what *Becoming Mother* is—a typical story of a woman becoming a mother. It is a reflective memoir that spans from pregnancy through the end of the first year postpartum. While I use the physical changes of pregnancy, birth, and the postpartum period to give the book structure, the central theme of this book is identity.

Becoming a mother is a metamorphosis—from individual woman to mother and baby. And in this memoir, you will watch me resist, deny, cope with, and ultimately embrace my identity as a mother. This isn't a comprehensive analysis of everything I experienced—not by any stretch of the imagination. But it does pull together and address some of the typical concerns that women have before giving birth: pregnancy weight gain and loss, the pain of labor, the reality of breastfeeding, the hidden tasks of caring for an infant, the struggle to maintain a social life, the tension between work and family, and the effects of sleep deprivation.

Before I go any further, let me assure you that if you are pregnant, you will not finish this book thinking, "Oh God... I've made a terrible mistake." My goal is to be honest with you—which means that I share with you the challenges alongside the rewards. The humorous with the sad. The darkness as well as the light. Both the chaotic and the monotonous. Depression, elation, and everything in between. To tell you that everything is wonderful is simplistic. And so is saying that everything is exceedingly difficult.

I've broken the process of becoming a mother into several main narrative pieces: pregnancy, labor and birth, the first days, feeding, the first weeks, and the first year. After each section, I reflect on how I experienced the changes in my identity during each stage—as well as a few other observations about motherhood. I chose to intersperse these reflections throughout the narrative to more closely tie together everyday experiences with their long-lasting influence on my identity.

To my knowledge, few published memoirs of first-time motherhood exist—and most of those precious few are told as humorous confessions. After all, everyone needs a good laugh when undertaking such momentous work. But I suspect that few first-time mothers have chosen to seriously write about this topic for two main reasons: lack of time when caring for an infant and lack of ability to verbalize the immense psychological and emotional forces that have pulled and pushed them from all sides throughout the first year of new motherhood.

It is true that you can easily find first-time motherhood blogs that recount experiences and milestones of the first year. But you need to weave together hundreds of posts to see overarching themes. And most of these blogs focus solely on the baby's development.

So if you're looking for a book about how you or someone you love may experience new motherhood, this is the book for you. It isn't a guide. It isn't a parenting book. Its goal isn't to convert you to a certain brand of motherhood. Its goal is to show you what becoming a mother can be like. Without sarcasm. Without boasting or martyrdom. Just the plain, messy truth of what it's like for one to become two.

Pregnancy

December 2012
Seven weeks pregnant
140 pounds
It's 4:30 p.m.

I'm curled on the couch in my fluffy robe in the darkness. I am at war with myself. A nauseating point of gravity sits in my stomach and launches wave after wave of attack. I fold inward in defeat.

The doorbell rings.

Oh my God...

I carefully roll off the couch and swing open the door. It's our long-time friend, Ryan.

Oh crap... What am I going to say to him?

"Hey, Bear," I pin my robe closed as the cold sweeps in. "What's up?"

"Got something for your husband." He waves a few packages of gourmet beef jerky from a local store, here in Dayton, Ohio. A Christmas gift.

"Oh, right. Forgot."

I'm back on the couch before he even shuts the door.

"So..." He looks around the dim living room. *Runaway Bride* is playing, but I've muted it. "You feeling okay?"

I shrug.

"Is this... the flu?"

I shake my head and roll my eyes.

"So, it's... babies?"

"Well... it's just one."

"A... singular baby."

"Right."

Just three days ago, the obstetrician pinpointed a tiny flicker on a black and white screen. Like a pulsar in the night sky, a tiny, silent dot. *See it? That's the heartbeat*, she had said.

"I guess... congratulations?" he says.

"Yeah, Bear. That's what people say when they find out a woman is pregnant," I joke.

I know this is weird for him. He doesn't want kids. Ever. Even to the point of a vasectomy. We had joked for years about how children ruin marriage. But Doug and I had still agreed that we were going to have kids. Some day.

"So I guess this means Doug was successful at Conception 2012."

"Barely," I kid. "It's December."

"Right," he chuckles.

My husband, Doug, is efficient at everything that he does in life—from his problem-solving in engineering to his systematized household—so we joked that baby-making would also be quick and sure. *We don't need months of "trying,"* Doug had said. *I'm one shot, one kill, baby girl.*

Well, he was almost right.

"So I guess you're not feeling too great," Ryan says.

"I feel like I have a terminal illness."

"Well, *that* sounds terrible."

"It's like my brain doesn't process hunger the same way, you know?"

"No, actually I don't." He laughs.

"I mean, whenever I'm hungry, my body thinks I'm sick. So I'm constantly eating. But I can't get *too* full because that makes me sick, too."

"Well... maybe it will get better?"

I realize that I haven't said one good thing about this pregnancy yet.

"You know I'm happy about this, right?" I tell him.

That makes us both laugh. But then, the nausea cuts me off.

"Things are going to look very different next year," I say.

He nods. "So when does this baby..."

"Escape?" I say.

He laughs. "Yeah."

"The due date is August 10."

"Hm... Okay. Are you guys still going to do Monday Night Dinners?"

"Definitely," I pause. "Well, maybe not for the first couple of weeks, but once we can leave the baby with a sitter, we'll be back in the rotation."

In our group of twelve friends, we rotate hosting responsibilities for a collective dinner on Monday nights. We are all hanging in that space between the end of college and the beginning of parenthood. Some of us aren't even sure that we want kids someday. No one has announced a pregnancy, but it's only a matter of time. Everyone knows about our Conception 2012 plan. Our friend, Ben, even checked to see if the Internet domain for www.conception2012.com was available. It was. Then, we started brainstorming what the site would look like. A large countdown clock, for sure. I think it was Sarah who had suggested an animated sperm should slowly make his way to the egg as the clock ticked down. And maybe the countdown would begin again every month? We never fully worked out the details.

We're both quiet for a moment, and I'm not sure what else I should say. Or can say.

"I hope this nausea stops soon," I say. "My mom had constant nausea from the end of the first trimester to the end of the pregnancy. For all four kids. She would vomit all day long."

"That sounds pretty awful. How's your mom doing lately?"

"Good. I actually just told them yesterday. They're excited."

"Your dad, too?" he asks.

I shrug. "He's excited as he can be."

We don't dwell too much on these points. It's not really what we want to talk about anyway—the possibility of my mother's cancer overtaking her and the certainty of my father's recent Parkinson's and bipolar depression diagnoses.

"I mean," I add, "he's still depressed."

Ryan nods.

"I guess I knew that he wouldn't be jumping up and down even with great news like this," I say. "But... I don't know. I thought maybe it might help. But depression is depression, I guess."

"Right," he says. "So... August... does that mean you won't teach for that whole semester?"

I nod. Teaching English to international students at a university doesn't pay a lot, but the benefits are quite good. Faculty maternity leave. Love it.

"I still need to talk to Human Resources, but I'm pretty sure I'll be out for most of the fall."

We talk for a few more minutes and then he leaves. When I lie back on the couch, I rest my hand on my belly and imagine what is going on in there.

I worry.

I think about last time. The red tendrils spreading in the water. The small, hot, concentrated fire. The burning and squeezing. It was August, the first month that we had tried. I told myself that it was just another period. But then I took a second look at the home pregnancy test. A questionable faint line. I hadn't known that I was pregnant until it was over and the nurse confirmed that the blood test had been positive.

It was September 11 and I had just gotten back to my desk after teaching all morning. I had been irritable all weekend and I told myself it was PMS. Mega-PMS. I snapped at my friends. I leveled their good jokes with sarcasm. I was the constant wet blanket.

But my body knew what was going on.

The nurse delivered the news in a voice mail. *The test results confirm that you are miscarrying. I'm so sorry for your loss.*

Loss? What loss?

I was pregnant?

I guess I was stunned that my body was capable of miscarriage. I knew that it happened to a lot of women, but I'm not a lot of women. I eat well and exercise and drink lots of water. I take vitamins and use sunscreen. I see the gynecologist once a year.

I barely talk about the miscarriage. I don't want people to ask me how far along I was so they can measure the amount of grief that I should feel. But more important, I don't want to see myself as a woman who has miscarriages. I still want to believe that I can carry a pregnancy without problems.

I know that Doug and I are headed in a direction where none of our close friends have been. And all of the stories that we've heard from other parents try to prepare us for an expensive, sleepless hell that people find rewarding because their kids are so awesome. Most of the time, at least.

But when other people talk about their kids, I feel lost. I have no points of reference for what they're saying. It's just a list of facts. *He's only four months old and he's already twenty-four inches! She still nurses five times a day. He has an October birthday, so that's rough with kindergarten.*

I want to know more than this. I want to know how they survived. I want to know what I can do to prepare for all of this. I want to know how being a parent is changing who they are, not just their daily habits and routines. But maybe they don't know how to talk about all of this. Maybe the words just aren't there. Or maybe they never think about it.

I feel like I'm going into this whole thing without any realistic expectations about pregnancy, labor, and everything that comes after.

Quite frankly, I don't want to be the pioneer among our friends. I'm much more comfortable observing a path that a close friend has traveled before and then deciding how I'll go down it. There's that and...

I'm scared of becoming a parent.

So much negativity surrounds parenthood that it all makes me wonder if this is what I want for my life. I like what I have—a decent job, a solid group of friends, time to write, a physically fit body. If we have kids, how will all of that change? Certainly, some things have to change, right?

Will I lose my friends? Will I give up my career to stay with my kids—and then have a hell of time getting back into my field? Will I never have time to write again? Will pregnancy and birth utterly destroy my body?

I am afraid of losing myself.

I'm afraid that I'll lose my creativity. That I'll stop working and then resent my kids for it later. That I'll gain sixty pounds and never lose it. That my husband will stop finding me attractive. That I'll lose my social life because I'm too busy raising children. That childbirth will destroy my vagina. Or that I'll die during childbirth because of some crazy problem. That the stress of children will damage our marriage.

I sense that once I come out on the other side of this, I will be forever changed. And what if I become someone that I don't like anymore? Will I be okay with that? What if I have regrets? Will my children know?

With so much uncertainty, I decide that I'm going to make it my mission to not fall down this hole of parenthood, where it seems some parents become trapped and live their days with resentment. I'm going to keep my social life. I'm only going to gain the recommended amount of weight and I'm going to lose it quickly because I will eat well and exercise. I'll go back to work and not feel guilty about daycare. I'll love my baby, but I won't let my baby dictate all the moves in my life.

I have a plan.

Of course, I know it is just a plan. I'm not so naïve that I see it as more than that. But plans give me something to work toward. They give me goals—and I *love* goals.

But the truth is, no one—not even I—can tell me what is going to happen to me or to us. And so I feel that the first step in this journey is a bit of surrender. A little bit of opening my hands to the unknown.

Eight weeks pregnant

140 pounds

Today, I'm in Target to buy yogurt and crackers, but somehow I've walked past the fitness section. (Target, how do you do it? Did you use some clever

7

algorithm that predicts the likely paths that pregnant mothers take in the store?) A shelf of pregnancy exercise videos calls out to me. I scan the titles until I see a section of pregnancy fitness journals.

Ohhh...

First, a confession: I'm a sucker for recording data, especially when it's about my health. It's geeky, I know, but it's true. Before pregnancy, I kept a food and exercise journal to help me keep track of my weight loss. Later, while we were trying to conceive, I charted my temperatures. I loaded my data into an on-line fertility tracker and *presto!* It predicted my ovulation days for that month.

I want the same reassurance about my diet during this pregnancy. I don't want to fall into the trap of mindlessly eating simply because I'm pregnant. I want to eat the right amount of food—and a variety of food.

I scan the pages. No places to write calories. I kind of like that. I don't want to be overly concerned about how many calories I'm eating. I care more about the quality of food. There are empty boxes for me to check off every time that I drink eight ounces of water. Love that. The journal also gives me a chart of nutritional information about foods that are loaded with essential pregnancy nutrition: avocados, sweet potatoes, chicken, almonds, and more.

I drop it in the cart.

I've had an ambivalent relationship with food for most of my life. As a teenager, I loved food to the tune of 195 pounds. In my senior year of high school, I crash dieted until I was 150 pounds. Then I crashed some more in college until I was 135 pounds. I did this because I thought it made me beautiful. And most people agreed. They complimented me on my new shape. But I was unhealthy. I had no core or muscle tone. I didn't know how to eat well, so I just denied myself food over and over again, believing that this was the only way that I could maintain my weight. I was constantly afraid of re-becoming that girl of 195 pounds. I couldn't shake her, no matter how much weight I lost. And if I gained the weight back, what would people think of me?

8

But then I fell in love with someone who built up my self-esteem. He cooked for me. Good, wholesome, healthy food. Not just food with few calories. He made me baked salmon, roasted potatoes, Italian chicken, and curried chickpeas. He said that I was beautiful. And I believed him. Later, I married him.

But then I swung too far in the other direction. *Ah, whatever. I'll have the whole piece of cheesecake.* On other days, I would think, *Man, that fried chicken was good... Maybe just another piece.* I wasn't a compulsive overeater—I just had a little more than I needed. A little too often. And over the years, it added up.

Two years into our marriage, I remember looking in the car's vanity mirror and sucking in my cheeks. They looked puffy. I asked Doug if he thought they were puffy.

"You look beautiful, Sweets."

It was sweet, but my reflection didn't lie.

When I stepped on the scale later that day, it was the first time I had weighed myself in three years.

172 pounds, the scale screamed.

"What the hell!" I screamed back.

It took a few rounds to the doctor to figure out what was going on. Not only did I have bad eating habits, but I also had an underactive thyroid. With medication, I dropped seven pounds. But that was it. Not one pound more.

I was happy to be 165 pounds for a long time. I started to work out on an elliptical machine three times a week because I thought it might help knock off some more weight. It didn't though. I stayed 165 pounds. But I wasn't *really* trying to lose weight. I never considered changing my diet. The food was too delicious.

And then we started talking about having a baby.

Thirty pounds—that was the average pregnancy weight gain for a woman of my height and weight. Thirty pounds. Which would bring me back to that dreaded 195 pounds.

I had dieted without exercise before and I had exercised without dieting. So I wondered what would happen if I just exercised regularly and ate normal portions of healthy food.

I was half-hoping it wouldn't work so I could throw it back in the faces of all those smug, hyper fitness gurus with their too-perfect abs. Okay, so I wasn't able to get the washboard abs, but, it turns out that you can lose a lot of weight by exercising and eating reasonably. And you keep it off.

After nine months of cardio kickboxing, weightlifting, and food journaling, I had lost thirty pounds. But I was also an eating machine. I would eat all day long and I kept the weight off because I had built a strong metabolism by adding muscle to my frame.

But I wonder how all of that is going to change. Right now, I am in the best shape of my life. I'm not looking forward to gaining weight, but I don't want this to be a battle either. I want to make peace with food during this pregnancy. I want to be more concerned that our child is eating well than I am with the changes that are happening to my body.

Nine weeks pregnant
140 pounds
The next few weeks suck. Big time.

I lie on the couch day after day throughout my Christmas break watching *Braveheart*, *The Lord of the Rings* (all three movies), and *Gone with the Wind*. I choose these movies because it doesn't matter if I fall asleep in the middle of them—I know them by heart. And I hate TV right now. Everyone is smiling and laughing as they buy things for Christmas: glitzy Old Navy sweaters, space-age My Little Ponies, and sleek Acuras. All I can think is, *I bet those people don't have nausea all day. I bet they feel fantastic! Look at them! Dancing around! Dancing and prancing around!*

Whenever I fill up my glass of water at the refrigerator, I stare at a picture of a friend's daughter. She teeters on one foot next to a well-decorated Christmas tree.

Is this really worth it? Ugh, it better be.

On the really hard days, I think, *We have made a big mistake. Why would anyone do this a second time? How does the human race go on?*

Every time I open the pantry, I superimpose giant red Xs over the foods that make me feel sick, give me heartburn, or sound unappetizing. When I log my food in my journal, I feel badly that I skip entire food groups on some days because I can't stomach the sight of another carrot or cracker. This is what I was trying to explain to Ryan. My brain no longer understands when I am hungry. Some connections in my brain have crossed and now, hunger isn't felt as hunger anymore. Now, hunger means sick.

And then there is the sad realization that even my favorite foods don't taste the same. When I nibble on a piece of dark chocolate, I recoil in disgust. Gone is the bittersweet taste. It is all sour. It coats my tongue in a sour mess as it melts. I scrape my tongue clean with a napkin, half-gagging.

So, so sad.

At my next prenatal appointment, my doctor rolls in the clunky ultrasound machine with that wonderfully uncomfortable internal probe. The first time they used it on me, I tried not to laugh as the nurse covered the probe with what definitely looked like a condom. *Too late for that*, I thought.

This time, the probe is even more uncomfortable because I haven't been able to completely empty my bladder whenever I pee.

"It's because of the position of your uterus," my doctor tells me. "You have a tilted uterus, so it's pointed toward your back."

"How do we fix that?" I ask.

Wahn-wahn. Wahn-wahn. Wahn-wahn. The sound is unmistakable.

My doctor turns toward me and smiles. "Do you hear that?"

"Oh my God!" I turn to Doug. "That's the heartbeat."

This time, we can *hear* life. That once distant, tiny, silent star has drawn closer. It speaks to us in heartbeats. It has taken shape. Tiny arm buds. Tiny leg buds. A large head. It floats slightly from side to side as my doctor pivots the wand.

"Everything is normal here," the doctor is still smiling. "And your uterus is fine. It will fix itself as the baby grows, so you should be able to empty your bladder more comfortably soon."

She flips off the ultrasound machine and sinks her hands into the pockets of her white coat, her smile still wide.

"So we should talk about whether or not you want to do any screening for Down's syndrome," she says.

"Okay," I say. "Um, well, I don't know. What's your advice?"

"It depends on how you would feel about the results. If it would change your mind about this pregnancy... then, you might want to do it. But I will say that I've had women do it, get a positive result, and then when they did the follow up amniocentesis, they found out the baby didn't have it. So they had all that anxiety for weeks when they thought the baby had Down's."

"Oh... Wow."

"Right. But if you know that you wouldn't change your mind if the test came back positive, I say, why have the screening? The screening doesn't carry any risks, but it could falsely flag you. And the follow-up tests *do* carry the possibility of miscarriage. So..."

We're talking about abortion, but the word is so heavy, neither one of us can say it. For a brief moment, I ask myself if I truly would want to keep this pregnancy if the child has Down's. The truth is, I don't want to have a child with Down's syndrome. But I also know that having an abortion and starting over with a clean slate isn't really what would happen.

It's not that I think I wouldn't be able to carry another baby to term. It's the fact that I would always know that I looked at that tiny person on the screen, that little life that was now depending on me and said, "No." The combination of guilt and grief would never come off me.

"So I guess we'll skip the screening then," I say.

"Okay then," she notes it on her computer. "Do you have any other questions for me?"

"Nope," I say quickly.

She keeps smiling and nodding at me. A few more seconds pass, as if she is giving me another chance to think of something.

Oh... Should I have questions for her? I've just been so happy that I'm still pregnant. But now I'm wondering if I've dropped the ball. I wasn't ready for this conversation about a Down's screening, and now it seems like she's waiting for some other big questions.

"Well," I say finally, "I guess I do want to know if there's anything that I should or shouldn't be doing. Do you have any advice?"

"Well, if you're looking for good books to read about pregnancy, I highly recommend *What to Expect When You're Expecting*. It's just phenomenal at answering all those common questions that women have in their first pregnancy."

As I drive home from the appointment, it hits me. I really don't have control over this process. All the charting, the well-timed sex, and the tests have created this illusion that I can control this pregnancy. But it is entirely out of my control. There is no process to follow to make sure that I don't have a child with Down's syndrome or any other genetic mutation. It is all a risk. No one can guarantee me that this will be a healthy, full-term pregnancy. All I can do is control how well I take care of myself, trust my body, and trust the process. And if that's not enough, I'm going to have to accept the hard truth that bringing life into this world carries risks—ones that not everyone can avoid.

A few days later, the head nurse calls me and asks for some information over the phone to complete some paperwork.

"Now, you realize that the doctor delivers out of Hospital A?" she asks me.

"Oh, um, no I didn't realize that."

At this moment, it occurs to me that I don't really have an option about where to give birth. I have chosen my doctor and my doctor delivers at Hospital A.

"Can she also deliver at Hospital B?" I ask. "I've heard great things about their facilities."

"No, sorry, she only has privileges at Hospital A."

"Oh. Okay."

And that is how the place where I give birth is decided.

January 2013

Eleven weeks pregnant

142 pounds

We share the news. Doug's family is ecstatic. This will be one of the first babies among his five siblings after a nine-year hiatus. My co-workers are surprisingly excited. I get hugs. Even bear hugs.

And then the questions start. So many come so fast that it is hard to know how to field all of them.

Where are you delivering? Who is your doctor? Are you going to buy a house? Will you go back to work?

And then the advice.

Don't worry about drinking coffee. I did—my kids are fine. What kind of car do you have? A Civic? You'll need a new car. Cloth diapers? Why not save the environment another way?

But when we tell our friends, they only respond with excitement. No advice.

None of them have kids yet.

February 2013

Thirteen weeks pregnant

143 pounds

The first time that I feel the baby move happens while I'm sitting on the couch eating a bowl of oatmeal on a Sunday morning before we go to church. A big sneeze overtakes me and then I feel it—a rolling motion, like a lemon pressing out and pivoting from one side of my lower abs to the other.

Whoa, that was a weird feeling.

I stand in front of the mirror and look at my stomach. I've never had a non-muffin-topped stomach. Well, maybe I did as a child, but I became a chubby girl around fourth grade, and from then on, I've always had a part of my belly folding over the waistband of my jeans. That was how I determined when I needed to buy new jeans. When my belly folded over too much. When I started assuming the shape of my menopausal teachers.

Even after all of the weight loss, that troublesome flap didn't go away. It shrank. It loosened. But it remained. I'd lose weight everywhere else. First, it would evaporate from my legs, hips, and butt. Then, my arms. If I pressed on, my back and shoulder blades would become more defined.

But the flap stayed.

So when I look at my stomach, that tender donut of flesh where my baby is growing, I wonder what shape my belly will take. Right now, I just look bloated.

I think that I'll be a curiously thin pregnant woman. Because I have the advantage of the flap.

My stomach has already been stretched from being overweight in my younger years. The key difference, however, is that it took me years of slightly overeating to reach my peak weight. Other thin pregnant women will reach my largest measurements in a much shorter time, and their skin will struggle to keep up.

But I've inadvertently trained for this.

Fifteen weeks pregnant

144 pounds

With a lot of effort, I've managed to exit the first trimester without vomiting—quite an accomplishment considering how much nausea I've been feeling and how powerful my sense of smell has become. (Talking with a student after his smoke break causes my stomach to lurch.)

But lately, my sense of smell has started to wane and I'm actually feeling hungry for a food that—just a week earlier—made me sick to think about: curried chicken with chickpeas. It is one of my favorite meals that Doug cooks.

At work, I eat a small container of chicken, chickpeas, and rice for lunch. It is absolutely delicious. Spectacular. I am officially the luckiest woman alive to be married to this man.

That night, I pull out the three large tubs of leftovers: rice in one container, chicken in another, and then chickpeas in a third. I lift the lid of the chickpeas and the smell hits me. Perhaps it's the fish sauce that is so pungent? I start to breathe through my mouth as I get a plate. My eyes land on the congealed coral-colored coconut milk surrounding the curried chickpeas. The spoon slices into its jiggly layer and my whole body recoils.

Oh God, is my thought as I run to bathroom.

I think I'm having a boy. So far, both Doug and I have had dreams that I gave birth to a boy. And then there are the physical signs. My nausea is abating, and people say that not much nausea is a sign that you're having a boy. A co-worker remarks on my excellent complexion. "A boy. For sure," she muses.

And it just really feels like we're having a boy.

Still, I don't want to know for sure. I love surprises and how often in life do you get a surprise like this? When I ask Doug if he wants to find out, he says, "Baby girl, you're running this show. I'm just here to support you."

Sixteen weeks pregnant

146 pounds

My colleagues joke that I'm not really pregnant. "Where? Where is this baby?" they tease.

I mostly agree with them. I don't really feel pregnant yet. Pregnant women are either burying their head in the toilet or rubbing their bellies like good luck charms.

My pregnancy falls somewhere in the middle of this range.

At first, the nausea made me feel like I was in chemotherapy. Then the excitement of sharing the news made me feel like I had just announced that I was in remission. And now, I just feel like I'm living in someone else's body. It can't really be my body because my body gets hungry at regular intervals and thinks there's nothing better than a good piece of pan-fried salmon. My body can empty its bladder completely and doesn't skip a day without pooping. My body doesn't find my most comfortable bras painful against my nipples.

March 2013

Seventeen weeks pregnant

146 pounds

"So you think you'll want to go back to work?"

It's not the first question that people usually ask when they find out that I'm pregnant, but it often comes up in the first few minutes, somewhere after *how exciting, when is the due date,* and *are you going to find out what it is.*

This time, it's someone from our church. A lady in her sixties, with a few grandchildren of her own.

"Yeah, that's the plan," I say.

"Well... things change," she winks. "You might feel a little differently once you get that baby in your arms."

"Yeah, I might," I admit.

I don't really think that my mind will change, but this seems like the only way to get out of this conversation without talking too much about philosophies of working and mothering. I'm pretty sure that I'll still want to have a career after this baby is born. I don't see myself as a stay-at-home mother. But I also don't want others to think that I disrespect that decision.

I love teaching. I've always been one of those teachers whose practice didn't stop at writing lesson plans and grading assessments. I've always done research in my own spare time, or mentored future teachers, or signed up for extracurricular activities to get to know our students. I loved to make brownies for my students at the end of a term. I would create blogs for my classes and post videos of in-class group tasks.

I never got paid more for doing any of this. It was never about the money. I did it because I loved my job. And I still find joy in lighting the path between where my students are and where they need to go.

But I have to admit that I don't know if I'll always feel that way.

Today, I've felt especially off. Usually, if something doesn't settle well after I eat, I add something else to the mix, and then I feel better. Yogurt doesn't sit well today? Add some granola. Salad causes the stomach to churn? Add a cheese stick. Crackers bring on heartburn? Try a scoop of peanut butter.

But after a whole morning of doing this, I stop and decide to limit myself to only water for a while. Hours and hours pass and I'm not hungry.

It's 8:00 p.m. While I'm sitting at my desk and grading papers, Doug asks me if I've eaten dinner. I lean back in my chair and say, "God, I just want to start over."

"Start what over? What are you talking about?"

"I just want to vomit everything I've eaten today and start over."

"You feel sick?"

"I think so."

"Well, go do it, Sweets."

"I'm not going to make myself puke."

"You'll feel better."

"I don't see how I have anything to throw up. I haven't eaten anything since lunch."

"Maybe you're hungry."

"Trust me. I'm not hungry."

"Well, then get to it."

"To what? Puking?"

He nods.

"I'm not doing that," I shake my head.

"You'll feel better."

I look down at my stack of papers, ungraded essays riddled with nonsense like, *most of white collar have huge work stress. They must to dispel work stress!*

"I'm going to brush my teeth," I say.

I'm halfway through my brushing routine when I feel it—my stomach lurching. I have no control over it. My body has decided to proceed without my consent.

While it's happening, I feel Doug pull my hair away from my face and rub my back. When it's over, I try not to look into the toilet, but of course, I do. What I see helps me make sense of the day.

"Huh," I say, after getting my breath back.

"What?"

"I believe that was my lunch... Maybe I didn't digest much of anything that I ate today."

"Is that normal?"

I shrug my shoulders. "My nurse mentioned at my last visit that I should expect slower digestion around this time. It means the baby is grabbing more nutrition from what I eat."

"Wow, that's crazy."

Twenty weeks pregnant

150 pounds

We have the twenty-week ultrasound performed at a branch of Hospital B because I can't make an appointment on the day that the ultrasound technician visits my obstetrician's office. Doug and I are ushered into a large dim room with a cushy chair like one you see in the dentist's office. The ultrasound technician rubs jelly on my little pooch of a belly and pushes the wand down against my skin. Instantly, a black and white image appears on a large TV screen on the wall.

"So, we're looking at the head here, but let me get a better look."

As she moves the wand back and forth over my stomach, I wonder if she realizes how memorable this moment will be for us. We're going to see our first child. Its legs, its arms...

She pauses with the wand over my right side and the image is crystal clear. We are looking at an unmistakable profile of our baby's head.

And it's moving. Its little legs fold over its chest so its feet are close to its face. It kicks and fidgets. A hand floats in front of its face. Just then, the baby's mouth opens in a tiny hiccup. It's the cutest thing I've seen in my life.

"Man, that kid is moving!" I say to the technician. "It's amazing that I can't feel all of that yet. I only feel flutters."

"Oh, soon enough, you'll be wishing you couldn't," she smiles. "So are you finding out the sex today?"

"No, we want to be surprised," I say.

"Okay, sure. I'll let you know when to look away so there's no chance of you seeing."

She walks us through a tour of the baby's body: brain, heart, lungs, liver, and bladder.

"So turn away for just a minute while I look at the thighs.... Okay, and we're done with that. Let's get a look at the face."

I didn't know that this was a possibility. She brings the wand to the baby's face and presses down. It's hard to see with all the shadows and the picture that she takes is not a good one. When she presents the printed pictures, I force a smile. It looks like I'll be giving birth to Skeletor.

But the other pictures are amazing. Little legs flipped over like the baby is riding a motorcycle at high speed. Tiny feet. Tiny hands. Little, little nose like me. And all of this happened without me thinking about any of it. All my other achievements—degrees, publications, awards, even my weight loss—I had worked hard to earn. I was used to that. If I wanted something, work was how I got to my goal.

But this baby grew so perfectly whether or not I thought about it. I didn't have to spend hours of thinking to make it happen. I didn't have to talk to the right people. All I had to do was live. Breathe. Eat. Repeat. And it helps me understand that babies, no matter how hard it is to conceive them, don't develop and grow from our hard work.

It feels like grace.

Now, I actually feel like I'm pregnant. I start to believe that I'm going to have a baby.

Twenty-one weeks pregnant

153 pounds

My mother wants to throw me a baby shower in Minnesota, where most of my aunts, uncles, and cousins live. So Doug and I buy plane tickets for a visit. A week before we leave, my mother tells me that my dad has been admitted to a psychiatric facility near their home. He has gone into a manic episode because his medication for bipolar depression needs to be adjusted or changed. He says that he doesn't feel safe at home.

We decide to come anyway.

I bring copies of the baby's sonogram to the visit. The receptionist removes the paperclip that holds the pictures together. Then she lets us in. My dad is lying on his side with his back to the door. When he rolls over, I can barely see his spindly legs in the folds of his baggy sweatpants. His face is gaunt. His beard is long. He looks like a mountain man, hid away in his cabin in the wilderness.

"You growing a beard, Dad?" I joke with him.

"Sharon?"

"Hi, Dad."

My mom helps him get up and he shuffles toward me in plastic hospital slippers. He stopped taking real steps a year ago as the Parkinson's worsened. He gives me a bony hug. When I pull away, I see food stains on his sweatshirt. Mom brushes at them with her fingers. They don't come off.

We leave Dad's room and move to the day room. We sit around a table and play a game of rummy. I take out the pictures of the sonogram.

"Hey Dad, remember when I said I was pregnant?"

He looks stunned. "Pregnant? You?"

"Yeah, Dad, I told you I was pregnant around Christmas. Remember that?"

He doesn't say anything, so I slide the sonogram to him. "That's your grandchild, Dad."

He is quiet as he looks at the printed pictures. He shakes his head.

"Well, I see it, so I guess I have to believe it... but I just don't believe it." His head is still shaking.

I stand up. "Okay, look at my stomach, Dad. See here?" I point to my bump and laugh.

He keeps shaking his head. "It can't be..." He looks out the window, but at what? I can't tell. "What day is it?" he asks.

"It's March 29," Doug says.

He shakes his head again. "It can't be much past February 15. Doesn't feel like it's much past that. It can't be March already."

After we walk with Dad back to his room, Doug asks my mom how much Dad has been sleeping.

She shakes her head. "He doesn't sleep. His apnea is so bad and I'm having trouble getting this place to get him to use the machine at night. They said he doesn't want to wear the mask, so they don't make him wear it."

When I turn to leave my Dad's room, I see him lying once again on his side, looking at the wall.

April 2013

Twenty-two weeks pregnant

153 pounds

A year or so ago, I saw a documentary on Netflix called *The Business of Being Born*. I saw that Rikki Lake was the director, and so I watched it because I couldn't imagine her as a documentarian. Then I realized that it was a movie about the benefits of homebirth and giving birth without medical interventions, including medication.

But, really, I thought, *what woman in her right mind would turn down painkillers during childbirth?*

By the end of the movie, I thought I might be that woman. I wasn't seriously considering giving birth at home, but the movie made me think more about the effects of medical interventions on labor and birth. It seemed that the more you tried to mess with labor and birth, the more things could go wrong. Perhaps with birth, "less is more" is good advice.

But as I listened to other women's stories about giving birth—both those who found it traumatic and those who felt empowered by it—I realized that the process of labor and delivery isn't just about giving birth to a child. It's also about the birth of a new mother. And while my bringing a baby into this world safely was important, that didn't mean that my rebirth as a mother was unimportant.

So now I'm looking more into how to have an unmedicated childbirth.

Some pregnant friends from my church have taken classes in a childbirth method called the Bradley Method. Classes meet for twelve weeks for a few hours each session. Couples learn more about pregnancy and the birthing process to help them labor naturally whenever possible. The father also assumes the role of coach in the birth. It sounds like the right fit for us.

So I search for Bradley instructors in our area. As I make the call, Doug asks me if I have checked with my obstetrician.

"What for?"

"To see if she's okay with it."

"Why wouldn't she be okay with it?"

"I'm just saying that we don't want to have conflicts in the delivery room. Why don't you ask the OB first?"

When the nurse at my OB's office returns my voicemail, she asks me to repeat the name of the class.

"It's the Bradley Method. Its focus is on natural childbirth... trying to keep the labor and delivery as natural as possible."

"Well, she's not going to care how you labor. She'll pretty much let you do whatever you want. But she will want you to have an IV. That I know for sure."

"So she's okay with the Bradley Method?"

"As far as I know, yes, but I'll double check."

The nurse calls me back within two hours.

"Sharon, actually, the doctor does *not* approve of the Bradley Method. She said that she has found that couples who follow the Bradley Method tend to be more focused on avoiding a C-section instead of being focused on a healthy baby."

"Oh... So... What type of classes does she approve of?"

"Oh, anything really. Hospital classes are fine."

"Okay, so classes at Hospital A are okay?"

"Sure, any of those are fine."

"Okay."

And that is how I choose childbirth education classes. I'm not happy with the decision, but Doug has a point about the possibility of conflicts in the delivery room. I like my OB even if I don't agree with her recommendation. As a compromise, I decide that I will still read some Bradley Method books.

Twenty-four weeks pregnant
156 pounds
I'm finally noticeably pregnant to others. My flap has filled in enough to be round like a pregnant belly.

At work, colleagues shriek on a day when I wear a close-fitting shirt and skirt that shows off my little bump. One of my bosses can't control herself and she lays her hand on my stomach as she coos about how much weight she gained with each of her pregnancies.

"I'm not even lying—fifty pounds each time," she pronounced. "I was the happiest pregnant woman around. I *loved* it."

When she leaves, I'm still marveling over the fact that she has clearly been able to lose all of that weight—twice.

Twenty-five weeks pregnant
160 pounds
"You've reached a milestone!" my obstetrician announces at my next prenatal appointment. "If your baby were born today, it would most likely survive."

Oh my God, I think as I lie back against the examination table. *It could have died before now. I could have given birth to a stillborn. I could have lost a baby that actually looks like a baby.*

"Oh..." I say slowly as she measures my growing pooch. "Well, that's good. Never thought about it like that."

"Now, you called earlier about the Bradley Method, right?" she asks as she prods my uterus.

"Uh-huh."

"So I wanted to explain about that more. I don't approve of the Bradley Method because in my experience the couples that go through those classes are overly focused on not having a C-section. I'll never forget... I once observed a delivery as a resident, and this couple *refused* a C-section. I mean, it was clear to everyone else in the room that this needed to happen, but they just *refused*. And then... the baby was born with mental retardation. I will never forget that."

She finishes prodding me and offers her hand to help me sit up.

"So I want to be very clear that my goal is for you to have a vaginal delivery... but I also don't want you to be so dead set against a C-section that it impairs your judgment about what's best for you and this baby. How does that sound?"

I smile and nod. It's a good explanation for her opinion and it reassures me that she isn't overly excited to perform a C-section.

"So, you're okay with me laboring naturally?" I ask her.

"Sure. You can labor naturally or you can have medication. I'm good with either way." She balances her laptop on one arm and then uses her free hand to enter information.

Then, I remember to ask her about midwives and doulas. I had read that these birth attendants could help me cope with unmedicated labor. But I was still confused about what roles each person would have in a delivery room. If I have an OB, do I need a midwife? How are midwives and doulas different?

"I've also been reading about midwives and doulas," I say. This gets her attention. She looks up from her laptop and then puts it down on the counter.

"Okay..." she says.

"I just really want someone with me the whole time while I'm in labor, someone who knows what's going on and who won't have to leave me to check on other patients. What do you think?"

"I'm not good with midwives because they tend to tell me how to do my job. I'm great with doulas."

"Should you meet whatever doula I hire?"

"I don't need to. You might want to tell me their name, but it should be fine."

Twenty-six weeks pregnant

160 pounds

When I research the difference between midwives and doulas further, I feel a little foolish about my question to my obstetrician. I was going to her with the intention of having her deliver my child. If I hired a midwife, she would have the same role as my obstetrician and then I would definitely be creating a power struggle in the delivery room. A doula, however, was not medically trained to deliver a child. Instead, her role would be to support me during labor.

I take to the Internet and search for doulas in my area. I make a list of seven possible choices and start calling around for their availability. I eliminate two of them this way. Then, I start setting up first-time consultations.

The first doula that I interview is a full-time licensed massage therapist who specializes in prenatal massage. And I *love* massage. But she talks for almost an entire hour about what she does and what her experiences have been. I don't open my mouth except for the last ten minutes when I'm finally able to ask questions. Once I hear that she will "join me at the hospital," I know that she is not the doula for me. I want to find someone who will labor at home with me during early labor.

The second doula is actually a group of doulas. Their website looks soft and inviting. Peaceful women, focused on laboring, a close-up of one hand comforting another. The links are informative and their "About Us" page talks about birth as empowering and natural. They are based out of Cincinnati, but according to their website, they are willing to travel as far north as Dayton. When I call for a consultation, one of the doulas tells me that they are having a meet-and-greet at a Panera in northern Cincinnati. Would I be able to come on Saturday?

I am able to go, but Doug has a prior commitment. When I arrive at the meet-and-greet, I feel like the ugly single girl who has shown up late to a party—and all the other girls have dates. Everyone is sitting in a circle with their scones and tea and they are introducing themselves. It feels like a reverse interview, where the doulas are interviewing their potential clients. The first couple is looking for a doula in September. The next couple needs one in August. Then another in August.

"We just found out that we're pregnant, so we're due in late November or December. But we weren't able to get these ladies the last time we got pregnant, so we're not messing around this time!"

Laughter among the couples. One of the doulas blushes.

Another couple for August. Someone else for September.

It's my turn and I reveal that, I too, am looking for a doula in August. "I feel silly asking this, but do you even have availability for August? I mean four of us are looking for August. Could you accommodate all four of us?"

The doulas look at each other. The older one defers to the younger one, who looks at her planner.

"Well... we still have availability for August, but it's filling up fast. So what I would do..." she looks around at the August couples, "...is talk with one of us immediately after this if you're interested and we'll go ahead and set up a consultation."

"Oh." *I thought this was the consultation.*

But I'm done with these ladies. They may be awesome, but I'm not going to feel like I'm the lucky one here. I'm the one having the baby.

I leave without talking to either of the doulas.

I find out that another doula on my list has retired, and another has gotten a full-time job. I have one left on my list and she is available and she would love to meet us.

Her name is Pam. We meet at a Starbucks and she comes in carrying a binder, her hair in a ponytail, her eyes complemented by dark-rimmed glasses. She is sweet and soft-spoken, but with some friendly banter we figure out that she is also not afraid to swear and tell you the way things really are. She has attended births with my doctor, and when we ask for some references, she lists a friend that we haven't seen in a while.

When I ask her what she thinks about birth she says, "I believe that women's bodies were created to give birth. He didn't make any mistakes when He made us the way we are. Now, also, I think that you should have choices. And there are times when medication is the best choice to help a woman get through a difficult birth. My job is to support your choices. I can tell you what I think, but I'll support whatever you want to do. Also, I'm not going to tell the doctor what to do. I can tell you what's about to happen and what different actions can mean for the birth and recovery, but you guys have to be the ones to make the decisions. That's not my role."

We love her. She's in.

May 2013
Twenty-seven weeks pregnant
161 pounds
The feeling of pregnancy is now noticeably different. That point of gravity— once lodged in my stomach—has turned inside out and now I feel that I'm blooming. Until recently, if I had to pinpoint a part of the body where I— my life, my individuality, all that I am—resided, I would have pointed to my heart. No question. But now, I feel the answer to this question is more complex. I feel movement and warmth in this new point of life in my core. A new expanding universe is housed inside of me, abiding by different rules and reacting to different forces. Every day, it grows.

We grow.

And this, I feel, is pregnancy. After fighting with each other for weeks and weeks, we are now dancing. Dancing while blindfolded. Each of us listening to different music. We can't see what comes next and sometimes we step on each other's toes, but we manage to keep moving.

I try to share these thoughts in a letter to the baby.

On the back of your baby shower invitation, I included a quote from Kahlil Gibran, a Lebanese poet. It said:

29

Your children are not your children
They are the sons and daughters of life's longing for itself
They come through you, but not from you
And though they are with you, yet they belong not to you

I put it there as a reminder to myself, before you are even born and before I can become extremely possessive over you, that I shouldn't expect that you will do everything that I want you to do and that whatever picture I have of who you will become cannot become the standard for whether or not I think you are successful in life. You are your own person. You are you and I am me. And your dad is your dad. And that's all.

I think that the measure of whether or not your dad and I did a good job of being parents will be if you are happy in life. And, truthfully, from my heart, I don't care what that picture looks like. I have seen enough pain caused in my friends, my family, and Doug's family to know that this is the best attitude to have toward parenting. Be who you are and if you don't know who that is, take some time to figure it out. And then take even more time because you will change year to year and decade to decade. The journey is never over. And it's your life. It's not my life. No matter how much I want to protect you from failure and disappointment, it is a part of life, and being an independent person means that you are able to weather those hard times so you can truly enjoy the times that are great.

As I write this, I can feel you kicking and turning. And this makes me feel like everything is going to be okay.

Twenty-eight weeks pregnant
163 pounds

I sit on the edge of the examination table at my next appointment. This sitting position is awful for pregnant women. Any seat without a back or arms for support is torturous. I struggle to get out of these seats of torture when it's time to stand up and then a backache sets in. I think about moving to the chair next to the table. Then, I decide to tough it out.

Reading and researching over the past few weeks has pushed me toward developing a new philosophy about this birth. I'm starting to believe that I can trust my body to do this because women have been having babies for thousands of years. So mirroring the way that most women have given birth throughout history seems to be the safest way to deliver this baby. That means no induction. No augmentation. No medication. Just give nature a chance to work on its own.

But in order to completely espouse this new philosophy, I will need to change the way that I think about my own body. Until now, I've seen my body as a machine. That was how I lost weight. It was simple math. Calories in, calories out. Good food in, good results out. As long as I was willing to believe in this equation, I would see results.

But after reading *Birth Matters* by Ina May Gaskin and *Childbirth Without Fear* by Dick Grantly-Read, I start to believe more in the mind-body relationship. I start to understand that while I can prepare my body physically for this task, I also need to change how I think about birth.

No more indulgent daydreams of worst-case scenarios of birth, fueled by movie dramas and television shows. Visions of barely making it to the delivery room, doctors swooping in with urgent news, nurses scurrying to hook me up to tubes—birth doesn't have to be like that. Those scenes make great entertainment, but no one is making a movie out of this birth.

So I will not be a damsel in distress. I will be strong. I will be powerful. I won't do this for admiration from others—I will do it because I want to offer this baby as much protection as possible from harm. Childbirth has risks—but I will do what I can to minimize them.

It seems that I'm creating a very strange space in dealing with my doctor. I don't want to make pronouncements about what I will and will not do during labor because—frankly—I'm not sure what I'll want to do once labor starts. And don't I trust that my doctor knows what she's doing? At the same time, I don't want to be a bystander in this process. I want to be an active participant, a person who knows what is going on and why. I want to be able to explain to her why it's important to me to have an unmedicated birth. And I want her to respect that.

I want to start engaging in a dialogue with my doctor, but I'm not sure how to do that yet. Making a birth plan is what all of the books recommend, but I haven't done that yet.

My doctor comes through the door and I start with the news that I've chosen a doula.

"Okay, great," she says.

"Would you like to meet her? She says that she has attended a birth with you once before."

"Oh, I'm sure she'll be fine."

I feel like asking some of my questions related to labor and delivery, but which ones?

"So is there anything else that I need to do? How am I doing?" I say.

"You're doing fine. You're a textbook case." She places her hands on my knees. "Relax. Go pick out baby furniture."

"What about this one?" I point to a car seat that looks hefty.

"What kind is that?" Doug asks from the end of the aisle.

"Um, Graco."

"No, I mean, is it a convertible car seat?"

"I don't know. What does that mean?"

He crosses his arms and starts reading a sign. I walk over to him and look over his shoulder. He is looking at a kind of car seat glossary. We use it to translate the information posted next to each car seat. It's *almost* helpful.

"Okay, so this one is good for babies that are five to thirty-five pounds. How old is a thirty-five pound baby?" he asks.

I shrug. "I guess it depends, right? Maybe we can find out how much a typical baby weighs at one year?"

I start googling height-weight growth charts while he looks at strollers.

"What kind of stroller do you want?" he asks.

"Huh?"

"A stroller. What kind?"

"Oh..." I pause, trying to imagine us pushing a stroller. We like simple. Less is more. But these are all so... complicated.

In the next aisle, a woman is talking to her toddler. "Mommy said sit down, Willow. Willow, sit down, honey. Don't eat that. Grossie, gross. What? What sweet girl? Hold on, honey."

Oh geez. Are we going to talk to our kid like that?

"Sweets?"

"Sorry, I... um..."

"What kind of stroller?" he repeats.

"I don't know." I glance at a brown and green model that seems more streamlined than the others. "This one looks good."

He pulls the model off the pedestal and starts test-driving it. He practices opening and closing it.

"It's clunky."

"I mean... I might not even need a stroller if I use a sling," I say.

"We should register for a stroller, Sweets. You're not always going to want the baby in a sling."

How do you know that, I think. *Maybe I'll love it.* I recently read a blog post with a new term: *container children.* These were babies who spent the majority of their time in car seats, strollers, bouncers, highchairs, and other baby furniture. The writer had even included research on the importance of bonding between parents, especially mother and child, in the first few months and that close contact played an important role in bonding.

"Come on, try a few out," he presses.

We settle on a model and add it to our registry using a handheld scanner. I guess it won't hurt to have one if someone buys it for us. It might even be useful for some occasions.

But I'm still going to hold my baby a lot.

After stopping by the bathing section, we decide to call it a day.

Our next move is to create an Amazon baby registry, especially for out-of-town family and friends. Now *this* feels like a shopping spree at my fingertips. Yes, we'll take one of those layette sets, although I'm not quite sure what a layette is. Yes, I'd love that top-rated bottle sterilizer.

Bottles... Hm... What kind of bottles?

Wait a minute... do I even need bottles? Everything that I've read says that breastfeeding is better for me and the baby. The general consensus among everything that I've read about breastfeeding is that I should be able to breastfeed—as long as I'm well-informed, dedicated to the process, and have good help. A friend sends me an invitation to a La Leche League meeting. I am unable to go, but I'm thankful to know that there are groups that exist to support breastfeeding mothers.

But maybe I can pump breastmilk ahead of time and let Doug do some of the feedings at night, I think. *That sounds like a good idea.*

Choosing a brand of bottles baffles me. This one claims to be more natural. This one claims to reduce colic. This one claims to be the most popular. I read a Consumer Reports article about bottles and decide to register for several starter kits to see what our baby prefers. I choose the kits that emphasize that they are similar to breastfeeding.

I'm beginning to see that this process is really about determining what kinds of parents we want to be. Every decision forces me to think about what we want to do or what we imagine our lives will be like as parents. All of my reading and research has coalesced into two themes: "natural parenting" and "informed consumerism." I subscribe to Consumer Reports and spend several hours reading car seat reviews and comparing their ratings. And as for the natural parenting, we decide to give cloth diapers a try, especially after some conversations with a colleague who cloth diapered three of her four kids. But we don't want to discourage people from purchasing disposable diapers as gifts—especially the newborn size. And we don't really know what type of cloth diapers will work best with our baby's proportions.

So we register for a few cloth wipes and one highly reviewed cloth diaper on Amazon.

My thought process is similar for deciding what to do about a crib. Some people say co-sleeping is best to maintain breastfeeding. Others say it's dangerous. The American Academy of Pediatrics doesn't recommend it, but those in favor of Attachment Parenting do.

"Sweets, there's no way we're bringing a baby into bed with us," Doug states.

I have to admit that I don't particularly like the idea either. But then, I'll be the one getting up out of bed throughout the whole night to nurse.

So I find an alternative that is a good compromise: a co-sleeper. It's like a bassinet with a side that can fold down. The idea is to secure it to the side of the bed and create a separate sleeping space for the baby. Doing so gives me the option of sliding the baby easily to me so I can nurse in the middle of the night.

"So we would attach that to our bed?" Doug asks.

"Yeah."

"How is that any better? I mean, the baby is still going to wake both of us up when it starts to cry," he points out.

"So I should be the only one who gets no sleep? I'm going to need help here."

"I'm going to help out, but someone is going to need to have it together enough to still do the shopping and pay the bills. Everyone I've talked to about taking care of a newborn has said that my job should be to do everything else and your job should be just to focus on taking care of you and the baby."

"Right, and I'm going to do that."

"How about this..." he pauses. "If you want to use that co-sleeper, let's wait to put the crib together. And we have the guest bed in the third bedroom... And the third bedroom is going to be the baby's room... So..."

"What? Attach the co-sleeper to the guest bed?"

He shrugs.

"It's not a bad idea," I admit. "But... I guess that means I'm sleeping in there with the baby while you get to sleep through the night?" My sarcasm runs thick.

"Look," he holds his hands out, level to the floor. "I will take care of everything else. Your schedule is going to be to sleep when the baby sleeps. My sleeping still has to happen at night because I'll be working during the day."

"But you're taking time off when the baby is born, right?"

"Yeah, I'll get... two weeks, I think? I can extend it out further if I go in for some half days."

We're both quiet for a few moments.

"Did you just convince me to sleep in the baby's room while you get to sleep in our bed?" I ask.

I can't believe it, but I failed my one-hour glucose challenge, the screening that identifies women who might have gestational diabetes. Now, I need to do the three-hour test to confirm the diagnosis. That means a night and morning of fasting, a blood draw to determine my blood sugar baseline, a concentrated sugary drink when the baby is expecting breakfast, and then three hours of waiting while technicians draw my blood at one-hour intervals.

Great.

When I arrive for the test at 7:30 a.m. on a Friday, I figure the line will be as short as it was when I came in on Tuesday morning. Wrong. When I walk through the door, I sigh at the thirteen-person-deep queue. Nearly everyone in the line is over sixty years old. A few older men turn toward the door when I walk in, but none of them offer to allow this clearly pregnant woman to go ahead of them.

It takes until 8:05 for the receptionist to check my orders. Then, she tells me that my doctor's office has not faxed the order for my glucose test. Unwilling to repeat this ordeal on a different day, I tell the receptionist that I will call my doctor's office when it opens at 9:00 and ask them to fax the order again.

It's 9:35 by the time I finally have my first blood draw and subsequently chug the tiny 100-gram bottle of what tastes like flat orange soda. These are the first calories I have consumed in twelve hours. For the first hour, I feel okay. Bored and still hungry, but okay. After the second blood draw, I return to the waiting room. And then, I start to feel lightheaded. My heart starts racing and kaleidoscope patterns scatter over everything in the room.

Oh wonderful, I think. This is what usually happens before I pass out after having my blood drawn. Beads of sweat pool at the back of my neck. Then, my hearing tunnels into a loud ringing.

My first thought isn't, *I should get help!* Instead, I think, *Shit! What if I pass out in this waiting room and then have to take this test again on another day?*

So I slump down into a secure position in my chair and breathe deeply through the episode. I can feel the baby turning and flipping from the onslaught of sugar. I have never fed it so much sugar at one time without anything else in my system. The baby is going absolutely nuts. Its movements trigger a wave of nausea and I concentrate to keep from vomiting. I close my eyes and ignore the stares from the two older men in chairs across from me.

As my hearing returns and my vision clears, I lift a hand to wipe the sweat from my face and neck. I check my watch. Ten minutes have passed and I have successfully coached myself through a fainting spell without calling enough attention to myself to void the test.

I make it through the next two needle sticks without a problem and then rush home to gobble a large brunch to make up the caloric deficit from the morning fast. When I finish, I lie on the couch and rub my belly. I tell the baby that I'll never do that again.

This time, the test comes back normal.

Twenty-nine weeks pregnant

163 pounds

Throughout this time, I've been exercising with precautions. I still do cardio workouts, but I don't push my heart rate as high as I once did. I raise my heart rate to a steady aerobic level and I listen to my body. Some days, I barely have enough energy to finish a short prenatal workout DVD. On other days, I feel fine. But lately, while I'm doing yoga workouts at home, I start to lose my balance more often. It's probably time to seek out other prenatal fitness options.

A small yoga studio near my work offers prenatal yoga classes on Wednesday evenings. I try out a session.

I am in love.

Women in the class ask for baby updates from each other as they unroll their mats and grab yoga blocks from a shelf in the corner. They trade advice on cloth diapers and slings for babywearing. They talk about doulas and many of them are giving birth at the hospital where I had wanted to deliver—before I knew that my doctor didn't have privileges there.

The teacher begins class with introductions, and this helps me to feel included in this community. I meet some women who have due dates close to mine and we trade pregnancy stories. And then, the yoga is also a great stress relief. The stretching aligns and balances me. I sleep so well that night.

I can't find much else in the area for prenatal exercise, except for Hospital A's prenatal fitness class. The price is forty dollars for twelve one-hour sessions. I sign up.

After the first session, I'm not sure that I'll go back simply because the exercises are not that challenging. The height of physical exertion is holding a bridge pose against a stability ball and climbing a hill outside. But then again, I'm meeting other pregnant women, and it has been nice to feel a little normal around other people who are also feeling abnormal. Once we start talking throughout the exercises, the time goes faster and it becomes more enjoyable.

When we arrive at the hospital for a tour that weekend, we see a few other pregnant women and their partners sitting on couches arranged in a circle in the center of the bright lobby. Our guide wears scrubs decorated with flying cartoon angels. She sympathizes with our pregnancy ailments and then shares a few stories with us about her cravings and lack of sleep. Then, she ends with, "But it's all worth it!"

She walks us to the Labor & Delivery Unit and stops at a massive set of double doors.

"So, our wing is protected by these doors. Only people who have clearance are allowed to come in." She presses the buzzer and identifies herself. The doors open. "Also, both parents and infants wear ID bracelets. The infant's ID bracelet has a sensor that will activate an alarm if it leaves this wing without approval. So you don't have to worry."

Worry? I think, as we advance through the doors. *What? Someone might try to steal my baby?* The thought hadn't occurred to me until now.

The nurse leads us into the first room on the right. We gather in a semi-circle around a bed where some woman will some day give birth.

"This is our typical labor and delivery room. We don't transfer you to another room to give birth. It all happens here, which is nice," she tells us. "One thing you'll notice about our rooms is that they are very spacious and welcoming. There are places for visitors to sit and relax."

She is right. There is a sofa, a rocking chair, and a few padded chairs. But I'm not really planning on entertaining while I'm laboring. A decent-sized TV is mounted in the corner as well. Next to it is a rack that holds a huge stability ball. That might be nice for labor.

"We also have all the necessary medical equipment to keep you safe, but it's not conspicuous like in other hospitals."

She shows us that a wooden cabinet next to the bed swings open to become one of those instruments with the heart-shocking paddles. An infant warmer is tucked away in the corner.

I notice that many of our gazes land on the TV and the chairs. A few people have the courage to open the door to examine the bathroom. But no one looks at the bed. Maybe it's because we're trying not to imagine what is going to happen on it.

But I can't look away from it. Why is it such a terrifying piece of furniture? It seems too small for something as important as giving birth. But no one else is giving the bed a second look. They are sizing up the shower and looking out the windows. Maybe these other women are having the same thoughts, but it's too large of a dose of reality to confront in the presence of strangers. Or maybe I'm obsessing. Or maybe both.

My attention drifts to the electronic fetal monitoring device next to the bed. I've read about these machines and I haven't found many reasons to like them. Books tell me that they can't accurately indicate a problem during labor, but they do allow nurses to manage more than one patient at a time. When I asked the teacher of my childbirth education class for her opinion about these machines, she pursed her lips and thought for a few moments before telling me that they were useful for malpractice cases. But nurses can't look at only an EFM reading and know what is happening with a patient. Still, they are standard practice. So if I don't clarify that I want to maintain my mobility during labor, I'll be hooked up to that machine for most of the time.

At the end of our tour, the nurse says, "Well, we'll being seeing you all soon!"

Really? I guess it is only about two months away.

June 2013

Thirty-one weeks pregnant

166 pounds

My obstetrician has a special surprise for today's appointment: a medical student. A nurse asks if he can come into my room with the doctor.

I grant him permission. I feel badly that medical students are relying on the whims of patients to get experience. And there's no internal exam today, so why not?

"So you're taking Hospital A's prenatal fitness class, huh?" my doctor asks as she reviews my chart.

"Uh-huh."

"I just love that class, don't you?" she blurts as she washes her hands at the sink. "Some people swear by prenatal yoga, but when I was pregnant, that was the *last* thing that I ever thought about doing, you know? I mean, you're already *huge* and you want me to do *what*? Balance on one leg? What? The hospital's class is just so much more practical." She chuckles as she dries her hands on some paper towels.

I chuckle with her. I'm not going to tell her that I'm taking prenatal yoga. What's the point? I fear that she might discourage me from taking it and I happen to love it.

"So how are you feeling these days?" she asks.

"I've noticed that I can't get my breath like I used to," I say. "I feel like this baby is all the way up in my ribs. Can you tell how the baby is positioned?"

"Well, let's see." She takes my hand and helps me lie back against the table. Then, she places her hands on either side of my belly. Her hands press in each side and then rotate. She moves one hand down to my pubic bone and pushes in. "So my guess is that this baby is lying in there sideways right now. Probably with the head here," she touches next to my right rib, "and the butt over here," she touches my left side. "Definitely, its back is facing us."

"Do you think it will turn?"

"Oh yeah. There's plenty of time for it to turn."

She motions for the medical student to examine me. He doesn't press down on me as firmly as my doctor.

"So you feel the baby's head here," she points as he manipulates my belly.

"Uh-huh, yeah," he gazes off to the side, seeming a bit uncomfortable looking at me.

"And see how you can't feel anything down here?" She pushes down next to my pubic bone. "See that?"

"Oh, yeah," he says. He quickly presses down next to my pubic bone.

I'm kind of happy that I'm helping this guy get some exposure to babies that aren't lying in the head-down position. Maybe I'm his first patient with a lying-sideways-in-utero baby.

Then, the examination is over and my doctor starts to pick up her laptop. "Okay, so we'll see you back in a few weeks."

"Oh, I have a few questions," I say, feeling awkward about stopping her from leaving the room.

"Okay," she turns back to me, keeping her laptop in her arms.

"So... I mean, I haven't got it written out yet, but..." I remind myself that there's nothing wrong with asking questions. This was one of those steps to being active in this process. "I wanted to talk about what I might put in my birth plan."

My doctor looks to the medical student with a smile that seems to say, *Oh, another one of those kinds of patients.* She sets her laptop down.

"Okay, before you go any further, let me just say that I have three requirements and beyond that, I don't care." She speaks quickly and decisively. "First, you have to have an IV. Secondly, you need to have some kind of monitoring. And last, you will get Pitocin if you don't make progress. And one more thing—Try to keep your birth plan as short as possible. I can pretty much guarantee you that the longer your birth plan is, the more likely it is that you'll have a C-section."

"Oh." Her statements have come so quickly that I'm trying to process what each of them means for what I want in my labor. My mind races to think of my questions. I repeat back what she has said to me and start asking my questions.

"Okay, so is it possible to have a Heparin lock? Like a port in my arm instead of an IV?"

She crosses her arms over her chest. "It has been my experience that women who *don't* get IVs usually become dehydrated. What happens is, you can drink all the water that you want, but it won't get to the tissues as effectively as it will with an IV. And truthfully, I haven't seen anyone chained to the bed because of an IV. They're mobile. They can follow you if you want to walk around."

I don't like her answer, but I keep going. "And the monitoring, can it be intermittent? Only twenty minutes of every hour?"

"That's the lower threshold that I'm comfortable with, but yes, twenty minutes per hour is enough for me, assuming of course that everything else is progressing well."

"And the third thing was... right, so what does it mean 'if I don't make progress?'"

She shrugs and says, "Just if you don't dilate very much every few hours. It's really on a case-by-case basis. I can't make any predictions for you now."

"Okay..."

"And like I said, you can labor however you want. You can get in the shower if you want. I don't require you to have medication and I don't care how you want to push. You're running the show. I'm just here to catch."

I'm nodding. So far, so good.

"But I don't want you to get your heart set on a certain way that this birth has to be. I've seen it before in other patients. They get all these ideas about... they want to do this and they want to do that, and then when it's actually happening, they just want to get some relief and lay down. And there's nothing wrong with that!"

"Oh, hm," I say, not sure about how to respond to this. I can't really argue with her experience, but I also don't like to be lumped together with all of her patients from the past. But she doesn't seem to be interested in why I want to labor naturally, so I decide not to push the issue.

"Okay, one more thing. What is your policy on inductions?"

"I'll let you go as far as forty-two weeks. After forty-two weeks, I'm probably going to insist that you be induced because after that, the placenta starts to deteriorate and we could run into more problems than if we just go ahead and do an induction. But I'll let you go pretty long if you want."

I leave the appointment feeling a little defeated, but not so defeated that I feel like I have to look for another doctor this late in the game. Even if she thinks I won't go through with an unmedicated labor, she seems to be okay with me having one. She just wants to avoid being sued. But I wasn't expecting her to shoot down my request for a Heparin lock. I thought for sure that it would be an acceptable compromise. I have read that having a port in my arm—instead of a traditional IV—would help me to maintain my mobility. But maybe I can delay getting the IV until later in my labor.

I try not to dwell on it.

Thirty-two weeks pregnant
166 pounds

I've hit a wall—the "I'm-okay-with-being-pregnant" wall. My belly is now rounded and protruding enough for people to assume that I'm pregnant. My skin has not stretched yet—I still have room in the flap to keep growing. But sleeping has become a challenge. I now have to heave my belly from one side to the other in the middle of the night when one side of my body has fallen asleep.

I had a vision of being that pregnant woman that gains a basketball belly and retains her toned arms, thighs, and legs. As long as I continued to eat well and exercise, I figured that I'd grow like that.

Ha.

My thighs have grown. My hips have spread. My butt is bigger. Still, I should acknowledge that having a long torso gives the baby a lot of room to spread out vertically, so I'm not torpedo-pregnant. I don't knock people over when I turn to the side.

Every sitting position that I find comfortable is far from professional, so when I am teaching, I find myself standing a lot. But then standing makes me tired, so I'm constantly alternating between sitting and standing. Before climbing the stairs at home, I carefully consider whether I'm leaving anything behind. Still, "pregnancy brain" makes me constantly forget why I've climbed the stairs once I get to the top. I'm starting to gain weight rapidly now—one to two pounds every week. The numbers creep up more and more and I assure myself that everything is okay. The baby is growing a lot now. My diet hasn't changed that much, so it's not like I'm packing on unnecessary weight. I can lose the weight later.

"Puppies, huh?" a fellow teacher asks as she microwaves her lunch. She is talking about my recent Facebook post announcing that I had a dream that I had given birth—to puppies.

"Yep," I say, leaning back in my chair. "I think it's my mind's way of making sense of all the movement going on in here."

I prop my hands on my belly. Yeah, I'm doing that now.

"What breed?" she smiles.

"Oh..." The question catches me off guard. "You know, I'm not even sure. I was just so happy that they were puppies."

"Happy?" she laughs.

I nod seriously. "Uh, yeah. I know how to take care of puppies. You think I know how to take care of a baby?"

She is laughing harder now.

"I mean, puppies... Come on. I got that. But a baby..." I shake my head.

She continues to laugh as she leaves the kitchen with her heated lunch.

Doug is blending a smoothie when I hear a thud. He turns it off. I hear him scraping the sides of the canister with a spoon. He turns it on. Another thud.

"I hate this blender," he says.

I already know what that means, but I don't say anything.

Two days later, a package arrives from Amazon. Doug opens it excitedly and pulls out a massive blender base. It's at least the size of a car battery. It lands with a thud against the counter. He gives a slow nod with a smile.

"Do I want to know?" I ask.

"It's a Vitamix, Sweets."

"Not what it is. Do I want to know how much it cost?"

He shakes his head with a smile. "Probably not."

"Okay..."

As I walk away, I hear his voice trailing off. "Baby food... Baby food..."

Thirty-three weeks pregnant
168 pounds

While I'm sitting in one of our childbirth education classes at Hospital A, I feel a kind of nudging against my ribs and I remember that the baby's head is still there, nuzzling my heart. When I'm sentimental, it makes me cry. At other times, it annoys me. I push down against the baby's head to relieve the feeling of baby on bones.

The content of this class is divided into three evening sessions, but none of the information is really new to me. It's all similar to what I've read on-line and in popular pregnancy books. Stages of labor. When to call the doctor. Methods of managing contractions.

The couples in this class are surprising. Doug and I are one of two married couples in the sixteen-person class. The other couples are a hodge-podge: boyfriends and girlfriends, engaged couples, a mother-daughter pair, and one couple that looks like they hate each other. If I had to guess, I'd say the guy got her pregnant and now she's forcing him to attend classes with her. He sits with his arms crossed, chair pushed away from the table. Her elbows are propped on it as she scrolls, scrolls, scrolls on her phone. She is still in her business attire—pressed slacks, blouse, and jacket. But he has been shoved into a tight, untucked dress shirt. He is pale with a spotty black beard and thick glasses.

We are also the only couple that is not finding out the gender. Everyone else knows whether they are having a boy or a girl. And almost everyone is decidedly overweight or obese—with the exception of a slender young woman whose boyfriend slinks into the first class thirty minutes late. He doesn't return for the second session. During the break at the third session, the instructor quietly gives the woman a bag of baby clothes and items.

At the end of the that last class, the instructor opens the floor for questions. No one bites.

"Come on, guys," she kids. "What are you concerned about? Anything?"

Still nothing.

I sympathize with her. I hate it when I'm teaching and I can't get students to participate. So I lift my hand.

"I think the thing that concerns me the most, aside from labor," I confess, "is how I'm going to cope with all the interrupted sleep in the first few months."

She crosses her arms and gives a friendly smirk before she answers. "You know, it's true what they say—you'll never sleep the same again."

Oh, well, that's awesome.

"And it might be longer than a few months," she adds. "You might not sleep well for the first year."

"Right, I've heard that. So I guess I'm asking if you have any advice on how to deal with that. I'm a person who really needs sleep. I mean... I *love* sleep. I *need* sleep."

There's that smirk again. As if to say, *You are sooo going to be schooled.*

I hate that look.

It's Saturday morning and most of our friends are gathered around the table for breakfast. I wrap my hand around my favorite multi-colored striped ceramic mug. Doug bought it for me on our honeymoon. We didn't buy a set—just the one mug. Later, we tried to buy more of them, but all of our on-line searches had reached dead ends.

I rest the mug on top of my belly and something nudges against it. It doesn't feel like the head this time. It feels smaller. I wonder if the baby has turned head down. I push the bulge with my hand. It nudges back and then settles.

Ryan sees the gesture and says, "You okay over there?"

"Yeah... just the old baby-on-bones problem, Bear," I kid.

Ryan's fiancée, Cate, asks, "Any thoughts on what the baby's personality is like?"

I think for a moment and I'm surprised that I have an answer. "Actually, yeah. This is the most laid-back baby you can imagine."

A few heads turn in my direction.

"Why's that?" Cate asks.

I shrug. "The baby doesn't move just to move. It moves if it's trying to find a comfortable position, but it doesn't kick me just to be kicking something. It gets excited when I eat, but beyond that... Oh, and it loves to listen to people."

"And you know that because..."

"When it's too quiet, it starts nudging around, like it's wanting to know what's going on out here. Maybe that's because it has been listening to me teach for hours a day for weeks and weeks. Probably also because I'm having conversations like this all the time."

"What about you?" Sam asks Katy, who is just out of her first trimester. She and her husband, Jarod, are the other couple in our group of friends that is embarking on the journey of parenthood this year. Our babies will be born about four months apart. "Any thoughts on what the baby is like?"

"Too early to tell, I think," she laughs. "But if I had to guess, I'd say I'm giving birth to a black hole. I just eat and eat and eat all day long..."

July 2013

Thirty-four weeks pregnant

167 pounds

At my next prenatal appointment, I walk into the exam room and sit in the chair next to the table. I'm not getting on that thing until I need to. My doctor comes in, smiling ear to ear, and announces, "Well, we're not going to let you go much past your due date because I'm going to Italy!"

I offer a perfunctory chuckle while I try to figure out if she's serious.

"Yeah, my daughter is in Italy now," she continues. "So my husband and I are flying out for a visit on August 12. So, just letting you know where we're at with your due date and all..." She trails off as she glances over my information on the screen of her laptop. She sets it on the counter and starts typing in information. Her back faces me.

"Um... So..." I wonder how serious this development could be. "Are you saying that you might not be here for the delivery? What happens if you're not here?"

"I wouldn't worry about that because I have a way of getting babies to come when I'm here." She turns toward me with a smile and makes wide gestures with her hands. "You won't even believe it. It's like they *know* I'm leaving or coming back! I should tell you stories. But..." she rests her hand on my knee, "let's just say that you deliver and I'm not here, it's not a problem. I have a group of doctors that I partner with and one of them could deliver you. Same hospital."

She is nodding steadily even though I haven't said anything yet.

"Will they be okay with my birth plan?"

Still nodding. "We're all pretty similar, so I'm sure they'd have no problems with it."

"Should I make any appointments to meet them?"

She shakes her head and turns back to her laptop. "Let's worry about that later. We're not there yet."

"Okay, so... what do I need to do now?"

She taps on the screen of her computer with a stylus. "Well, we're going to take a swab for a Strep-B test. It's simple and you don't even have to worry about the results. It's not important until you're in labor and then if you're positive for Strep-B, we'll just give you some antibiotics during labor to make sure nothing transfers to the baby."

Thirty-six weeks pregnant

172 pounds

My prenatal appointments are scheduled for every week now. The baby is finally head-down and its back is facing outward, a good indication that my body is getting ready for labor. The cervical checks begin. My doctor digs her hand up into me and circles it around my cervix. It's uncomfortable, but I bite my lip through it.

"Well, that's about what I thought. Not dilated. Not effaced. And that's okay," she smiles.

This week, I've started to notice that my underwear doesn't fit like it used to. As I've been gaining weight, I've grown steadily into larger sizes, but this change seems so sudden.

I grab a measuring tape and wrap it around my hips, connecting the tape underneath my belly. My hips have spread one whole inch. Wow. It's a surprising change, but I'm not angry about it. In fact, I decide that I will be happy for the extra inch once labor sets in.

Cardio exercise has become more and more difficult. The baby is pushing my lungs upward, so I can't take a full breath anymore. And now that my hips have spread, I've finally developed the "pregnancy waddle." I still go to prenatal yoga, but the hospital exercise classes finished weeks ago. I make the decision that I'm at the point in my pregnancy when I should consider walking to be good exercise.

The last class that I take at Hospital A is a breastfeeding class. The teacher is a nurse who is certified as a lactation consultant. As I shift in my chair to find a comfortable position, I look down at my belly and see that it is asymmetrical. A large knob shifts to the right. I push at it. It pushes back and then shifts over to the left. I have no idea what body part it is. A foot? I have trouble imagining how the baby is folded up, so it's hard to tell.

The breastfeeding class is the most helpful of the classes that I've taken at the hospital. The nurse shows a video of a newborn baby that crawls to his mother's breast and latches just minutes after birth. The video came from a Swedish study that found that infants who were born from unmedicated births were more likely to latch successfully in the immediate moments after birth. I feel good about the results. Another reason to try to avoid medication, if possible.

We practice nursing holds with dolls and fake boobs (a bundled sock covered in pantyhose) and I learn that I'm supposed to hold my breast like a hamburger when offering it to my baby. I should line up my nipple to the baby's nose, tickle its chin, and then when its mouth is open at its widest point, I should pull the baby onto my breast. If the latch is painful, I should break the latch with my finger and try again.

For the last twenty minutes of the class, the nurse fields questions and there are many. *How long should I wait between having a beer and nursing? Is nursing painful? Is it really that bad to offer the baby a bottle of formula sometimes? When should I wean the baby? My sister got mastitis. How can I avoid getting that? What's a good nursing bra?*

The conversation is lively and interesting. An older mother who is attending the class with her daughter even joins in with her advice. "Don't go out and buy a bunch of nursing bras all at once. Let your milk fully come in, ladies! You will keep getting bigger and bigger and you'll ask yourself, 'When does it stop!'"

As the conversation dies down, the nurse asks, "Okay, any last questions?"

A woman on the left side of the room raises her hand. "I'm just wondering if it's possible that I might not make enough milk."

The nurse noticeably stiffens in her chair. "So the bottom line is—Feed your baby. Absolutely, feed your baby. If that means you use formula, then use formula. Having said that, ninety-five percent of women will have no problem making enough milk for their babies, provided that they feed the baby whenever the baby wants and for as long as the baby wants in those first days and weeks. All that nursing is going to tell your body how much milk to produce."

She pauses for a moment.

"Now, a lot of women think they don't make enough milk because their babies lose weight in the first week, but they usually regain it within a week. Your body will jump into action and rise to the challenge of feeding your baby. It's really amazing to see it happen. Just be mindful about granting uninterrupted access to feedings in those first days. I'm not saying that there aren't challenges or that it will be easy, but if you stick with it, it will get easier."

I feel great about her advice. I will stick with it. I can do this.

Thirty-seven weeks pregnant

173 pounds

I'm almost afraid to say this because I know I'm going to eat my words later, but...

I am so bored.

This is the first span of time in fifteen years when I haven't been working or moving to a new place or otherwise occupied. I had been looking forward to my annual teaching contract ending on June 30—no more heaving myself around all day long, sitting in uncomfortable chairs, or walking to and from the parking lot in the summer heat. I was going to finally have time to get everything ready for the baby. I was going to work on revising some short stories that I had been working on before I got pregnant. Until now, I had convinced myself that the reason I haven't touched them lately is because I've been too busy.

But now that I have the time, I'm starting to see that there is a strange suspension between who I am now and who I'm going to be. I don't feel that I can imagine or create anything until I know what this birth will mean in my life.

It's weird.

So I check out a stack of movies from the library. I Netflix. I read about signs of labor on-line and find a lovely matrix with the odds that I'll go into labor by certain dates. It's discouraging. *Only a fifty percent chance that I'll go into labor by the baby's due date? Geesh.* The good news is that I have a ninety percent chance of not being pregnant by August 23. But that is still five weeks away.

And then I start knitting. A wool diaper cover—newborn size. It's not my own pattern. What do I know about newborn diaper covers? But I pick up a pair of needles anyway, read through the directions, and start casting on. Each stitch is so small that focusing on each one makes me feel like giving up. (*It will take too long. This will never end. The baby will be four years old by the time I finish.*) So instead, I get lost in the motions of the needles. I find my rhythm and I keep going. I focus on three rows at a time, then five rows at a time. I take breaks. Sometimes I hammer out fifteen rows. And when I see a mistake, I stop and fix it. No matter how much I need to unravel to return to the problem, I go back and I fix it.

As the cover takes shape, I nod in satisfaction. Maybe I'll do a few more rows.

My doctor's cervical check at my thirty-seven week appointment yields more encouraging results. "Okay, you're doing something here." I feel her hand swiveling and probing. I dig my heels against each other to cope with the discomfort. "That's one centimeter, about fifty percent effaced... and your cervix is moving to the anterior position. All great signs!"

As I leave my appointment, my doctor happily points to all the possible dates when I could have my baby while she is in town.

"Any day of this week. This weekend, but not that one. I'm not on call."

I wonder why she is telling me this. As much as I believe in the mind-body relationship, I don't think I can tell this child which day to start labor.

Thirty-eight weeks pregnant

175 pounds

My doctor is still positive at my next appointment. "Two centimeters, seventy percent effaced," she announces during her cervical check. But something is different this time. This probing feels deeper, gruffer, and I'm shooting through the roof in pain. I wince and dig my heels against each other as my knees are bent, feet pressed together. My hands grip the sides of the table. When she pulls her hand free, I feel compelled to ask.

"Did you do something different or am I just becoming more sensitive to these checks? That was really, really painful."

"Well," she sighs. "That's because I'm getting more aggressive. I just stretched out your cervix manually, so you're a full two centimeters now."

"Oh..."

"You should expect some spotting after that." She types something into her laptop and the nurse hands me a pad. "Should we talk about inductions?" she asks without looking at me.

"I... really don't want an induction." I instantly hate my words. It sounds more like a request or a preference rather than my decision.

"I can tell you that you are not at an increased risk for a C-section if you have an induction right now." She turns back to face me.

"Right," I try to put together my rationale. "But I want to have a natural birth and everything that I've read about inductions says that an induction will probably make my contractions unmanageable without medication."

"Well, let's talk about this again next Monday, if you're still pregnant."

The cramps start on the way home from the appointment, and I think back to what my doctor said, *I just stretched out your cervix manually.* What did that mean?

When I start to browse the Internet, I realize that what she had really done was called "sweeping my membranes." She used her hand to manually separate my amniotic sac from my cervix. This releases prostaglandins—hormones that can trigger labor.

I have a way with getting babies to come on time, I remember her saying.

Indeed.

The cramps strengthen. They are like menstrual cramps and the only way that I know how to cope with them is to lie on my side on the couch and try to nap.

I didn't want an induction, but I guess it doesn't matter to my doctor. I don't want to rush this baby. If the baby needs more time, then I'll give it more time.

It's really hard to sleep at night. I keep heaving my belly from one side to the next, trying to find a good position. I get up about four times throughout the night to pee.

My belly has now reached my flap's capacity. It is a taught drum. When I look down at it, I see a few blue veins that I've never seen on my stomach. The stretching has brought them to the surface.

It's also really hard to move now. When I take walks, I wear a brace that wraps around my belly and supports it. If Doug drives, he helps me get in and out of his car. I look down at my legs and realize that I haven't shaved them in well over a week. The last time I shaved them, it was a struggle to manage it by myself, sitting on the edge of the bathtub, trying to see around my huge belly. Doug offers to help me. So I find myself standing in the bathtub, legs covered in shaving cream. I rotate like a rotisserie chicken while Doug shaves swatches of my long legs.

This guy...

August 2013

Thirty-nine weeks pregnant

178 pounds

When I return for my next appointment on a Monday, my doctor's first words are, "You were supposed to have your baby this weekend!"

"Ha." I give a forced laugh, but I'm not amused at all.

She turns to me and I get into position for a cervical check.

"Can you please not sweep my membranes this time?" I ask. "That was really painful last time." *God, I hate my words.* I don't want to be polite. I'm angry at her for not asking for my consent to do that. And yet I'm still making requests instead of just saying what I don't want.

"Sure, no problem," she says as she probes me. "Three centimeters, seventy-five percent effaced," she announces. She turns away from me and toward her laptop, which is resting on the counter.

"So what I'll tell you is that if you have an induction this week, you don't have any factors that would increase your risk of a C-section."

"I really don't want an induction," I say. *Ugh! My words! Why can't I be assertive?*

"Okay, but what I can tell you is that I won't be able to deliver this baby past Friday afternoon, which is August 10."

"But I still have five days for the baby to come, right?"

"Yeah..." she trails off.

"So... let's say you're not here for the birth. Should I meet with these other doctors?"

"If you go past your due date, you'll need to schedule an appointment with them for a non-stress test to make sure that the baby is okay. So you'll have a chance to meet them then. But you know, these doctors may not want to let you go all the way to forty-two weeks, the way that I would. They may not let you go past forty-one weeks. And then you may have to have an induction anyway."

"Right..." I think about what she is saying. *But you won't let me go to forty-two weeks because you're not going to be here anyway. So my choice is be induced at thirty-nine weeks with you or be induced at forty-one weeks without you? What if I go into labor naturally? Isn't that still an option?*

"But whatever you decide," she crosses her arms, "I hope that you also respect the desires of these doctors and not go past the timeframe that they are comfortable with. Okay?"

"Oh. Okay." I say quickly.

I feel like an inconvenience, like I should feel badly that I'm creating a hiccup in this plan, but I'm starting to care less and less about what this doctor and the other doctors think about me. Who is having the baby here? What should take priority? Having the baby by a certain date or having the baby when the baby is ready?

August 10, 2013

Forty weeks pregnant

177 pounds

It's Saturday, my due date, and my doctor is officially out of the country. Yay. I will have to check in with this new practice on Monday.

We decide to take a trip to Whole Foods. We walk around the store. Or rather, Doug walks around the store, while I waddle slowly from aisle to aisle. An employee is demonstrating the power of a Vitamix blender. He tosses in vegetable after vegetable, all obliterated by the Vitamix.

Next to the demonstration booth is a pyramid of these amazing blenders with a sign announcing their sale price: $500 each.

I see Doug across the produce department. He's looking at pomegranates. I point to the sign. He makes an O with his mouth. And then shrugs. Then he mouths, "Baby food..."

Oh my God...

I turn down the snack aisle and consider the cookies. We meet up again at the end of the aisle, where a woman is offering samples of yogurt from a local dairy, Snowville Creamery.

"Would you like to try some?" she asks me.

"Sure." I take a sample. "Wow, that's really good!"

As I'm selecting which variety of yogurt to buy, she asks me, "When's your baby due?"

"Today," I say. I've been waiting all year to say that.

"What!" she looks at my belly. "You're kidding me! Wow, you carry it well."

"Ugh," I put my hand on my lower back. "This baby is so low in my hips. It just knocks around in there, all day."

"Boy or girl?"

"I don't know. We're going to be surprised."

"Good for you! Isn't that the best kind of surprise?"

I nod. "Yes! Yes, it is!"

"So you feeling anything going on yet?"

I shake my head. "Not really. I mean, I have some contractions on and off, but nothing regular."

"Well, maybe it will be today!"

"Maybe," I smile. Then, I realize what I'm actually wishing for. Labor. Pain. Major pain.

"Well, I just wish you the best. To you and your baby."

"Aw, thanks."

Before we walk away, Doug picks up a second tub of yogurt for me.

We walk down a few more aisles, and I start to feel a contraction. I pause for a minute to feel it. I tell Doug that I'm going to sit down in the café area until he is ready to leave. As I sit there, I feel a few more contractions. Nothing painful. Just tightness. I put my hand on my belly, waiting for the next one.

Doug walks up. "Ready?"

"I'm having some contractions."

"Really?"

"Yeah, but maybe it's because I was walking around so much."

"Well, let's keep walking and see if they go away."

The contractions continue, even as we get in the car and drive away. While I'm sitting there, I feel one wrap around my lower back.

"Oh... That was a different one."

"Do you think this is it?" he asks.

"I mean, that one was really different, so..."

We start to get excited. I give him constant updates as we drive home. We time them. Four minutes apart. Six minutes apart. Five minutes apart. Then, ten minutes apart. Then nothing.

"Well, maybe that was it," I tell him as we are putting groceries away.

"Is that normal?"

I nod. "It could just be my body getting ready."

But later that night, they start up again. Five minutes apart. Six minutes. Five minutes. Ten minutes.

"Maybe this is it," I tell him. He is smiling. I look at the clock. It's ten. "I'm going to go ahead and sleep while I can."

"Okay, I'm going to go clean the car."

"Your car is already clean."

"No, I mean, take it to the car wash."

"What?"

"I'm not bringing a baby home in a dirty car."

"Whatever," I laugh. "Go do what you're going to do."

August 11, 2013

Forty weeks and one day

I woke up this morning with no contractions. Nothing. I sit around the house again, wondering what is going on in there. I take a walk. Nothing happens.

Doug helps me take my mind off labor by inviting Ryan (a.k.a. Bear) and Sam (a.k.a. Toad) to our house. We watch *The Neverending Story* and laugh at the creepy way that Falcor groans, *I liiike chiiildreeen.*

The laughing helps. A lot.

August 12, 2013

Forty weeks and two days

I start getting more and more questions about whether the baby is coming. Friends and family start sending more messages, Facebook posts, and emails. I realize that I'm now retreating into seclusion because I don't want to deal with the barrage of opinions about what I should do to get labor going. My parents have planned to drive from Minnesota on August 17. A few weeks ago, I liked this plan. But now I'm wondering just how much time I'll have to cope with a new baby before they arrive.

I still believe that this baby will start labor when it's ready and I won't interfere with that process until I have medical evidence that says I should be induced.

So far, the reasons for me being induced are 1) I'm tired of being pregnant and 2) my doctor is going on vacation. Nothing medical about that yet.

I schedule an appointment with the new practice to which I've been transferred. The office is located in a building adjacent to the hospital. When I walk in, I have the distinct feeling that I have entered a machine, gears turning, chugging, and advancing in regular intervals. The waiting room can easily hold forty people. There are four receptionists and a constant stream of nurses and doctors moving to and fro. Patients are checked in and checked out, sometimes two or three at a time.

But the office's efficiency comes at the cost of accuracy. It takes the receptionists some discussion to understand how to process and bill a transferred patient—me—who has never seen any of these doctors. Doug and I are eventually shuttled back without explanation to a tiny room with a window and a machine. The nurse tells me to have a seat.

"Can we at least talk to a doctor at some point?" I ask.

The nurse seems puzzled. "I thought you were just coming in for an NST."

"I literally don't know what you're talking about," I say. "What is an NST?"

"Okay, so you're... whose patient?" she asks.

I tell her the name of my doctor and explain that I've been transferred to this practice.

"So you've never seen any of our doctors before?"

"No, never."

"Okay, you will. Sorry about that. We just need to do this non-stress test before you see the doctor. You'll get to see her though."

She attaches some cords around my belly. They look like the EFM machine that I saw on the hospital tour. Then, she hands me a cord with a button attached to the end of it, like one of those controllers on a game show. She explains that I should push the button whenever I feel the baby move. Then, she leaves us alone in the room.

The chair that I'm sitting in is large, cushy, and reclined. In this position, the baby has tons of room to relax and spread out, which poses a problem for this test. The baby moves mostly when it's in a cramped position. Then, it will shift from side to side, as if trying to make more room. But I'm not sure if I'm allowed to sit up. Maybe the chair is reclined this way for a reason and I might throw off the results if I'm not positioned in a certain way.

Time passes. A small stream of paper advances every few seconds from the machine and the paper is slowly spooling onto the ground. It seems to be recording the baby's heart rate.

The nurse comes back about five minutes later and reviews the spooled paper on the ground.

"Do I have to stay in this position?" I ask.

"No, you can move around if you need to." Her eyes scan the data on the paper.

• "Yeah, because I don't think the baby is going to move unless I sit up."

Doug asks, "Are we allowed to talk to it or touch her belly to get it moving?"

The nurse looks up from the paper and says, "Oh, yeah! Of course. Are you calling the baby 'it' because you didn't find out?"

I nod. "I love surprises and this is the best kind."

"Wow, you're strong. I couldn't wait that long to find out. I wanted to paint my baby's nursery and get ready."

I smile politely. We have painted the baby's room, but it's a neutral theme: forest friends. We have a lot of neutral newborn clothes and I figure that there will be plenty of people showing up with boy or girl outfits after the baby is born.

"Yeah so," the nurse continues, "whatever you want to do. We just need to make sure the baby is moving enough."

When she leaves, I wonder about the validity of this test. *We can do whatever we want? What's the point here? Just to make sure it's not dead?*

Once I sit up and we start talking to the baby and prodding my belly, the baby responds. It kicks back and nuzzles to the side. Doug points out that when I tense up, the baby's heart rate speeds up. *Great*, I think. *I'm stressing my child out.*

When the nurse returns to view the newest results, she is positive.

"Did you feel like you had any contractions during this time?"

"Yeah, but they come and go like that. They're not regular."

"Okay, great. Let's get your urine sample and get you in an exam room."

The hallway is bustling with activity. Nurses are shuttling patients from room to room. When they close the door behind the couples, they hurry to another location. My nurse hands me a clear tiny cup. There is no lid or place to mark my name. At first, I wonder if I asked for water.

"There's a bathroom right there." She points to a door.

"Oh, right." *I'm supposed to pee in this?*

When I finish the task, I open the bathroom door and the nurse is gone. I'm holding my cup of pee while new couples whiz by me into new rooms. Doug is gone, too. I look around for someone to help me.

Just then, my nurse comes around the corner. "Oh! I'll take that."

Then she takes me into the exam room where Doug and one of the doctors are waiting.

Dr. M seems to be just a few years older than me. She wears her hair in a ponytail and she pivots around the room in tennis shoes. I like her casual nature. Maybe she'll be okay with my birth plan. She does the requisite cervical check. It's uncomfortable, but not nearly as painful as the last few with my own doctor.

"The baby's head is literally right there." She tells me as she washes her hands. "It's low. But the baby seems fine. Everything looks good. You're three centimeters, about seventy percent effaced. This appointment is mostly just to see if you have any questions for me about what to expect."

"So it's you and four other doctors that might be delivering me?"

"Right."

"I do have a few questions about the birth. I just want to make sure that we're on the same page."

"Okay."

"Like, do you care if I have a Heparin lock instead of a continuous IV? I want to stay as mobile as possible."

"Assuming that everything is going well, I don't see a problem with that."

"Okay," I start listing my other questions on my fingers. "And the monitoring. Is it okay to have intermittent monitoring? Like twenty minutes out of every hour on the monitor, forty minutes off?"

She shifts from one foot to the other. "Well, again, assuming everything's okay, that would be possible. But we'd need to have some kind of monitoring for sure."

"Right, yeah." I nod. "And inductions. My other doctor was willing to let me go to forty-two weeks before inducing me. Is that also okay with you?"

She draws in a breath before answering. "So... Really, we don't want you to go much past forty-one weeks. I mean, you're already at forty weeks and two days. And the longer the baby is in you, the more weight it's putting on. And a larger baby can cause problems for you."

I look down at my belly and think back to all the comments from others when I would tell them how far along I was. *Really? You carry it so well!*

"So forty-one weeks? Is that what I'm hearing?" I ask.

"I wouldn't want to go much further than that. But, if you really want to go all the way to forty-two, I think we'll let you do that."

Let me? Wow, thank you for your permission, I think.

"I think just one more thing then," I think about all my questions. "Oh, right, what about progress? Will you want me to have Pitocin?"

"Um... Do you mean will I have you on Pitocin right away?"

"Or, just if I don't make progress. In your judgment."

She casts her eyes downward and shifts again from foot to foot. "Look, we're going to try to let you labor as naturally as possible, if that's what you want. But at the end of the day, we have to be concerned about your health and the baby's health. And if the baby needs to come out sooner, then I want you to be open to interventions to help the baby out."

"Oh, I am. I mean, if it comes down to the health of me and the baby, I'll do whatever needs to be done..."

Am I coming across as too pushy, I wonder. *Hell, I don't care anymore. I'm going to be as direct as possible here because I don't know these people. I need to know what I'm in for.*

"So, Pitocin?" she repeats. "It depends. I'll try to follow your birth plan as you want it, but we have to keep an open mind."

I leave the appointment feeling that at least she knows where I stand on my birth plan. And hopefully, the other doctors will too.

August 13, 2013

Forty weeks and three days

Today is Tuesday. I feel like a ticking time bomb. It's like all the pieces have been moved into position and I'm just waiting for my water to break. But it feels like it's going to be a slow labor. My body has slowly been ramping up the efforts for this delivery over the past three weeks, so I shouldn't be surprised that this baby isn't dying to get out.

I keep a legal pad next to me as I watch movies and read some short stories by Joyce Carol Oates. I write down when a contraction starts and ends, and record the time between them. Ten minutes apart. Then twenty minutes. Then six minutes. What does it all mean? All I can determine is that it means I'm not going to the hospital yet.

I decide to not spend another day sitting around the house, waiting for something to happen. I exercise even though my hips are sore and my lower back aches. After I shower, I look at my nails and decide to go get a manicure and pedicure. Because, why not?

While I'm sitting there and my manicurist is massaging my feet, I daydream.

I try to visualize not being pregnant. No giant belly. No forty pounds of extra weight. No more of the baby digging its head against my cervix and the sharp jabs of pain that ensue. No more shallow breaths because I can't take a full one. No more people telling me to enjoy life now... *because once that baby comes out...*

Then, I imagine the moment when everything settles down and I am finally in the recovery room. I will have earned a lovely, non-pregnant nap. Nurses and visitors will say, "Wow, she did an awesome job! Ah... Poor thing. She's tired. Shh... Let's not wake her." And then I'll sleep for a solid, uninterrupted three hours. No getting up to pee all the time. No heaving myself from side to side.

Ahh... So nice...

The Flux

R obbie Davis-Floyd, an anthropologist who pioneered the academic exploration of birth within American culture, observed that, "the near-constant inner and outer flux of pregnancy keeps the category systems of pregnant women in a continuous state of upheaval as old ways of thinking change to include new life" (2003, p. 24). In other words, pregnancy is all about flux. Not only do you feel and look differently, but you think differently.

I thought differently about birth. After reading and researching, I found myself abandoning my perceptions that birth was inherently dangerous and therefore required the highest technology possible for good outcomes. And then I started to think about how to preserve birth as a natural process.

I also thought differently about myself and about Doug. What kind of parents would we become? Would we push strollers and engage in toddler talk, too? Davis-Floyd insightfully describes the magnitude of these thoughts and concerns: "Hopes and fears from the past and for the future merge at the surface of [the pregnant woman's] daily consciousness, as time compresses in the physical experience of pregnancy, and past, present, and future together are carried in her womb" (p. 24).

Whoa.

So pregnant women find themselves in a strange limbo of being— yet not being. Kind of a mother—but not really.

Flux drives us to cling to certainty. Throughout my pregnancy, I felt an ongoing internal struggle between my desire to maintain control and the necessity of my surrender. As an individual, I wanted to feel in control of the pregnancy. I wanted to believe that I would bear the responsibility for conceiving and delivering a healthy baby. But it took time to acknowledge that this desire for control could never really be fulfilled. If I ever thought that I had control, it was an illusion. Although anything I ate, drank, or breathed could influence the baby, I could not completely control all of the variables in pregnancy to make sure that we would both survive the journey.

So coping with the flux becomes a central theme throughout my pregnancy narrative, and as I reflect on my experience, I can see several ways that I did this.

Dealing with the Flux as an Academic

I'm an academic. There, I've said it. I've managed to find that one vein in the field of education where I can receive both the most prestige and the lowest salary. But, hey, I'm an addict. I could have gotten out a while ago, but I keep coming back. There's just something hopeful about being surrounded by people who care about exploring and learning.

So as an academic pregnant woman, I was driven to read. I researched. I pondered my role in childbirth. I wondered how to have the healthiest birth possible. I took classes. I hired a knowledgeable doula to help me through labor. And after having acquired all of this knowledge, I was able to be at ease, so I could surrender to the process of labor. Acquiring knowledge helped me build confidence in the ability of my body to give birth. It helped me to develop expectations for the birth. It gave me a voice to use with my doctor. Knowledge made it possible for me to experience peace in surrendering.

Dealing with the Flux as a Health Advocate

I've never been much of a health advocate for myself. I typically followed whatever course of treatment a doctor recommended. And if I didn't like the advice, I didn't take it. And if refusing a treatment made my health worse, I just blamed myself for not following advice. It's my life, in my hands.

But—whoa—then I started making decisions for another person. A person who couldn't disagree with me. A person whose life depended on my good judgment. So I started to take on the role of health advocate. In fact, becoming my child's health advocate was the first robust role that I experienced as a new mother. It was a natural extension of my quest for knowledge. As I researched information about how to have a safe pregnancy and delivery, I began to see how closely connected my health was to my baby's health.

I didn't anticipate that becoming my baby's health advocate would create conflict with my doctor. I can see now that my doctor was a good choice for the woman who I was at the beginning of my pregnancy—but she was not the doctor for the woman that I had become by the end of my pregnancy. She had served me well as my gynecologist for ten years, probably because there wasn't much to disagree about. Since I was healthy, my annual gynecological visits involved a pelvic exam, a Pap smear, and a breast exam. And that was it.

But then she became my obstetrician.

Suddenly, there was a lot to discuss.

I sense that my doctor knew about this jump from gynecologist to obstetrician. At the end of my nine-week appointment when she asked if I had "any other questions," she paused for a while, as if giving me time to ask something profound. This would have been the perfect time for me to start the conversation about her philosophies about giving birth, but—quite frankly—I was not prepared for this conversation. I was just beginning to accept that I was pregnant. I didn't have the desire yet to read and research beyond conception and the first trimester. So I certainly was not ready to assume the active role of being my baby's health advocate.

After the twenty-week ultrasound, I started to feel the urgency to become more educated about labor and birth. Until that point, I had mostly just gawked at the cut-away diagrams of a baby's head pushing through a vagina and researched how to avoid tearing during delivery. My first instinct had been to preserve myself. But a new instinct started to emerge after I saw that squirming baby on the ultrasound. This wasn't a tiny flicker on the screen anymore. This was our child. And so, I started to feel those first pangs of maternal instinct. I started to care about protecting the baby.

For me, this instinct fueled my desire to increase my knowledge about birth. It helped me to move from passive patient to active, birthing mother.

Around thirty-one weeks of pregnancy, I felt that I had learned enough about my options in childbirth to talk with my doctor about a birth plan. Unfortunately, I found that my doctor's approach to labor and delivery works best with women who prefer to take on a passive role in the process—the "doctor knows best" approach. Although I did value my obstetrician's expertise and advice, I often felt that she regarded her experience as more important in decision-making than my own desires for the birth. My personality and temperament seemed to have no bearing on how she counseled me about what might happen during labor and birth.

This seemed very strange to me.

At moments when I tried to position myself as an active participant in the process—for example, when I asked if I should schedule appointments with any of the other doctors who might deliver my child in her absence—she encouraged me to slip back into the passive patient role: "I have a way with getting babies to come when I'm here" and "Let's worry about that later."

But I didn't stay passive. Knowing about the risks of a medical labor induction led me to do something uncharacteristic—I questioned my doctor. I even resisted her when I believed her recommendations were not in the best interest of my baby. To my own embarrassment today, I didn't use strong language to show how I really felt, but I said enough to voice my dissent. And when my doctor transferred me to another practice, I became even more vocal about what I wanted during labor.

In hindsight, I should have discussed my birth plan with my doctor much sooner, perhaps right after the twenty-week ultrasound. Still, I wonder how realistic that timeframe is for a first-time mother. It takes time to cope with the flux of pregnancy. It takes time to accept that labor and delivery will happen. So it is hard for me to imagine being ready to have this conversation earlier than I was.

Dealing with the Flux as a Consumer

As I reflect now on how I changed throughout pregnancy, the most surprising reflection is that the active process of figuring out my identity as a mother started with decisions about what to buy. "Go pick out baby furniture," my obstetrician recommended.

I didn't realize it then, but the process of putting together a baby registry helps expectant parents enter an unfamiliar world by asking them to put on their comfortable, well-worn hats as consumers. We may not know how to be parents, but by God, we know how to read reviews on Amazon. And adding things to a baby registry feels like a shopping spree—until you realize that it's also an exercise in determining how you will be a parent.

After we finished putting the registry together, I realized that the products that we had chosen actually conveyed messages to my family and friends about what kinds of decisions we had already made about parenting. The products suggested that I would be breastfeeding, that we valued organic products, and that we were going to use cloth diapers. But then the registry also reflected the decisions that we weren't sure about: soft carriers *and* strollers, multiple car seats, and multiple types of bottles.

But the hard truth is that forging a new identity takes time and experience. It requires that you actually live in that new role. And therein lies the struggle. Pregnant women desire to forge their identities as mothers, yet they are unable to do this as long as they are pregnant. So taking on smaller, definable tasks serves a purpose. It helps pregnant women to try out the shoes of motherhood even if they are still a size too big. They can still learn some of the steps for walking in these shoes. They can try to imagine the patterns and rhythms of motherhood. And those rhythms help pregnant women to find comfort in following a process, even when the big questions remain unanswered.

Labor and Birth

Wednesday, August 14

6:00 a.m.

I stir in bed. Something doesn't feel right. Then, something dribbles out of me.

Now, I'm awake.

My water has broken! It's time!

I run to the bathroom and drop my pants.

It's blood.

"Doug," I call. "Doug, wake up."

"Huh?"

"I'm bleeding."

That gets his attention. He flips out of bed while I grab my cell phone and call my doula.

Pam tells me to not panic. "It could just be cervical blood which means your cervix is changing. How much is there?"

"Kind of a lot. I'm still bleeding. Like I'll probably need to wear a pad."

"Okay, I would call the doctor and see what they want you to do."

I reach the doctor on call. She asks me if my ultrasounds have been normal (yes) and if I have recently had sex (no). She groggily orders me to go to the hospital to be checked. I change into new pants, but we bring the bloody pajamas in case they want to see them. We leave without bags, expecting to come home. Before I leave the house, I grab a granola bar because I have a feeling it will be a while before I eat again. On our way to the hospital, I realize that the doctor didn't really tell us where we should go, but I assume that we should go to Labor and Delivery and not the emergency room.

6:45 a.m.

We arrive at the double doors in front of the Labor and Delivery Unit and Doug presses the intercom button. The doors open.

"Weren't they supposed to ask for our names?" I ask.

Doug shrugs.

The halls are quiet, except for the light banter between the nurses at the front desk. Some nurses are typing information at computer stations, periodically pushing back and forth in their swiveling chairs. A receptionist greets us and I explain why we are there. No one seems alarmed that I'm bleeding. They even take a few moments to make sure that my pre-registration forms are accurate. Then they admit me to the triage area.

The triage area is a row of five hospital beds, each separated by a light curtain. A nurse shows me to my bed. "I'm your nurse. My name is Sharon."

"Oh, me too."

She gives a simple smile and nod. She doesn't seem unkind—just too practical to find humor in coincidence. I also wonder if working as an L & D nurse has raised her threshold of what qualifies as a surprise.

The bed has what looks like a larger version of a dog pee pad. I assume its purpose is to catch whatever comes out of me.

"Here's a gown," the nurse offers me along with a clear, plastic drawstring bag. "You can put all of your clothes in this bag here. I'll give you a minute and then I'll come back."

I don't really want to be in a hospital gown already, but the doctor will probably want to do a cervical check whenever she (or he) arrives. I go ahead and change into it. Should I leave on my underwear? I guess so. Otherwise, I'll be bleeding all over the floor. But isn't that what the human pee pad is for? That seems a little gross though. I decide to keep my underwear on. Still, I feel pretty naked already.

After I put my clothes into the clear bag, I add the bloody pajama pants. Then, I take them out and fold them so that the blood is hidden.

When the nurse comes back, she picks up some cords and stretchy bands that look like colored Ace bandages. They are attached to the electronic fetal monitor. I cringe.

"Will I have to wear these the whole time?" I ask.

"For now, yes, because we need to get a baseline and see how you're doing. Later, you may be able to take them off."

"All right..." I sigh.

She wraps one around my hips and positions the monitoring device close to the right side of my pelvis.

"This one will pick up the baby's heartbeat," she says.

And it does immediately. *Wahn-wahn-wahn-wahn* enters the conversation.

She wraps another monitor around what used to be my waist and rests it on the top of my belly.

"And this one will measure your contractions."

Once she leaves, I realize that I have to pee. I look at the cords and bands and wonder how problematic it would be to unplug them to go to the bathroom.

"I have to go to the bathroom," I tell Doug.

He calls the nurse back and she shows me how to unplug the cords and wrap them around my neck. Doug holds the back of my gown closed as we amble toward the restroom next to the triage area. In the bathroom, I see that the bleeding hasn't slowed yet. I take in a breath and try not to think about it.

Once we return to my bed, Nurse Sharon takes my vitals, fastens an ID band around my wrist, and asks me a list of medical questions. It's hard to pay attention because behind the adjacent curtain, a woman is talking to two nurses who are prepping her for a C-section. I eavesdrop on their conversation between questions.

"Yeah, the last time I had a C-section, I was nervous, but now I'm like... let's just do it." She and the nurse talk about how to celebrate the birth. They list their favorite restaurants in the area.

Nurse Sharon finishes with the questions and tells us that some lab techs will be in to take my blood and then it will be about an hour before the results are back.

"Would you like to watch TV?" she asks.

"Um, okay. Where?"

She pulls a monitor that is attached to the bed in front of me.

"Oh, I thought that was some kind of medical equipment."

She smiles and shows me how to change the channels.

A Baby Story is airing on TLC and Doug and I watch two episodes. In one episode, a woman labors freely in a tub of water with midwives. She cries out in pain and doubts herself, and when the baby finally emerges, I'm moved to tears. In the next episode, a woman says her birth plan is, "littered with the word *epidural*." Her pregnancy diet is full of Dairy Queen and Taco Bell, and the camera follows her there to prove it. When she goes into labor, it lasts for days, both at home and in the hospital. When she finally pushes, she does so for six hours with an oxygen mask attached to her face. She exhausts herself with ineffective pushes. The baby is finally extracted with a vacuum and all is deemed well. I am horrified.

Time passes and Doug seems a little concerned.

"Look," I motion to the reception desk. "No one is jumping to do anything for us, so it can't be that serious. And I still prefer this over the boredom of yesterday. That was driving me nuts."

"Yeah..." He looks around the tiny triage room. "You think we might need our stuff? We might be here a while."

"Go ahead and get the bags," I tell him. "Can you also call Pam and ask her to come?"

9:30 a.m.

I hear a cart rolling down triage alley and it stops at my curtain.

"Are you here to take my blood?" I ask in my friendliest voice. Maybe if I act like drawing my blood is not a big deal, my body will believe me. I really don't want to pass out right now.

"Yes, ma'am," the older technician says. She is accompanied by a younger tech, who stays with the cart.

"I have to tell you," I confess, "I have little veins that are hard to get."

"Is that right?" the older one asks. "Which arm is better?"

"My left."

She prods my arm a little and then returns to the cart. I look away.

"You excited to meet your little one?" the younger tech asks me.

"Yes," I smile. "I don't know if I'm having a boy or a girl, so it's extra exciting for me."

"Oh, girl, I couldn't do that. I like to be prepared."

The older one is prodding my arm again. Then the tourniquet. Then the stick. A pause. Then a dig. I wince. The younger tech comes over and talks her through it. I realize then that the older tech is still in training. I start to take deep breaths as the digging continues. Then I take small, shallow breaths.

"Are you having a contraction, hon?" the younger tech asks.

"No, I'm trying not to pass out."

"Oh, we got it now. Okay, relax honey."

She switches in a new vial. Then another new vial. Then another. I keep breathing.

When it's all over the older tech attaches a green ID band around my arm, loose enough to slide to my bicep. Two bands already. If I'm lucky, maybe I'll get a third one.

9:45 a.m

I call Nurse Sharon.

"I'm really, really hungry," I tell her.

"Okay, we have all kinds of clear liquids to eat. Chicken broth, some Italian ice, Jell-O, soda. Do any of those sound good?"

"Do I have to be on clear liquids already? I don't even know if I'm staying yet."

"I'm sorry sweetie, but yes. For the time being."

"Then I'll have one of everything."

She brings a small tray of tiny treats and I devour them all.

10:00 a.m.

Pam arrives and we chat a little about what might be happening with my labor and a lot about other things happening in our lives. She and her family will be going on a camping trip soon. I tell her, "As unpleasant as this is, I still prefer sitting in the hospital rather than sitting at home waiting for something to happen."

11:00 a.m.

The Price is Right is on and Pam and I watch it together, hoping for Plinko. I see a pair of rubber clogs moving below the edge of the curtain.

It's Nurse Sharon.

"So just wanted to let you know that the final results will be back around noon, but the preliminary results look good. And I've been watching your contractions and they're fairly regular, about six to seven minutes apart. Things are looking good."

11:45 a.m.

Doug has returned.

"I mean, what kinds of tests are they doing?" he asks.

I shrug. "I have no idea. She said things look good so far."

He presses the call button and within a minute Nurse Sharon is back.

"So the test that they're doing," she explains, "requires them to separate all the maternal and fetal cells and count them. That's why it takes so long. The test will show whether or not the placenta is detaching."

Doug asks a few more questions about the test, but I start zoning out. Food is on my mind again. My body knows that it's lunch time and it's expecting something sizable.

"Can I have more snacks?" I ask.

1:00 p.m.

Dr. M finally arrives and, as I expected, she wants to do a "quick" cervical check.

I get into position: legs against the bed, knees bent out, feet together. It's a standard exam—a quick in, check around, and out, but it's still uncomfortable enough that I push my feet together to get through it.

"Still three centimeters," she reports as she tosses a slightly bloody glove into the garbage. "The test results came back normal, and that's good. You're having regular contractions, and that's good. But I just..." she shifts from one foot to the other. She positions her hands like there is an invisible box between them and she's turning it around so we can see every side. Her gaze lands on this box. "I would be so much more comfortable if we could keep an eye on you here. It's just... if your placenta *does* detach then... just, terrible, terrible things could happen. I don't even want to tell you what."

"Okay..." I look at her and she makes eye contact. Then, my eyes wander to this invisible box that she has created in her hands. "So the test results are normal, but you want me to stay?"

"Yes."

"All right, but my concern is that I can't stay in this hospital throughout my whole early labor without real food. I mean, I could be here until tomorrow, right? So how can I have a natural labor without food?"

She blinks a few times. *Did this really not occur to her*, I wonder.

She says to my nurse, "Okay, so let's get her meals for today and get her a room."

I guess I have given my consent to be admitted.

Then, she continues. "I'll allow you to labor as you want until tomorrow morning at six. But if you haven't made enough progress, we'll need to talk about augmentation. It's not an induction because you're already in labor."

"Well, what does that mean? What would you do?"

"We'll either give you Pitocin or break your water. But let's just see how it goes today."

After she leaves, I ask Pam which is the better option.

"Have them break your water. It's the more natural of the two."

When Pam leaves to make a phone call, Doug takes my hand into his and just holds it.

I stare down at my belly beneath the green gown. Whose belly is this? This isn't what it looks like. Where is my cute shirt? I'm not in hospital mode yet. I start to cry.

"Hey... What's going on?" Doug asks.

I look at the triage curtains around my bed, all the beige, the pastels, the grays beneath fluorescent lights. Where can I relax around here? Where can I get some food? What can I eat? Are the pillows going to be comfortable enough? What do I need? I feel like I've just been placed on the conveyor belt of delivery, chugging away toward my stamped delivery date: tomorrow, 6:00 a.m.

"I thought we'd be able to go home. I don't want to stay here the whole time. I want to go home."

"We're going to get you comfortable here and we'll get this going," he says. "You're going to be okay. And if something happens, we're here and we're close to help, okay?"

I nod, but something else still bothers me.

This is the beginning of the end of me—at least the *me* that I know right now. I haven't wanted to fully accept that my life is going to change. All this time, I've been trying to make plans for how I would work a baby into all the contours of my current life, but I know now that plan will never work. These aren't modifications coming down the line. This is real change. Real, life-shifting change.

This is it. And I'm not ready.

1:45 p.m.

Nurse Sharon moves us from triage to a Labor and Delivery room. As we unpack our bags, we realize that Doug didn't bring the baby book for the baby's footprints. A white dry-erase board hangs on the wall. The nurse writes *Sharon* on it. She pauses, and then writes *Sharon* again. Then she adds labels next to each: *Mother* and *Nurse*.

Hm. Mother. Wow.

"What are you having dear? A boy or a girl?" she asks, marker posed against the board.

"We don't know. It's a surprise, but I think it's a boy." I smile.

She writes, *Boy?* Then she asks, "Did you bring your birth plan?"

We look for it in the bags, but we can't find it. Pam has a copy and gives it to the nurse.

"Great. I'll make sure to give this to the doctor."

I'm surprised at how pleasantly she asked for it. I thought there would be a little bit of an attitude about having a birth plan, but she seemed happy to deliver it. I feel better about having created one.

2:30 p.m.
Doug leaves to get the baby book.

2:45 p.m.
I tell Pam to go home and that we'll call her back once we need her.

"It could be a while before things really get going," I say.

"Okay, but really," she picks up her bag and slings it over her shoulder, "you need to sleep as much as possible. You're going to need your energy for the end, so please, please, please, don't exhaust yourself now. Sleep!" She draws the blinds closed before she leaves the room.

And that is what I do.

3:00 p.m.
I nap.

Doug returns and quietly organizes our bags and belongings: a small roller suitcase, a diaper bag, a nursing pillow, and some snacks. Nurse Sharon arrives with a fat, movable, folded mattress for Doug. When he unfolds it, I see a huge black bar that will dig into the middle of his back as he sleeps. Poor guy.

When I'm hungry, I order a cheeseburger, a baked potato, a salad, a yogurt parfait, and some juice.

7:00 p.m.

Our night nurse arrives. Her name is Karen and she speaks with a serious, furrowed brow, but then breaks into smiles and sarcastic humor to lighten the mood. She says that she has seen my birth plan and she likes it. She tells me that we're going to get my labor going.

"The bed is your enemy!" she jokes.

I like her already. We make a plan to do some walking after I get some rest.

Doug takes a call from his brother and gives him an update. The only people that know that we're in the hospital are my parents, my sister, and Doug's immediate family. We tell them not to come to the hospital, and they stay away. I am so grateful. It's not that I don't want to share our baby, but I know that I would be constantly thinking about the people in the waiting room and pressuring myself to hurry the process along. This is also why we haven't even told our friends that we're in the hospital. I want to be relaxed throughout this process and feeling like people are waiting on me is not what I need.

10:00 p.m.

Before we have a chance to lie down, Karen comes in and comments on the focal point pictures that I've asked Doug to post on the walls.

Doug tells her that they are pictures from our vacation to Maui last year. Then the two of them chat about Hawaii for what seems like forever while my contractions come and go. They feel stronger than this morning, but I feel only mildly distracted while they are happening. If I were feeling more talkative, I would like to tell them why I chose these pictures.

I chose a sunset because it was just one beautiful moment in a series of moments. It wasn't necessarily the most beautiful, but it is the one that we were able to capture. It is true contentment.

I chose a landscape with mountains in the background because the land is calm after years of upheaval. In a college geology class, I learned that Hawaii was created by an underwater volcanic eruption that reached the surface of the water and cooled into islands—but you would never know this by just appreciating its beauty. You have to peel back layers of lush vegetation and color to see the scars underneath. It is true beauty.

I chose a tall tree because of its deep roots that reach into the earth for nourishment and its branches that reach out to God for growth. It draws power from the earth and offers its fruit to everyone else. It is a conduit, a vehicle. It is immovable not because of vanity or pride, but because of its purpose. It is true strength.

I chose a night sky, studded with diamond stars because it is the vast unknown beyond human comprehension. I am about to participate in the act of creation, and in that sense, I am about to feel a fraction of how God must have felt at the birth of the universe. To bring order to chaos. To fashion a living being and then set it into motion. There is as much mystery in it as the purpose and nature of the trillions of stars that surround us. But I trust in God's hand in creating them. It is true faith.

Finally, they finish their conversation and I'm ready to lie down. It's difficult to sleep in this bed because I have to lie on my side and I don't want the monitoring bands to slide away from the spot where it detects the baby's heart rate. That would probably send out some kind of warning to our nurse. But the *wahn-wahn-wahn-wahn* is starting to get on my nerves. I ask Doug if he can turn down its volume. He figures it out and I'm able to rest a little more easily.

Thursday, August 15, 2013

1:00 a.m.

I can't really sleep anymore. I walk around the room. I roll around on a stability ball and keep my eyes closed. I think about all the advice that I've read about what to do during early labor and tell myself that I need to relax as much as possible right now. But it's so counterintuitive. When the pressure comes, I naturally tense. I have to concentrate on not fighting it. Doug helps me into positions to go completely limp. The contractions have become stronger and more regular, every three to four minutes, but they are still not what I would call painful. My belly tightens enough for me to want to concentrate on relaxation, but it's not beyond my tolerance.

Around 2:45 a.m., Nurse Karen asks us if we've called our doula yet. "Now is the time that I would want to be here if I were your doula." So we call Pam.

3:00 a.m.

Doug and I walk up and down the hallways. Another pregnant woman walks toward us, escorted by two middle-aged women, perhaps her mother and aunt. One of them is guiding the rolling IV attached to the mother's arm. The other woman says, "Oh look! You have a walking buddy!" I'm too uncomfortable to really acknowledge them, so I move on. As we pass them, I am thankful that I don't have an IV yet. We walk down an adjacent hallway and that's where I see a framed poem, its words cross-stitched carefully on cloth. It reads,

> *It is important that I spend*
> *the next few hours alone*
> *with you in the darkness.*
> *You and I will never be*
> *this close again. By morning*
> *you will be a tiny person*
> *all your own. No longer*

the kicking bulge in my
body that I have grown to
love so well. I pray that
God will safely guide you
on your journey tonight
I ask for the strength to
help you all I can.

I burst into tears. That word: *you.* There is a *you* living in me. There is a *you* that I will meet soon. I'm here because of this *you.* I'm doing all this for this *you,* someone that I haven't even met yet.

3:30 a.m.

Pam arrives as labor progresses to contractions every three minutes. She seems very alert despite the early hour. Nurse Karen comes in and tells us that she has noticed that the baby's heart rate has been dropping after contractions.

"It's a warning sign that you're not getting enough fluids."

I believe her. I drink from a twenty-four ounce water bottle every day, and I know that I haven't refilled it enough today.

"Let's put in an IV for an hour to get you some fluids and then I'll take it out. We'll leave in the port like you wanted in your birth plan."

"Okay, let's do it," I agree. "But can you put it in my arm, not my hand? And is there a way for you to cover it up so I don't have to see it stuck in my arm?"

"Sure. I can do that."

Karen is a pro at getting the IV going. There is not much pain at all.

And she keeps her word. After an hour, she tells me that the baby is doing better and she removes the IV. She covers up the site with some gauze and it helps me block out the fact that I still have the port.

I look up at the whiteboard and see that Karen updated it. It now says: *Karen-nurse, Baby boy*!

Well, then, a baby boy it is.

Karen and Pam rub lavender lotion on my hands during contractions while Doug rubs my back with a massager. They play my "Laboring Music" playlist in the background, and I hope they like it. I had planned to listen to my music through headphones, but Doug plays it through my laptop's speakers.

5:30 a.m.

Doug falls asleep on the mobile mattress. Before he lies down, he says, "Baby girl, I'm running out of gas. I've hit my wall."

I continue to labor with Pam, and Nurse Karen comes in to check on me intermittently. Between contractions, I tell myself that I'm strong. I tell myself that I can do this. I only think about right now.

It's difficult to totally rest during this time because I have to be cautious about how I move with the port in my arm and with each band around my belly. I have been unplugging the cords more and more to take full advantage of my mobility, but when I rest in bed, I keep the bands on. I lie on my side, but sometimes the baby's heart rate detector slips too much and then it flatlines on the monitor. And then there's the fact that maneuvering in a hospital bed with a huge belly, bands, and an IV port is just plain hard. I can see why the rails of the hospital bed have different shapes cut out of them—to help women grip them in a variety of positions. I use these rails to make minor adjustments after I find a position that is mostly comfortable.

At one point, Karen comes in and tucks in pillows all around me to help me sleep. And while I don't fall completely asleep, her arrangement of pillows helps me doze off for a while.

6:15 a.m.

Karen asks if she can check me to see my progress. She is certain that Dr. M won't arrive until at least 9:00 a.m. even though she said 6:00 a.m. yesterday.

"Okay, sure. Let's see where we're at."

The exam isn't terribly painful, but the news doesn't help.

"Four centimeters, ninety percent effaced."

My heart sinks. I had been hoping for five centimeters at least. Ninety percent was good. That was progress.

Still, I am certain Dr. M will want to break my water now. *What will that do to my labor? Will the baby be okay?* I turn over on my side and stare at the buttons on the bedrail. *Up, down, channel, volume.* I trace the button that says *help.*

6:45 a.m.

Karen and Pam wake up Doug and encourage him to lie behind me as I lie on my side in bed. He climbs into bed with me and holds me.

I start crying. Doug whispers, "It's okay. Let it out. I got you."

7:00 a.m.

I am mostly awake, but lightly resting. Karen tells us that she has recommended the next nurse because she will help us have the birth that we want. Her name is Nancy. She comes in to introduce herself and then she asks me if I've eaten.

"I thought I wasn't allowed to eat breakfast." She looks at her computer monitor. "Well, let's see what we can do..." She taps a few places on the screen.

"Go ahead and order what you want, dear."

I do. Oatmeal with raisins, a banana, scrambled eggs, toast, turkey bacon, and orange juice. When the food arrives, Doug asks how it is. I tell him the eggs are terrible compared to his eggs. He leaves to get some breakfast for himself.

9:00 a.m.

Dr. M arrives and glares at me as I'm eating breakfast.

"Why is she eating?" she asks Nancy. "She's supposed to be on clear fluids."

"Oh really?" Nancy says. "I didn't know."

I'm not an idiot. I see what Nancy has done for me. She got me some food. She got me some energy for labor. I realize that I might throw it up later, but I am thankful in the moment for this food.

"Well the damage has been done," the doctor waves her hands at me. "Might as well *eat*."

Shame washes over me, heavy and cold. Eating has never been such a dirty word for me. A lump grows in my throat.

I finish my oatmeal but not the eggs or toast. Suddenly, Dr. M seems a lot younger. Is it her ponytail? Is it how quickly she has become unhinged? Is it the way she indecisively waves her hands in the air? Is it the fact that she is averting her eyes?

A sinking feeling overtakes me.

I position myself on the bed, feet together and knees bent as I've been trained. *Maybe she has been up all night. Yeah, maybe she's just tired,* I reason. *Maybe she's not really angry with me. Or Nancy.*

But Dr. M is still not looking at me. She has placed some metal instruments on the hospital bed between my legs. They clink against each other as she fidgets with them. I look away so I can't see them. Then, she asks, "Do you want to do internal monitoring? We can get rid of these bands for you."

I know what she's talking about because I've read about it in books. She wants to attach an internal probe to my baby's scalp. But I'm surprised that she's bringing this up now, when her hand is inches away from my vagina and I'm moments away from an experience that terrifies me.

"What?" I ask weakly. Pam is holding my hand.

"We just put a monitor on your baby's scalp. It doesn't hurt them."

I can barely utter an audible *no.* I shake my head.

"It doesn't hurt them," the doctor repeats, but she's still not looking at me. She's looking to Nancy and asking for different instruments.

"She said no," Pam repeats for me. And I am thankful.

With that, the doctor pummels into my vagina, and I suck in air at the piercing pain. I am so tense that I'm sure that it's making this whole procedure worse. So I chide myself. *Get a hold of yourself! Suck it up! You're making this worse than it has to be.*

Dr. M pulls her hand out and motions to Nancy to give her a different instrument.

Oh God, she didn't get it. She's going to do it again. She's going to do it—

She plunges in again. This time, I lose total control and I'm arching my back in pain. I scream.

Oh my God, just do it already! Get it over with!

She pulls out and then shoves her hand into me again. I scream more. This time, it feels like her whole hand is twisting inside of me.

Why are you doing this? When is it going to be over? Fucking, get it over with! Why!

When she pulls out the third time, I am sobbing uncontrollably and Pam is rubbing my hand.

Dr. M stands, snaps her glove inside out, and says to Nancy, "She's five now."

And then she leaves.

Nancy quietly says to Pam, "Well, that was unnecessary."

Pam is silent and just rubs my hand.

Now Doug is at the door, holding a paper bag. When he sees me, he asks, "What happened? What's going on?"

I just shake my head, the sobs still overtaking me.

"The doctor was just in and broke her water," Nancy says quietly.

"It was so awful," I tell Doug. "It was just awful."

"What the fuck happened?" He drops the bag and walks over to me.

"She was so rough with me. She didn't even care that I was crying. She just left."

He shakes his head. He is silent. That's how angry he is—he's gone silent.

"It's a good thing you weren't here because I think you may have punched her in the face," I say.

He looks to the door and then looks back at me. A few moments pass, and he's still silent.

"Where were you?" I ask.

"I was downstairs in the cafeteria," he tells me.

"Did you get some food?" I wipe some tears off the side of my face.

"No, it looked disgusting. I went there to ask if I could make you some eggs."

I laugh. "What?"

"Yeah, I asked if I could go back into the kitchen and make you some eggs."

"What did they say?"

"They just gave me a weird look and said that they already had eggs made. I tried to explain that you were in labor and that I wanted to make some special eggs for you, but they wouldn't let me back there."

I laugh more. This guy.

Doug helps me out of bed and to a stability ball. I sit on it, lean against the bed, and continue to sob. Heaving sobs. Until I feel that I've emptied as much of those horrible moments as I can. I need to get back to neutral—even though I feel that I've just been attacked. And this is the only way that I know how to do that.

Nancy gently asks me, "Are you crying because you're hurt or because you're discouraged?"

I manage to say, "I'm crying because of what just happened. I'm just trying to get over it so I can move on."

"I think that's best. You don't have any reason to be discouraged. You're moving along just fine. Five centimeters is great!"

10:30 a.m.

I try different laboring positions as the contractions grow stronger. I no longer want to lie in bed. I'm walking, clutching the rail on the wall, and leaning over the side of the bed. Pam elevates the bed so it comes up to support my chest as I lean over. She suggests that I get on hands and knees and lean over the back of the bed. I do this. My eyes land on a series of stick figures that show me what I shouldn't be doing on that part of the bed. *I think I'll do whatever I want, thank you very—*

A powerful contraction overtakes me before I'm ready for it. *Whoa... that was too soon.* I breathe and breathe and try to refocus. And then another one comes. *Oh man...*

"I think I'm going to be sick," I tell Pam.

She grabs a basin and places it in front of me.

"Not yet," I tell her.

I ask to go to the bathroom, but halfway to the bathroom, I'm in the midst of another contraction and I clutch the wall until it has passed. As soon as I make it to the bathroom and sit on the toilet, I start to throw up. Doug quickly slides a garbage can toward me, but only some of the vomit lands inside. The rest of it splashes on sandals. He doesn't recoil or even complain. Instead, he holds my hand, gathers my hair at the back of my neck, and wipes my mouth.

I don't deserve this man.

Nancy asks me if I would like an anti-nausea medicine, Zofran. "It won't hurt the baby," she says.

"Bring it on," I say.

11:00 a.m.

My sister, Holly, comes in and I am too exhausted to even talk to her and the contractions are too close together to make eye contact. She has come in at the worst possible time. She leaves within minutes.

I think about where to move next and I ask to lie on the bed to recover from the nausea for a moment. I hate laboring in bed because it hurts more, but I can't stand until the nausea passes. Pressure is building in my pelvis and as soon as I can stomach the idea of moving, I ask to go back on hands and knees on the bed. As soon as a contraction passes, we rush to get into position before the next one. It's like paddling into the ocean. You know another wave is coming, so you try to get into the best position to help you ride to the top of it so you won't hit its wall and fall into the undertow.

Now, I'm so grateful for each break between contractions. The pressure and pain are so intense throughout the contraction that the breaks are like heaven. An empty, painless heaven. I love them. They make me believe that I can go on. They are like amplified versions of those moments of gratefulness that I feel after a strenuous cardio workout—repeated over and over after each wave of pressure and pain. In those glorious, pain-free moments, I no longer waste my time telling myself that I'm strong. Instead, I try to think of nothing. I try to savor.

The hospital gown seems pointless right now. I'm so out of it, that I couldn't care less who sees me naked. I don't even bother to keep the back of the gown closed. But as I lean forward against the bed, Pam drapes a blanket over my back to keep me from flashing everyone.

12:00 p.m.

As I'm leaning over the back of the bed, still reading about what I should not be doing on that part of the bed, a doctor comes in to introduce himself. He stands beside the bed, but not close enough for me to see him. He doesn't try to get closer. I think he has said his name, but I'm actively trying to block him out. This is my moment of heaven and he's interrupting it.

"So I've reviewed your birth plan," he says. "And we can do what you want. You can have a natural birth. Not a problem. Or we can give you the epidural now and make all of this go away."

Another contraction starts and I realize that my heaven is over too soon. I descend into my low moans and dig my head into the pillow.

And that's how he leaves me. Hanging off the side of the bed, his disembodied voice now playing and replaying in my ears throughout my moments of heaven. *Make it all go away. Make it all go away. We could give you an epidural and make it all go away.*

Huh, an epidural. What a thought. That sounds good.

The contractions start piling on top of each other, but the thirty to forty seconds between them are still enough for me to rally strength for the next one. I'm so full and heavy that I feel like a planet is pushing deep in my pelvis and I'm going to give birth to a new world. I'm so caught up in the sensations that I can't interpret what is happening to me.

When I glance to my left at the contraction monitor, I see that the contraction that I just finished had two peaks and was long. I had no idea. But now I know.

I'm in the worst part—the transition phase.

And then the doubt creeps in.

I'm not strong enough for this. It's too much. Maybe there's nothing wrong with getting the epidural. Maybe it won't slow my pushing phase. Maybe my blood pressure won't drop if I'm hooked up to the IV. Maybe I won't have any negative side effects. Maybe it won't cascade into a C-section. Maybe—

A contraction grips me from all sides. I groan. I moan.

As the contraction fades, I escape the bed, looking for another place to go. I can't decide. The countdown to the next contraction ticks on and I know I don't have enough time to decide what I want to do. As another contraction descends on me, I lean over the side of the bed and tell Doug to squeeze my hips together to counteract the pressure.

Who were these women that made it through labor without medication? They must have been insane! Or they must have felt less pain than this. Or maybe they had short labors. Or maybe they lied.

As the contraction passes, I think about how I might describe this feeling to someone else. I wish there were another word besides *pain* that I could use. Pain makes me think of a localized sensation, sharp like a knife. It might be throbbing or steady, but it lasts for a period of time and then fades. But this sensation is like a wave of pressure that I can't see coming. It's as if a balloon were inflating from inside, pushing down and out. Then it deflates. Then it inflates larger and wider. Then it deflates. Then, even larger and wider. As it pushes down and out, my lungs launch a primal counterattack. I vomit sounds now—deep and low growls and groans that leave my throat dry and raspy. The pressure encompasses everything that I am. I no longer have a stomach, lungs, arms, legs, or head. If I didn't know better, I would guess that one of these waves could shatter my pelvis and split my hips wide open. In fact, I think I would prefer that.

I feel something like a bulge pushing out from me. I think I'm peeing.

Doug points to something on the floor and Nancy looks at it.

"Oh, that's more of her amniotic fluid. Let's see... Clear. Good. You're doing great, Sharon!"

I don't feel great at all. When the contraction ends, I think about where to go. All the while, I hear in my head, *make it all go away, make it all go away.* I climb onto the bed and clutch the bedrail and start begging Doug, "I need the epidural. I need relief. I haven't slept in so long. I can't do this anymore."

Pam rushes over to my side. "Listen, I know what you wanted and I know that you can do this. The worst part is over, I promise you!"

"I can't... I'm so tired... I can't keep going. I need relief."

Pam continues. "You only have about forty-five minutes left before you can push. You can do this. I know you can. I think we should get you in the shower."

My eyes are fixed on the bedrail again with the buttons. *Up, down, channel, volume. Help.*

"I'll try. But I can't walk."

Doug and Pam lift me underneath the arms. Nancy says that she needs to wrap my Heparin lock. The only part of my body that I'm barely controlling is my legs. Nancy is wrapping my arm in something, but I don't turn to look at it. They let me clutch the wall during the next contraction. Someone pulls the gown off me so I can get in the shower unencumbered.

When I'm finally in the shower, I sit on a plastic stool, spread my arms, and let them rest against the steel rails that line the shower. I bow my head forward and rest it against the cool steel. I tell Doug where to spray and when. "Back... Belly... Back... Belly."

I turn my head to the left and see that Nancy has wrapped my arm in a plastic bag. *Biohazard*, it reads. That feels about right. When I look down at my belly, I don't see the EFM bands anymore. Someone must have taken them off. Not sure when that happened.

"Baby girl..." Doug says as he sprays me. "I'm so proud of you."

The steam rises in my face and I say, "Fuck pride. I don't care about pride anymore."

But then, the water helps dissipate the pain. It's true what I've read: The body processes feelings of pleasure over feelings of pain. The heat of the water confuses the signals in my brain. The pain comes on, but the water keeps me from feeling the peak. Like a surfer, I ride inside the tunneling waves, skating through without flying to the top or falling underneath. *If I can keep this up... If I can just keep this up...*

And it's here in this steaming shower that I stop thinking about whether or not I can do this or where to move next or where to escape. I refocus my attention back to the moments of heaven between contractions. Now, I let each contraction come toward me and I take it. I accept it. I flow through it. With each contraction, I feel myself unhinging, creeping open. I close my eyes and descend into an empty, peaceful darkness, a place where there is no more body and no more mind.

I only sense one thing right now, but I don't know what to call it. At first, it feels like a heartbeat, but that's not quite right. It's beyond that. It's a silent pulse, a rhythm, something that is so foundational to who I am and to what all of this is that I've never recognized it until these moments when everything else has been muted. I don't even like to use the word "sense" because this feels beyond my senses—but now I have become aware of it.

The only word that I can give it is God. And God isn't just close to me. God has infused me. But then, maybe God has always been here and this is only the first time I've ever noticed. Because now that everything has been peeled away—both my mind and my body—something else remains.

My spirit. And the spirit of this child.

And in these moments, we are united.

So, I don't fight it anymore. I accept it. I surrender.

Minutes pass and soon Doug pushes a cup in my face. A straw swivels among liquid and ice. "You have to drink, baby girl. You need sugar for energy."

It looks like soda. I refuse it. I feel like I might throw it up. But he doesn't relent.

"Drink it. You have to drink it. Drink it for me."

I give in and drink some. It goes down easily and I'm surprised that I like it. I drink the whole chilled cup, about twelve ounces. I ask for more. I drink another full cup. Doug tries to push a third one on me, but I only drink half of it. He keeps offering me the soda between contractions.

"Relax your shoulders," he reminds me every time a contraction comes. It's starting to really annoy me, but I don't want to interrupt my moments of heaven to tell him to stop.

Time passes, but I'm not sure how much. I feel like I'm going to pass out from the heat and humidity. Then, I remember that Doug despises heat and humidity and I feel sorry for him. He hasn't asked for a break. I wonder when he will reach his breaking point, but then the contractions return and I refocus.

"I can't breathe," I tell Doug. He opens the bathroom door and asks Pam to fan it open and closed. She does. The cool air comes in and I feel revived for a short time. When I finally can't take the humidity anymore, we leave the bathroom. I am completely naked, but I don't care anymore. I have no pride left. It is gone.

A contraction grips me. I clutch the side of the bed and start wailing.

"Help me!" I'm crying out. "Help me, please!" I've become irrational and I know it. Doug and Pam can't make this pain go away. But then, I'm not crying out to them—I'm crying out to God. Why does it have to be this way? Why?

WHY?

And then that silent pulse, that foundational rhythm comes to the forefront as the contraction passes. It's not a voice. It's not even words. It's just awareness entering my body between contractions. And if this awareness could speak, it would probably say something like this:

This is not punishment. And this is not a mistake.

Then Doug and Pam are right there. "We're here." Each of them says.

"We've got you, baby girl. We've got you." Doug says as he squeezes my hips together to counteract the pressure.

"What can we do to help?" Pam asks.

"I don't know..." And I don't want to waste my moment of heaven on figuring it out.

Another contraction comes and I moan low and deep. It's then that I decide that I need to get on the back of the bed again. Once I'm there, I start to feel the urge to push.

I tell Pam, "I think I'm going to poop."

"Go ahead and do it," she says. "Don't let anything hold you back. Do whatever you need to do right now. You know what needs to be done to help this baby come out."

I can't tell if I'm pooping or not. Now, it just feels like immense pressure. My moans are choppy and punctuated. My throat is raspy. Nancy asks if she can gently check me. In my next moment of heaven, I quickly lower down to the bed so she can check me before the next contraction. Her exam is the gentlest one that I've had so far, but it is still uncomfortable.

"Nine and a half centimeters. There's just a little lip left to go, and I don't want you to tear your cervix. So try not to push until just a little while longer."

In my head I scream, *What? Who cares if I tear my cervix! I'm not having any more babies after this!*

But as the next contraction approaches, I recall Ina May Gaskin's advice to blow raspberries and breathe like a horse to relax through a contraction. Women who made these noises were able to open up more quickly. I try this over and over and over again. My groans are lower and louder, uncontrollable now. Still, the urge to push is incredible. It's extremely frustrating.

"Sharon, does it just feel like that baby wants to come out?" Nancy asks. I nod ferociously. "Let's check you again." She does so and says, "Okay, she's ten. Let's go."

She flips the bed into an inclined position with the stirrups up and the end of the bed lowered. I don't even object. I had thought about squatting to push, but I have hardly any energy left. Doug offers me more soda and I take it. Nancy gives them directions. Pam takes my left leg and Doug takes my right. They hold them as I draw my knees back toward my ears.

I remember a natural childbirth book's advice to take two deep breaths as the contraction approaches and then push twice before relaxing again. But I'm pushing three and sometimes four times in each contraction. I'm a pushing machine. Nancy tells me to push in my abdomen when I feel the urge, but I don't need this direction. I feel possessed. It's like I'm throwing up, but instead the movement is down and out instead of up and out. Each time a contraction comes, the pushes are strong and I can feel the baby moving down each time. When the contractions end, I feel genuine relief. Lovely, heavenly relief. During some pushes, I feel Nancy reach in and massage open my perineum. It feels fantastic. She does this three times in a row and I feel much more open.

My screams start high-pitched, but Nancy reminds me to make them deep and throaty. I realize that I'm pooping while this is happening, and Nancy says kindly, "Let me clean that for you, sweetie. I got it." She does this a few times between contractions.

"Hold on, let me get a light to see if I'm seeing this right." Nancy swings a light down and says to Doug, "There's the head. See it?"

I can't believe what I'm hearing. Nancy calls for the doctor.

He arrives, takes one look, and says, "She's not ready yet. Call me back."

After two more contractions, Nancy says, "Little breaths now, sweetie."

"I want to be the one who finds out... what it is..." I hear myself groan.

"Okay, honey, I hear you." Nancy hits the call button. "Get the doctor back now and an extra nurse if you have one."

Pam tells me to reach down to touch my baby's head. I shake my head no. I don't deserve that yet. This isn't finished. I have to finish this. And then there is part of me that still can't believe that this is all happening.

The doctor arrives and Nancy tells me to push in the next contraction.

"She wants to find out what it is. Don't tell her what it is," Nancy says loud enough for the doctor to hear.

I feel the head crowning, the ring of fire that everyone talks about, but it is short-lived. I feel something hot and slippery on my stomach and I look down. It is bluish-gray. Its legs and feet are pointed toward me.

What?

There is a little person on top of me now. How did that happen so quickly?

And that is *not* a penis.

"It's a girl!" I am crying. No, I'm sobbing. "I can't believe it! Oh my God! It's a girl! It's a girl!"

"What's her name?" the doctor asks.

"We're not sure yet," I mutter. I think I should double-check with Doug before declaring it. We have been so prepared to have a boy that we haven't talked about names for girls in a while.

But then Doug shouts, "Her name is Felicity!" Then, he runs to get his camera.

Now, I'm crying even more. Total. Shock. Grips me.

I. Have. A daughter.

Here she is, warm and slick against my chest, screaming and then nuzzling my breast. Her screams diminish as I hold her. She is quiet now. I feel imbued with new magical powers. I kiss the top of her head, such pain and joy in my heart.

"What's the time?" the doctor asks.

"4:10," a nurse calls out.

"It's okay, it's okay," I'm whispering to her. "We've been through so much today. It's okay."

I ask Doug to call my mom. When she is on the phone, all I can say is, "She's here! Her name is Felicity and I'm so happy!" I'm crying so much that I can't say good-bye.

Nancy asks if she can take Felicity to clean her and I give permission. When Nancy lifts her, she says, "Oh honey, she went all over you." I look down and see a placemat-sized streak of thick, brown, shiny goo swiped across my side.

"After what I've just been through, I couldn't care less," I say. "That's the least traumatic thing that's happened to me all day." I look at Pam and say, "I'm so glad it's over... It's over. I'm so glad. Thank you for being here."

The doctor is now walking me through his procedure: delivering the placenta and showing it to me. His hand holds the top of it, like a hunter showcasing his kill. It droops like sagging skin—shiny, veined, and gray in the light. Then come the stitches.

"We don't usually see tearing like this in women who get epidurals," he says aloud.

But to whom? Me?

I guess he is trying to make me feel badly for not following his recommendation, but I don't even care. I am in a cloud of complete and absolute bliss. It is over. All that pressure is gone. The waves of pain that come now are like soft ebbs against the shore. I barely even feel them. My eyes set across the room as I see Doug holding our daughter. She is screaming and he quietly says, "Hey... Hey... It's okay" in his deep, soothing voice, the way he did when he talked to her through my belly.

I want to hold her again, but the doctor is injecting my bottom with anesthesia and beginning the first stitches. I just keep looking at her as I feel him stitching in a circle. As he stitches, I occasionally wince and dig my heels into the stirrups to distract myself from the sensation, but I mostly don't care. When he finishes, I look over his shoulder. The clock reads 4:30. Time for him to go home and he's gone. I wonder if twenty minutes for a delivery is a record for him. Probably not. It's probably only ten minutes for women with epidurals. Ha.

I cuddle with Felicity for a few more minutes while the nurses clean up the aftermath of the birth. I look at Felicity's scrunched face and hold her close to my heart. Her face relaxes. And then I remember something the lactation consultant had said in the hospital's breastfeeding class. *Get that baby skin-to-skin with you as soon as possible. She'll hear your heartbeat and remember that that's her home.*

I am home to her. I am where she has lived for her whole life. She is home. This time the tears come because I realize soon enough she will have a new definition of home. My heart doesn't want her to need anything else but me. Then, my mind argues that I don't want her to need me more than anything else. But these thoughts are not meant for now. This moment is far too precious to waste in the past or the future.

So I live in the present and hold her close. Home is here for now.

The Oneness

For months after I gave birth, I pondered the question about the best way to give birth. I was pretty sure that I had found it. I felt that surrendering to labor had opened that unexpected door into the experience of being completely united with this child and—at the same time—God. I wished that same transcendent experience for all new mothers. I believed that giving birth without medication was the key. I wanted all future mothers to know what an amazing experience unmedicated childbirth could be. Maybe if they just knew, they would change their minds about getting the epidural.

Maybe.

Then again, I'm not every other woman.

And this took time for me to acknowledge: that there are thousands of different factors that can limit a woman's options for labor; and that not all women desire such an experience; that some women are just happy that their babies are alive, regardless of what happens in the delivery room; that some women can be just as happy with a C-section; that an epidural is the right choice for some women. It may have even been the right choice for me if I had labored differently.

Each woman has her own way of experiencing labor—and we often don't know what we'll do until we're actually doing it.

But let's step back for a moment and ask a bigger question. Where did my need to find "the best way to give birth" come from? Undergirding this question is the modern assumption that women have options and choices in labor and delivery.

This certainly hasn't always been true. Two hundred years ago, women's birth experiences almost always involved a midwife, no pain medication, and no option of a C-section. But with the advent of medical technologies, there are choices—and choices reflect our values. As Tina Cassidy asserts in her book, *Birth: The Surprising History of How We Are Born*, birth is no longer simply a biological process. After a hundred years of obstetricians doing their damnedest to move childbirth out of homes and into hospitals, they have succeeded in adding another layer to the birthing process—a technological layer. And through our use or refusal to use this technology, birth has also become, "an expression of our lives—both an act of self-discovery and an extension of our management skills" (p. 250). Cassidy goes on to call our modern birth plans—our literal expression of our childbirth choices—"perfect time capsules of postmodern maternity, for... birth always reflects the culture in which it happens" (p. 250). Anthropologist and childbirth educator, Sheila Kitzinger agrees with this assertion, although she uses more cutting language: "The way a woman gives birth and the kind of care given to her point as sharply as an arrowhead to the key values in the culture" (as cited in Davis-Floyd, 2003, p. 38).

And so I need to acknowledge that this question of "the best birth" is a recent notion that emerges from a culture that has reframed birth as an experience that can be manipulated through choices. And those choices send implicit messages to others about our perceptions and values.

But for me—in my specific place and time—giving birth wasn't a medical procedure for which my doctor was responsible. Instead, giving birth was a natural process for which I was responsible and one which my body could handle. I told myself that my doctor was there in case of an emergency.

So I chose to approach labor as a difficult task. I broke the process into smaller units of time and focused on doing what I needed to do at that time. I didn't think about the whole process. I didn't think about the baby at the end. What worked for me was one hour at a time. Later, five minutes at a time. Then, one minute at a time.

For me, laboring was the most effective, the most peaceful, and the most satisfying when I was able to shut out the world and all its external noise. The more I looked inward, the easier it was. The more interruptions from the outside world, the more distracted I became. And the more I wanted to escape.

When I focused my attention inward during labor, I felt differently than I had at any other time during pregnancy. Throughout pregnancy, I was engaged in the exterior world while my baby was engaged in the interior world. But the process of labor synchronized us. I was not struggling with her anymore. I was not even *me* anymore. I was a vehicle that was undergoing a process. And so reading the poem in the hallway was jarring. It reminded me of our separateness—and yet this was the last time we would be so united. I felt those first real pulls of motherhood on my psyche. But I wasn't ready for it. I wasn't a mother. *I was just having a baby.*

But other women approach labor differently. A meta-study of 137 studies related to intrapartum interventions and women's satisfaction with childbirth experiences determined that there is not one method of childbirth that most women find satisfactory. An even more interesting finding was that providing pain relief during childbirth did not necessarily improve a woman's satisfaction (Hodnett, 2002). Rather, a woman's satisfaction about her birth experience came from her feeling cared for and feeling that she had some control over decisions about the birthing process. The more unexpected interventions that a mother experienced and the more decisions that were made without her approval, the more likely she was to be dissatisfied with her birth experience.

Throughout my narrative, these unexpected interventions are clear—when my doctors criticized my birth plan, suggested an induction, advocated that I stay in the hospital for my whole labor, decided that I have my water broken, and recommended that I have an epidural. All of these deviations from my birth plan instigated moments of fear, uncertainty, and doubt. And none of my doctors delivered their recommendations with convincing concern for my well-being.

In fact, what disturbed me the most was that these conversations turned my body into a battleground upon which my doctors would actively exercise their authority over mine.

You will get Pitocin if you don't make progress. You will have an IV. You are not at an increased risk for a C-section if you have an induction today.

We don't usually see tears like these in women who get epidurals.

Much to the chagrin of my nurse (but none at all to my doctor), I became collateral damage in their sparring match—over the question of whether I should be allowed to eat breakfast while laboring.

Why is she eating?

She. Not even "you."

It took the experience of delivering in a hospital for me to understand some of the many forces that push and pull birth in opposing directions. The mother has a picture of what a safe delivery is. The doctor might have a different idea. And the nurse just wants to support the mother without being chewed out by the doctor.

But does it really matter whether or not a woman is satisfied with her birth?

Yes. It does.

The human mind has a tendency to hold on to memories that stand out from typical everyday experiences. And sadly, we remember the most painful and soul-crushing moments even more than the most ecstatic and uplifting ones (Kensinger, 2007). Childbirth is full of both kinds of moments, placing women in labor in an especially impressionable position. Although doctors can scarcely recount the details of—what is for *them*—a typical delivery, mothers can often recount in great detail all that they remember from giving birth. And those who attend women in labor should be aware that their presence—however positive or negative—will live on in the memory of those mothers for years and years.

What moments do I remember from my labor?

First, the bad.

I remember how Dr. M looked when she saw me eating breakfast on the day that I gave birth. I remember her curt words, telling me to "go ahead and *eat*," as if she were telling me to "go ahead and *smoke*." Then, the sound of clinking metal instruments as she asked me questions, her eyes averted. Then, her angry fist in my vagina. The pain. Pulling out. A different instrument. Then, her frustrated fist. My shrieking, my legs tightening, toes pointed and scraping the hospital bed. Pulling out. Then, her exasperated hand again, twisting and turning. The hot tears pouring down my face, sobbing. Pulling out. I remember every moment of it.

I remember the tone in my doctor's voice as he stood beside my hospital bed and talked about my birth plan as if I were asking for a pony.

I remember looking across the room at my husband holding our daughter, tears streaming down my face, my hand in my doula's hand, my heart full, and the feel of the doctor's fingers stitching me. Then, his snide comment, "We don't usually see tears like this in women with epidurals."

But then, the good.

I remember the kindness in my nurse's voice as I sobbed after the doctor pummeled me in order to break my water. Then, her soft hand on my shoulder when she reassured me that I was making great progress.

I remember hearing my husband's voice in my ear. "I'm so proud of you," he said as he sprayed water on my back, my belly, my back, my belly. I remember him fanning the shower door open and closed to circulate air. I remember him lifting a glass of soda to my face and telling me to drink, drink, drink. I see his bare feet against the brown tile as I rested my head against the cool steel of the shower bar.

I remember the feel of my doula's hand in mine as I pushed. She held it right back through the contractions and then brushed my hair away from my face as I rested.

I remember these moments. They line the box of memories that have become my labor and delivery experience. They give my experience structure, flavor, and meaning. I try to relive these good memories instead of the bad, but the bad ones are still there. These memories shaped my identity about what kind of woman the trial of labor had proven me to be— a dissident of unnecessary hospital policies, a believer in my own strength, and a survivor of one of nature's greatest challenges. It gave me the courage to step forward each day as a new mother and say, "Hey, I know I can do this." And that means a lot for a first-time mother, especially in those first days when you feel like you'll never be yourself again and you'll never be able to take care of the baby without help.

And so, yes, we should care about whether or not a mother is satisfied with her birth experience.

And what do I say to people when they ask me if I am happy with Felicity's birth? I tell them that if I could erase the doctors from my memory and give birth with only my nurses and doula, it would have been perfect.

What about next time? Will I still give birth in a hospital?

Yes. Because I need the certainty of knowing that if I had a postpartum hemorrhage or if my baby experienced some kind of distress, I would be close to experienced doctors who could help us. I would give birth in a hospital again—hands down.

But if I could have a frank conversation with these doctors today, I would say this: Look, I get it. You're a doctor. You know a lot. You have a lot of experience. You've seen a lot of births. But you've never seen *this* birth. You've never seen *me* in labor. If there are one hundred women giving birth on this floor and ninety-seven of them want epidurals, that doesn't mean that I want one, too. You should still respect my wishes even if they don't match the vast majority of the births that populate your memories.

Doctor, I only came to you to help me if something goes wrong. I didn't come to you so you would take control of this process. Yeah, I know. Some women want that. But I'm not those women.

Let's talk to each other. I'll listen to you if you listen to me. I'll listen to your words of caution if you listen to my questions. And together, we'll ride this wave as it comes in.

The First Days

August 15, 2013

 4:30 p.m.

Pam starts to gather her things and I thank her one last time. Her eyes are ringed with dark circles, but she smiles. As she starts to walk toward the door, I say, "I love you."

"I love you, too," she laughs.

Nancy tells me that we need to get ready to move to the Mom and Baby Unit. I hand Felicity to a nurse's assistant. Nancy says she's going to push down on my belly one more time. When she does, I feel more warm fluid flowing out of me. Then, she and Doug hook their arms under mine so I can hobble to the bathroom. Everything in my crotch feels sore and tight. Why tight? Is it the stitches? And for some reason, I'm leaning to my left to take pressure off my right foot.

I sit on the toilet and another onslaught of fluid and chunks fall into the water. I don't want to stand until it completely stops, but then I'm assuming that I can keep this bathroom clean. But I'm already leaving a trail of blood. So I stop caring and stand. I feel faint and my legs are shaking, but Doug supports me from the side while Nancy dabs me with a towel and shows me how to use a clear squeeze bottle to flush water through the area. She unfolds a pad long and wide enough to cover me from the top of my butt to the top of my genitals. She positions the pad in a pair of disposable stretchy underwear that feels like loose pantyhose. I step into them and she covers me with a gown.

Oh. Right. I forgot that I'm still naked.

Nancy puts her hands on a wheelchair and aims it toward me. *She must be crazy*, I think.

"I can't sit in that. Can't I walk?" I ask.

"No, I'm sorry, sweetie. You have to sit and we have to wheel you down there."

"Okay," I sigh. "I'll try."

I wince as I lower myself to the chair. Sitting is agonizing. I'm not sure exactly what hurts so much in my bottom, but I end up leaning entirely to my left to take pressure off my right side. I place my feet against the steel foot rests. Then, Nancy hands my swaddled newborn to me.

"Are you kidding me?" I say as I use every muscle to lean to the left. "This hurts bad enough."

"I'm sorry, sweetie," Nancy says. "But you have to be the one to hold her in order to be transferred to the Mom and Baby Unit."

I take my baby in my arms and say, "Well, let's get there fast then."

I can't believe how quiet it is in the hallway. Where are the screams of women in transition? Is no one else pushing? It's like a library, and I don't feel any solidarity to the women in these rooms. We have been separated from each other, corralled into large, soundproof rooms, and left to believe that we are the only ones experiencing this pain.

Some visitors are sitting in chairs in the hallway. I decide to mess with them, so as I pass them, I say, "I've just been through hell."

5:10 p.m.

We arrive in the Mom and Baby Unit and are ushered into a private room. It is large and welcoming with faux wood floors. Unfortunately, the bed is inferior to the Labor & Delivery bed. There are not as many options for positioning, but the window overlooks the surrounding wooded suburbs. It is not like the small, colorless hospital rooms that I've seen on sitcoms and television dramas. This is bright and cheerful.

A nurse introduces herself. Her name is Erica. She tells me that she wants to help clean me up. She lifts Felicity from my arms and places her in a glass bassinet by the bed.

I ask, "Can I lie down first?"

"You'll feel better once it's over and then you can lie down, okay?"

I don't argue.

She and Doug help me hobble to the bathroom. The shakiness in my legs has gotten worse. As I lower myself to the toilet, I'm afraid that they will give out completely. I lean to my left and grip the rail next to the toilet.

Doug asks, "Is this normal?"

She nods. "Yeah, for some reason, right after birth, a lot of women have this shakiness. Not completely sure why, but it's normal."

I don't feel normal at all. More fluid and chunks are dropping out of me. Erica hands me the squeeze bottle, which she calls a "peri bottle." Then, she watches my technique as she squats in front of me. A stranger is squatting in front of me, intent on watching whatever is spilling out of my swollen vagina. But it doesn't feel strange. She shows me a can of Dermoplast spray that I can use three to four times a day to numb my bottom. The effect is immediate. She helps me climb into a new mega pad and stretchy panties. I wash my hands at the sink. When I look into the mirror, I am shocked. My pregnant belly has dropped into a droopy low pooch. I'm not angry or saddened by this—I knew I wouldn't look like my pre-pregnant self for a while. I'm just amazed that so much of the pregnancy shape has disappeared.

"Look at that," I point to my stomach. Doug nods. He helps me hobble back to bed, which is lined with another large pee pad.

Now that I'm sitting in bed, I don't like it. With my back against the bed and my legs stretched in front of me, the pressure in my bottom builds. I decide to lie on my side for the moment, but even this decision takes strength. I grab the bed rail on my left, being careful not to aggravate the IV port, and pull myself toward the rail to alleviate the need to activate any muscles in the painful areas. I wish this part of the experience were a lot like TV. When a woman gives birth on TV, in the next scene, she is sitting upright, glowing, and holding an infant. The only indication that she has given birth is that her hair is in a ponytail. They're not hugging the rails of the bed just to sit up.

"I heard that you went natural!" Erica beams. "That is so awesome! That's exactly what I want to do when I have kids."

I manage a smile, but I immediately say, "Thanks, but let me tell you... I completely understand now why women get the epidural."

Erica is doing something on the computer now.

"Can you take this port out of my arm?" I ask. "I'm afraid I'm going to hit it every time I move."

"Well, the doctors usually require that we keep IV access for at least another 24 hours, if not longer. Just in case."

She checks my vitals and then asks me if I want my dose of Motrin. I think about it. What is Motrin really going to do for me? I feel a lot better than I did when I was in labor. I'm swollen, but I also feel numb from the Dermoplast. "You know, I really think I'm okay."

"You sure?" She raises an eyebrow.

"Yeah, I'll wait on it."

I finally have my time to cuddle with Felicity skin-to-skin for a long time. My sister, Holly, arrives and I ask her to take some pictures and make the Facebook announcement. When it's Holly's turn to hold Felicity, she brightens. She holds the swaddled body close to her face. I think I see tears.

Once I am sitting up again, Doug asks to take pictures as well. Before I allow him to do so, I ask Holly to put my hair back. She gathers my hair like a pro and says, "I can't believe your hair is dry! Didn't you sweat?"

"I sweated everywhere else, trust me," I tell her.

Doug takes this picture.

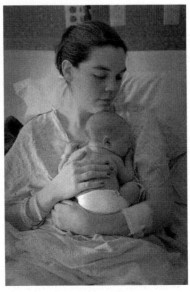

As he takes this picture, my eyes settle on Felicity's back. Her skin is red and covered with downy, light yellow hair. Light comes through the window and falls upon these tiny hairs, the feathers of a newborn chick. Her hands are completely unwrinkled and unaged. Her face is creaseless except for the tiniest lines at her mouth and eyes. I am witnessing her very beginning.

After Holly leaves, the nurse's assistant, Rebecca, comes in to meet me.

"You're the one who had the natural childbirth! That's great!"

I wonder if I'm becoming today's legend.

"Are you sure you don't want the Motrin though?" Rebecca asks.

That's the second time they've mentioned it. Maybe I should take it. Still, I feel pretty good, so I shake my head. "I really don't think I need it yet."

"Well, are you ready to try nursing her?" She asks. I nod. It's time to get serious.

I hold Felicity in my arms and think about what the books and breastfeeding class have taught me. *Line her up, nose to nipple. Tickle her lip with your nipple and then wait until her mouth is wide. Then pull her to your breast. If the latch is painful, unlatch her and try again.* I follow these steps and the pain is incredible. I try for another ten minutes, but latch after latch is painful. I try the other breast with the same outcome. When I look down, I see red bite marks and bruises on my nipples. I know we have not established a good latch, but I cuddle her anyway and whisper, "It's okay. We'll try again later. We're learning right now."

Every two hours, a nurse or nurse's assistant reminds me that I need to be nursing her at least every two to three hours. If she goes six hours without eating, they will need to do a blood sugar test. Sometimes, I try to wake Felicity to eat, but she doesn't wake up. I try everything— tickling her chin, tapping her feet, patting her back. It's an exercise in futility.

August 16 and 17, 2013 (one and two days postpartum)
The next thirty-six hours go by in a whirl: pediatricians, nurses and nurses' assistants every two hours and at shift changes, photographers, obstetricians, a nurse manager, people who drop off and pick up my meal trays, people who explain the birth certificate process, and on and on. Rest and sleep are impossible between 7:00 a.m. and 7:00 p.m. I can't imagine what the day would look like if we had more than our one visitor, Doug's brother, John.

There are a few memories from these days in the Mom and Baby Unit that will stay with me, and they all concern breastfeeding.

After Felicity chomps on my breasts on the first day and night, a lactation consultant, Jill, visits me on the second morning. She observes how I have been nursing Felicity.

"Have you tried hand expressing your milk?"

"Yes, but I can't get anything." I show her how I've been massaging my breast to express the milk.

She nods and then presses the edge of her hand against my chest and draws it down toward my nipple.

"You've got inverted nipples. And they're flat. But they're not the worse that I've seen," she pronounces.

Inverted? Really? I look at my nipples. They don't look deformed— just not... nipple-y. *Okay, so they don't point out nearly as much as the nipples on baby bottles.*

I think about the breastfeeding books that I've read, with the cut-a-way pictures of a baby's mouth latching onto a breast. I think about how far the nipple extended into the baby's mouth. I had wondered how my nipples would do that, considering that they never stood out that much. Ever. But then, I believed that my body would figure it out. This whole thing— pregnancy, birth, feeding. All of it.

Jill hands me a nipple guard and shows me how to put it on. It suctions my nipple, pops it out, and gives it extra length so that Felicity can latch well. Immediately, I start to cramp.

"Oh, that's different. I'm cramping."

She nods. "That means she's got a good latch and you're doing it."

"Oww... this really hurts. Not the nursing. The cramps."

"Are you on the Motrin?"

"No, but I'll take some now."

"Yeah, you'll want to be on Motrin around the clock until the cramps subside. How often are you nursing her?"

"Well, I don't know how often actually. I've been looking for her cues like the rooting around and her cries and every time, I've been offering her the breast."

"Good. Keep doing that."

Minutes later, my nurse comes by with the Motrin. "So you're ready for Motrin now?"

"It's not like I'm a glutton for pain!" I kid. "I didn't need it until now."

She happily hands me the Motrin and then tags me with another ID band. I look at the collection on my arm. One that says who I am. One that says what blood work I've had. And one that says which drugs I've taken.

The nursing cramps are accompanied by more gushes of blood, but I'm all right with it. Maybe the faster it comes out, the faster my recovery will be. Felicity nurses and nurses while my toes curl and my legs twitch to counteract the cramps. Doug watches me sympathetically from his corner futon. When she finally finishes, I pull off the nipple guard and see just a bit of light-colored milk pooling in the guard.

I feel like we're moving in the right direction.

Later that afternoon, after a thirty-minute feeding session, I set Felicity in her bassinet to sleep and I hobble to the bathroom, relieved for the break. As soon as I sit on the toilet, I hear her cry. My heart sinks. I try to hurry in the bathroom, but there are so many things to do: peri bottle, Dermoplast, new pad, and new underwear. *Hurry up! Respond to her cries!* I chide myself. As I'm working to get myself together, I hear a nurse talking with Doug. When I come back in, the nurse is holding a pacifier.

"Would you like a pacifier?" the nurse asks.

"Um..." I look at Doug, who has a blank look on his face. "But doesn't that interfere with her breastfeeding?" I point out.

"It could..." she says. "Have you fed her recently?"

"She just ate for thirty minutes. And I had cramps the whole time, so I know she has a good latch."

"She might just need this to fall asleep."

I look at Felicity, her tiny body squirming, her persistent tiny cry. *I just fed her...*

"Go ahead," I say.

Once the pacifier is in, she falls back asleep. And I think maybe it wasn't a bad idea after all.

That night, Felicity starts to nurse at 10:00 p.m. I sit in bed with a pillow propping up my right hip, and I feel pretty comfortable. At 11:00 p.m., I think she will probably stop soon. Then, midnight approaches and my back is tiring of this position. Doug helps me move from the bed to the glider, with Felicity still latched and chugging away. The glider is even more painful. We go back to the bed, but this time, I sit on the edge of it. 1:00 a.m. approaches and Felicity has fallen asleep. I put her down and congratulate myself. *That was tough, but you did it!*

But just five minutes later, she's crying again.

Doug comes over to shush her. He picks her up and gently bounces her. He stops for a moment. Then, he bounces her even more gently. She is still wailing away.

"Felicity... Hey... Give your mom a break," he says.

"It's okay," I sigh. "I'll take her."

She continues to nurse and nurse and nurse. At 2:00 a.m., Doug looks at me and says, "Sweets, we should think about sending her to the nursery so you can get some sleep."

The nursery. Red flags fly out from every direction. The nursery is dangerous. The nursery is for quitters. The nurses might give her a bottle. Then, I will miss the chance to respond to her cues. I need to buckle down and devote myself to this process. I need to trust that it will work. I can do this.

"I'm not ready to give up on her yet," I say.

About twenty minutes later, Felicity falls asleep and I put her down again. I sigh and hobble back to bed. Once I'm lying there, I hear her tiny grunts again. *Wa...ahh... Waahhh... Ahhh...*

Doug gets up and tries to shush her again. It doesn't work.

"Felicity! Ugh! Shhh!" He pauses. "Come on, Felicity, give your mom a break."

A wave of anxiety passes over me at the thought of Doug becoming so frustrated with her that he leaves us. *I can't do this alone,* I think. *I can't lose him right now. I have to do something.*

"I got her. It's okay." I haven't really slept in almost seventy hours, but I pick her up and help her latch again. Doug is at his limit, but I think I still have a little more to give. It's irrational to believe that he'll leave us, but the fear is still there.

Soon, Doug is completely asleep on the futon. But now, I need a glass of water and I don't have enough energy to stand up while holding the baby. I call his name. I call his name louder. I yell. I yell louder. As a last attempt, I grab the only object within reach—my camera bag—and launch it at his head. He jumps and looks around frantically.

"I need water," I say.

After he hands me a glass of ice water, he falls back asleep effortlessly. I turn away so I don't fixate on my jealousy. I need to think positively. I need to commit to this.

Throughout the night, my nurse, Erin, witnesses this nursing marathon. Her eyebrows arch when she walks in at 2:45 and I'm still nursing Felicity.

"She hasn't stopped?" she asks.

I'm so close to tears that all I can manage is to shake my head as I look down at Felicity. Is this some kind of cruel test of my commitment to her? Do all mothers go through this crisis of whether to care for themselves or care for their children? One thing is for sure: this is consuming me. From the inside out, I have been reduced and reduced and reduced.

Suddenly, emotion seizes me. *Mom, did I do this to you? How much did you give up? How much of you did we consume? And were you ever able to be whole again?*

"Is this normal?" I ask.

"She could be cluster feeding to bring in your milk... or she's going through a growth spurt... or both."

I continue to look at my baby, working hard to eat. "How will I know when she's had enough?" I ask.

"She'll unlatch herself."

I'm not sure how much longer I can go on like this tonight and Felicity shows no signs of slowing. It could be another hour. Another two hours. The cafeteria doesn't open until 7:00 a.m. and I'm starving. My thoughts spin on and I estimate the number of these feedings that are ahead of me. Thousands.

How am I going to do this?

A moment passes. "You know," Erin says, "If this is what you want to do, it does get easier. It does."

I hold on to these words as she leaves the room. The door clicks behind her, and I'm crying. Fifteen minutes later, Felicity falls asleep.

I turn over on my side, feeling a wave of pin pricks as the blood rushes to the other leg and hip. I shrug my tears into the shoulder of my gown. I hear the door open, but I don't move. I'm too exhausted. I hear Erin place something on the tray next to my bed. When she leaves, I turn to see what she left.

Graham crackers. And three packets of peanut butter.

I cry a little more as I eat them.

Felicity stays asleep until morning.

The next morning is Saturday and we are ready to go home. After Felicity fell asleep last night, it took me another hour and a half to calm down enough to sleep. Soon, it was time to get up again. We have to go to a discharge class and then wait for the discharge orders from the pediatrician and the obstetrician on call. And where is this discharge class? Down the hall on the left.

I make a bold decision—I will get dressed.

I pull on some pajama pants and a nursing tank top and I instantly feel more human. The movement of climbing into my pants and pulling the shirt over my head feel like feats worthy of applause.

Doug is changing Felicity in her glass bassinet. She straightens her legs in frog-like bursts.

"Look at your little Kermit legs!" he laughs.

Just as he tries to fasten the diaper, her legs go rigid. The tabs slip and he has to refasten them.

"Kermit, work with me!" he kids.

As I amble down the hallway, Doug pushes freshly-changed Felicity in her glass bassinet. I am so slow, holding onto the rails along the walls. Although the soreness in my bottom slows me down, I feel that the major culprit is my complete exhaustion from not having slept since Tuesday. It's hard to believe that just days before, I was walking normally. Weeks before, I was still lifting weights. Months before, I was still doing forty-five minute cardio workouts. How did women who didn't exercise during pregnancy manage recovery? How were they faring?

The nurse of the discharge class sits at the head of a conference table around which all the other parents are gathered. She hands us a single-spaced outline full of information about taking care of ourselves and our babies—then she reads it to us with her commentary. The only thing that I learn is that I look worse than every other woman in the room by several degrees. I can't figure it out. They don't have rings underneath their eyes. Two of them are grinning ear to ear as they hold their newborns. The couple on our left looks like they have just come from a salon. Did these women give birth or is this an adoption class? How long ago did they give birth?

From our introductions, I learn that, besides me, the woman in the hospital gown is the only other woman who has given birth just two days ago. One of the grinning women has undergone a C-section three days earlier and the other had a preemie at thirty-four weeks. They are finally being discharged today. The salon couple has stayed an extra day because their son was circumcised.

The woman in the gown just gave birth to her second child. She leans against her hand, like a bored college student in the back of a lecture hall. Did she have an easier delivery? Did she tear like me? Maybe it was fast? My labor lasted two days and I haven't really slept at all.

It's at that moment that I realize two of the couples are no longer holding their babies. I look for their bassinets. Gone. Where are they? No one seems concerned. It takes me a few moments to realize that the parents have sent their babies to the nursery. The father of the preemie raises his arm and I see an impressive sleeve of tattoos. I lose myself in their designs: dragons, fire, yin and yang.

"I have a question," he announces. "What can us dads do to help out our wives when we get home?"

His partner smiles and nods. Her cheeks glow.

Oh, shut the fuck up, I stew. *Stop showing off.*

I turn my attention back to the single-spaced handout. I have absolutely no desire to prove to a group of strangers that I am happy to be a new parent or that my marriage is strong or however else the story is supposed to go. And I'm out of patience for those who feel they need to.

My eyes scan the words on the page over and over again, but I can't understand them. Words shift in and out of focus. A curtain of tears starts to blur all of them.

Not in front of these strangers. Hold on.

But once I have ambled back to the room, back to the safety of the bathroom, alone with Doug, I let it all go.

What is wrong with me? Why can't I be healed like they are? What is broken inside of me? How had I failed? I exercised. I ate so well when I was pregnant. I took all the classes and read the books. I was smart. I cared. I was following directions. I did this naturally. I trusted my body. I did what I needed to do at each stage. I expected this to all be hard, but I hadn't expected that everyone else would act like it had been so easy.

But I can't explain this to Doug yet. I don't have the words for it. All I can manage to say is, "I just want to go home."

We find out that the pediatrician has cleared Felicity for discharge, but the obstetrician on call still needs to discharge me.

"And it's a Saturday..." our nurse trails off.

As we wait, a nurse's assistant chats with us. Doug asks her about the difference between giving birth in Hospital A compared to Hospital B. He asks what the obstetricians are like, what the nurses are like, and where she would like to give birth. We determine that there are two other obstetricians at Hospital A who would have been much more supportive of my birth plan.

Our conversation dies down and Doug starts to load the car. I hobble around the room and drop our belongings into different bags. I start to feel a little lightheaded and I decide that I should rest.

I sit on the edge of the bed and carefully swing my legs up. Lying on my side, I close my eyes and revel in the quiet moment.

After a few minutes, a click-clacking approaches my door. A quick knock, the door opens, and someone is in my room. It's the obstetrician on call.

"How are you doing, dear? Ready to go home?" She is looking at her clipboard as she shifts her weight to one hip. I notice her three-inch heels first. Then my eyes follow her toned legs up to her pencil skirt and her tucked-in blouse. *Ah, I remember having a body that could fit into a pencil skirt,* I think. *Wonder if those days are over.*

"Yes, very ready."

She glances at a computer monitor next to my bed. "Hm, does your bottom still hurt? You haven't moved from that spot, have you? You were all curled up like a cat just like that the last time I was here."

"Yeah, it hurts, but I've been moving. This is actually the first time that I've been like this all day."

"Okay," she keeps going. "So you're going to be in quite a bit of pain for a while dear, with a tear like that. So you'll need to take a stool softener to help with bowel movements. You don't want to strain when it happens. You'll also need to do a sitz bath four to five times a day. The nurses will give you one before you go home. You don't need to fill the little bag up. Just the basin. Soak in it several times a day. I'm also going to write you a prescription for Motrin. You should take it regularly until the pain subsides. Any questions?"

My head is spinning. I just want to get her out of here.

"No, I'm fine."

She click-clacks her way out of the room. *Thank God.*

Our nurse comes by with a packet of information. I flip through it as she talks, scanning headings like, *Call 911 if you... Self-care...* and *Congratulations!* She hands me a basin, a tube, and a clear bag and tells me it's a sitz bath, but she has different instructions on how to use it.

"Oh, but the doctor said that I just needed to use the basin," I point out.

The nurse bites her lip and says, "Well, we've always been taught that you want to keep the water flowing and that's what the bag and the tube do. But the doctor said... Okay, well, I guess go with the doctor's advice."

Doug appears in the doorway with the car seat in hand. That is when I realize that Felicity's going-home outfit is already packed in the car. So she's going home in a hospital side-snap shirt and a diaper.

Doug carefully maneuvers Felicity's tiny body in the car seat and starts asking the nurse's assistant questions. "Is this good? Too loose? Can you check this?"

"I can't be the one to put her in and buckle her," she tells us. "You have to do it."

Doug manages to shorten the straps enough to hug Felicity's tiny body. Then, it's time to go.

The nurse's assistant pulls a wheelchair up to the door. *This again?* I would rather take my time and hobble out of here without the pressure on my pelvic floor.

"Hospital policy. You have to be wheeled out of here," she says.

I sigh. "Okay, as long as it's fast."

After I settle in, she lifts the car seat and swings it over to my lap.

"What are you doing?" I ask, blocking the seat from landing on my lap.

"You have to be the one carrying her out," she says.

"Can't we take her out of the car seat to do that? That thing is heavy!"

"I'm sorry," she frowns. "She has to be buckled into the car seat and on your lap."

You have to be fucking kidding me, I think.

"Oh my God," I rub my hands over my face, feeling the tears rise again. I bite my lip. "Let's just get this over with."

She tries to be gentle with the car seat, but the weight is unbelievable on my swollen everything-in-my-crotch. *I can't believe that this is what they do to women who just gave birth. What's the point? God... I'm so fucking tired. I just want to get out of here. Yeah, keep looking. I know I look like hell. Can't you see why? I've got a newborn baby. In a car seat. On my lap. Which is next to my vagina. Which is so swollen it probably doesn't even look like one anymore.*

The thoughts run rampant until we are at the door of the parking garage where the nurse's assistant drops us off. Doug immediately swings the car seat off my lap and offers his arm to help me up.

She waves good-bye to us. I wave back. It's not her fault. I don't want to be mean to her.

August 17, 2013 (two days postpartum)
We arrive home from the hospital around 3:00 p.m. Five days in the womb of the hospital, now released to a bright world of buzzing back-to-school traffic. August in Ohio is usually hot and humid, but this weather is an unexpected gift. Large, white, puffy clouds. Low humidity. Seventy-three degrees.

Despite my lack of sleep since Tuesday, I'm starting to feel awake again. It must be some magical hormone cocktail that drives me forward. I think back to that childbirth education class when I asked the nurse about how to deal with the lack of sleep. Her smirk is etched into my memory and now I know why—there is no *dealing* with the lack of sleep. You're so busy dealing with everything else that worrying about how to get sleep gets shoved to the bottom of the list. I guess sleep will come when I'm good and ready. My body will tell me when it's time to power down.

After he parks the car, Doug unloads all of the bags. Then, he unlatches Felicity's car seat from the base and takes her inside. When he returns, he helps me out of the car.

We walk arm-in-arm into the kitchen, as slow as I imagine we would if we were eighty years old. I'm surprised that everything looks the same. I shouldn't be surprised, but I am. How can the world still be the same? It was only a week ago when I laughed with our friends as we watched *Neverending Story* over there in the living room. Only a week ago, we were sitting at that table, eating hazelnut pancakes and maple sausage. We were swapping stories about the worst weddings that we had been to, and we agreed that it was the public park wedding that relied on a blaring car's speakers for the ceremony's music.

Now, there is a baby. In a car seat. In our kitchen.

A baby.

Time has undergone a kind of watershed—before and after. It is jagged and uneven. Our whole lives fall on the side of *before* and life on the *after* side is still so new. The memories are still crisp, light, and unfaded. And they are too few. There are not enough experiences to guide us. There are no signposts or hints about what comes next, so as we stand in the kitchen we face this huge, unanswerable question—*What do we do now?*

Doug chooses to busy himself with unpacking. He tells me to sit down and take it easy.

I look around the apartment and think about where I can sit without feeling pain. Not the glider. We already tried that at the hospital. And not the couch. After I sit down, I won't be able to get back up. So I decide on a chair at the dining room table. I wince as I sit down. Then, I scoot to the edge. Better.

It looks like someone has robbed us. A mound of papers covers the dining room table. As I sift through it, I realize that it's not all junk mail. There are official immunization records, discharge papers with warning signs for me and Felicity, business cards, along with a folder of brochures about why babies cry (*Never shake a baby!*), an online immunization database, and a list of help lines for new parent questions. I read through the postpartum depression brochure carefully and answer the questions. *No, no, no, no.* Looks like I'm good so far.

We spend the rest of the afternoon and evening feeding Felicity, changing diapers, trying out burp cloths, fielding phone calls, and hanging a black-out curtain in the nursery. Doug tells me to sleep in our bedroom while he sleeps on the twin bed next to the co-sleeper in the baby's room. I'm relieved.

Finally, it's time to sleep.

I congratulate myself on a job well done. *You did it! Without medication! You're amazing!*

Yeah, that was pretty hard. I can't believe I made it through all that. Doug... he was amazing. God, I'm so lucky to have him. That guy... I picked a good one. And I didn't even know when we got married that he would be like this... I didn't know how wonderful he could really be.

That face that Felicity makes in her sleep—so cute. She looks a lot like him.

Okay, really, go to sleep now.

I settle in, turn on my side, the way that I always slept when I was pregnant. *Maybe I need my body pillow.* I wrap it around me. *That's better.*

But I'm waiting to hear her cry. That tiny cry. I think about what that cry means to me. Before long, I'm composing a poem.

I hear you cry, as I try to sleep
But it is only in my head—
that long wail, the gasps, the oscillating tones
And the me of yesterday could never have imagined
The beauty of a shrill cry
It was in a language I couldn't understand.
But now, I hear it and it means—Listen! I am Alive!

I turn in bed and pull out the tiny memo pad from my nightstand. I once used it to chart my temperature in the morning to track my ovulation. Now, I write the poem as quickly as I can.

That's better.

Time passes.

I turn in bed carefully, but it is still so difficult. I chuckle when I remember that fantasy about dropping into an effortless three-hour non-pregnant nap after giving birth. Now, here I am, lying on my side, no one complimenting me on my amazing performance during the birth, so tired that I can't go to sleep.

As I lie on my side, my hand slides from my hip to my stomach. My mind knows that my belly is gone, but it's my heart that starts to understand that my center has shifted again. There is an emptiness. Something is missing.

Life.

She is not there anymore.

She. Wow.

I want to get out of bed, pick her up, and place her on my chest.

But you need to sleep!

I try.

I look at the digital clock next to the bed. 2:45 a.m.

I wish I knew how long it will be before Felicity is hungry again. She fell asleep an hour ago, but I can't stop thinking.

I shift from my side to my back as I lie in bed. I have to pee. And I know I don't have the strength to pull myself up. I reach for my cell phone and call Doug's phone. I hear it ringing in the next room.

"I need help," I tell him.

He comes.

"What's wrong?"

"I can't get up. I need to pee."

He leans down and lets me loop my arms around his neck. He is my crutch as I hobble to the bathroom, leaning on my right foot. Sometimes, it feels like my crotch is on fire. Sometimes, it feels frozen. Right now, it's on fire. I try not to think about what the muscles must look like after having a human head push through them—but I do.

When I'm next to the toilet, I start to wiggle out of my disposable underwear and Doug helps lower me to the seat. I'm still leaning to the left, so he stays there while I pee.

Is that really the sound of me peeing? It sounds sloppy, sporadic. *I hope that's not permanent.*

I haven't bled that much, so I think about reusing this pair of underwear. But Doug is already ahead of me. He has thrown it in the garbage bag next to the plastic tub where we have stored all the afterbirth care. It's full of supplies: giant maxi pads from the hospital, Dermoplast spray, several boxes of Depends, witch hazel pads, moist toilet wipes, a squeeze bottle to flush water over my perineum, Lysol disinfectant, some cheap towels, and trash bags.

Going to the bathroom has become quite a production.

Doug hands me the squeeze bottle and I start flooding the whole area with water.

Something falls out of me.

"Oh..." I say.

"What?"

"I think... something just came out of me."

"What do you mean *something*?"

He helps me stand up and we look into the toilet together. And there we see a hunk of blood. I think about the discharge class. What did she say? Call the hospital if you pass a clot the size of... a golf ball? An orange? I can't remember. We can't see it very well because it has fallen to the back of the toilet, almost out of sight.

Doug leaves and returns with a flashlight. He squats in front of the toilet and casts some light onto the clot. This looks to be the size of an egg.

"That's... kind of big," I state the obvious.

"Stay here. I'll call the hospital," he says.

"Can you help me set up the sitz bath first?"

"Yeah, okay."

I wasn't sure how this whole sitz bath was going to work, but now I understand that it's basically a shallow tub that sits down into the toilet and holds water. When you sit on top of it, your entire crotch is immersed in water. The first time I do it, I'm won over by how much better it makes the whole area feel.

I've been sitting in the sitz bath for about five minutes while Doug communicates with the nurse's station. He has news when he hangs up.

"Should be fine. As long as you don't pass another one."

He helps me stand, and I gingerly pat myself with a towel. My finger rubs against something foreign. It doesn't feel like a part of me.

"What?" he asks. I must have made a face.

"This doesn't feel right."

"What doesn't?"

"*All* of this," I circle my crotch. "The whole enchilada. I think something's wrong."

"Okay..." he yawns and rubs his eyes. "Do you want me to look?"

"Yes, just tell me if something looks... I don't know... wrong, I guess."

Oh my God... What if the OB stitched me up wrong? It only took him twenty minutes. What if he lined up the skin wrong? That's probably why it's so tight. Oh my God. Will they have to do surgery to fix it? Will I ever be able to have sex again? Oh my God...

Doug kneels in front of me and checks me over. So we are now at a point in our relationship where he is examining my swollen everything. A part of me that he once found arousing—now, surely not. That last shred of privacy in our marriage is gone. Childbirth didn't take it away. I didn't have a choice then. I was caught in the urgency of pushes. But I have a choice now—and I'm choosing to put myself out there.

"I mean, you look swollen, but you're clean," he says.

I guide his hand to the area in question. "What's all this?"

He looks. "Hemorrhoids. A couple pea-sized ones."

"They feel larger than peas."

"They're not. They'll go away," he assures me.

"So everything else looks okay?"

"You're fine, Sweets."

He empties the sitz bath into the toilet, rinses and disinfects it, and hangs it in the shower. Then, he lines a new pair of underwear with a maxi pad topped with witch hazel pads, sprays me with Dermoplast, and helps me pull up the whole ensemble. We wash our hands. Then, he helps me hobble back to bed. I loop my arms around his neck and he helps lower me back to the bed.

He kisses my head. "Night, Sweets." Then he returns to bed in the other room.

It's 3:30 a.m. now. My body feels heavy with sleep, the kind that sinks you deeper into the mattress. I feel ready. I start drifting off. And then...

I hear Felicity cry.

Oh my God...

...Okay...

August 18, 2013 (three days postpartum)

My parents arrive to meet Felicity at 11:00 a.m., and the timing is perfect. Felicity is awake, but not yet hungry enough to cry. My mom has tears in her eyes when she walks through the door. The last time I remember seeing her like this was at the end of my wedding reception when she hugged me before we left for our honeymoon. Then, my dad shuffles through the door, his arms hanging at his sides, his face still frozen in that emotionless stare.

I hug my mom first. Ever since the cancer came back seven years ago, I've wanted this for her—to have grandchildren. I try to hold back my tears as I transfer Felicity from my arms to hers. Time compresses. The last moment that she held a newborn couldn't have been thirty years ago. It must have been yesterday. One of Felicity's hands escapes the swaddle blanket and Mom tenderly wraps it around her finger. Then, she helps my dad hold Felicity.

He looks down at Felicity, the corners of his mouth lifting.

"Well... Hello there, Felicity!" he says.

We spend an hour catching up and then we have another visitor, our friend, Cate. I'm starting to feel lightheaded, so I lean back against the couch and pull my legs up to rest on the cushions.

"Sweets, I need to go to the store and stock up on food," Doug says.

"I'm hungry," I say.

I hear him open the pantry behind me. Then, he drops something into my lap.

A jar of peanut butter. And then a spoon.

I shrug and open it. Cate laughs.

After I eat a few heaping spoonfuls, I turn to read the nutritional facts. Two tablespoons is 190 calories. *How many calories do I need to eat if I'm breastfeeding?*

"I'm not sure how much of this to eat," I confess to Cate.

"I think at this point... just keep going," she says.

"Right." I sink another spoonful into my mouth and lean back against the couch. It's quiet as Cate rocks Felicity in the glider. I want to talk about the birth, but I don't want to overshare. But how can I talk about anything else right now? How can I talk about the news or the weather when something like *birth* just happened to me? But I think that Cate certainly doesn't want to know all of the details of birth, especially since she doesn't want to have kids.

Another moment passes before we say anything.

"So what happened with your OB?" Cate asks. "Was she here for the delivery?"

I roll my eyes.

And then I tell her everything anyway.

It's the middle of the afternoon and I've just finished nursing Felicity. I tell everyone that I'm taking a nap and they are happy to watch her.

But as I'm lying in bed, I think about my parents. I think about how happy it makes me that they are here, that they are both getting the chance to be grandparents. I think about what I will write when I'm finally able to sit at a computer for a period of time. I think about Felicity's baby book.

I don't sleep. Again.

My parents leave that evening and Doug and I get ready for the next feeding, whenever it may be. There doesn't seem to be a pattern to when she's hungry. We haven't really been keeping track of it either. We have just managed to change her when she needs to be changed and feed her when she needs to be fed. Was she getting enough to eat? All the baby care books kept saying that it depended on how many diapers she had each day.

Shit.

We should have been keeping track. But we were so focused on getting settled in and I was so tired. We decide to start tracking her feedings and diapers roughly on a piece of paper.

That night, Felicity starts nursing at 10:00 p.m. She unlatches at 10:45. *Ah, sweet relief,* I think as I lay Felicity in her co-sleeper. I hear the clanking of pots coming from downstairs. Then, the blender runs. Doug must be in food preparation mode. I smile as I gaze at Felicity.

Her mouth twitches. Then, she's rooting around again, searching for my breast.

Oh, what is this! I've given birth to a bottomless pit! I take a deep breath and gather my strength. *Okay... here we go again.*

I help her latch again. I sit on the edge of the bed with a foot rest beneath my feet, but I don't want to stay in the same position. I consider moving, but I'm still too sore in my bottom to sit in the glider. Doug brings me food. I suck down fruit-veggie smoothies and split pea soup through straws. Then, he returns with a thick peanut butter and jelly sandwich.

At 11:55, she unlatches again. I sigh and then smile.

Yes! You made it! Two whole hours!

I tenderly return Felicity to her co-sleeper and lean against the mattress. I sink deeply into it, a total bedgasm rippling out from my core and escaping through my head and toes. *I am so done.*

...ahhh... uh. Uh...

Those grunts are unmistakable now. She is *still* hungry. I gaze over at her tiny mouth gasping at the air and I swear I can feel my fingers reaching all the way down into the bottom of my soul and grasping at the last remaining fibers of my being that haven't become threadbare. The red numbers on the clock announce 12:15.

Another hour passes. My back and arms ache as my baby nurses and nurses and nurses. I think about what all of this nursing must be doing to my metabolism. My waking and sleeping rhythms have been obliterated. As she nurses, I feel my body revving. Every feeding session throws more logs on the fire, the calories burning and burning, and I am awake again. *Am I keeping up? How do I know if I'm eating enough?*

"You need to eat at least 300 calories every three hours," Doug advises.

"Yeah, well, you're going to need to remind me. I'm not going to realize how much time has passed."

"It's every time you feed her. Every time, you need 300 calories."

"So what happens if she nurses for three hours like this? Every time?"

His lips pull down into a frown. "She can't still be hungry. Maybe people were holding her too much today."

I look down at her face as she sleeps. "No, I'm pretty sure she was hungry. I think I can tell when she's hungry now."

"Maybe she's going through a growth spurt?" he suggests.

"I don't know. Maybe." I sigh.

"You need to get some sleep, baby girl."

Anger bubbles in me. I bite my lip. That's all I hear anymore. *You need to eat. You need to sleep. You need to eat. You need to sleep. Why are you awake? You should be sleeping when the baby's sleeping!*

"I can't sleep now. I'm all wired. It takes me a while to unwind and go to bed."

"Yeah, but you don't know how long it will be until she needs to eat again."

Tell me something that I don't already know. God, lay off, I fume. *I've just been destroyed by a seven-pound creature.*

"Just... Let me..." I shake my head, unsure of how to finish.

"Okay, fine."

Days as a unit of time don't mean anything to me anymore, so I see the future in terms of three-hour intervals. One twenty-four hour period has eight three-hour intervals during which I need to completely finish a meal for myself and a feeding for her. If she manages to lower her nursing time to just thirty minutes, and I can eat in ten minutes, and we change her and get her ready for sleep in ten minutes, I'll have as much as two hours and ten minutes to sleep until she needs to eat again. But it will probably take me an hour to unwind, and then I'll have a whole one-hour stretch of sleep before she's crying for me again.

And around and around we go on this sick carousel of feeding, eating, and sleeping. I manage to keep up with the rhythm of the feeding and eating. But I keep missing my chance to grab on to sleep and then it's floating away from me again, not to return for another three hours.

August 19, 2013 (four days postpartum)

I still can't sleep by 2:00 a.m., so Doug suggests that we relax downstairs with *The Office* playing in the background. I rest my feet on an ottoman and stare at them. *Whose legs are these?* They are so bloated that arches in my feet have disappeared. I poke at my skin and my fingerprint lingers. Gross. Really gross. Throughout my whole pregnancy, I never retained water in my legs or feet. The nurses kept checking me at every doctor's visit, pinching my skin, and approving with a surprised nod.

"Look at my feet. Do you see this?"

Doug frowns. "You're retaining water. Probably because you were nursing for so long in one position."

I stand. As I walk toward the kitchen, I feel tingling sensations in my feet, like pins and needles. I'm walking in a swamp that is trapped underneath my skin.

Before I lie down for sleep, I weigh myself. 173 pounds—only four pounds lighter than I was when I went into labor. How is that possible? She weighed over seven and a half pounds at birth! Did I have that much water retention?

I look in the mirror and I barely recognize myself. My face is pale and puffy. My hair is pulled back into a messy, knotted ponytail. I turn to the side. My pregnant belly is gone, but a large pooch droops and jiggles as I move. Below my rib cage, I see a glimpse of my pre-pregnant body. I'm not sad that I don't weigh less—just extremely puzzled. Besides Felicity, I lost a placenta and buckets and buckets of fluids. What did I still have left to lose?

I lie down and close my eyes, hoping that I'll sleep before the next two feedings, presumably around 4:00 and 7:00 a.m. But I don't really sleep. I finally drift off for forty-five minutes before she starts crying.

I don't hate nursing her—as long as it doesn't last longer than an hour at a time. I thought I might hate the act of her pulling on my nipples for nourishment. But then her brow lifts and her eyes flip open in a look of true surprise and elation when some milk reaches her mouth. And I am doing that for her. When I pull the nipple guard off, I see milk pooled in the plastic end and I feel satisfied that she's getting food.

When it's over and I've selected another 300 calorie meal that Doug has prepared for me in the refrigerator, I lie down for sleep. But it still doesn't come. Each feeding that passes feels like more reassurance that I'll never sleep again.

I look over at the digital clock in our room. 8:45 a.m. Doug has taken the most recent sleep shift in the baby's room.

Time passes. I don't sleep.

Doug opens the door and says, "She's ready baby girl. After you feed her, we'll get her ready for the pediatrician's office."

After I feed her. Feed her. Feed her. I curl into a ball and cry.

"What's wrong baby girl?" he asks as he sits on the bed next to me. "Is this hormones or something else?"

I shake my head. "I feel like..." I choke on the sobs. "Like... I'm coming apart on the inside. Everything's coming apart."

I shuffle into the waiting room of the pediatrician's office, eleven pounds of fluid sloshing in my legs. The only pants that fit me are drawstring pajama pants, so that's what I'm wearing out in public today. Pink, black, and gray-striped pajama pants. I haven't washed my hair in two days, so I bundle it in a ponytail. Doug carries the car seat to the front desk and signs us in.

It's not the first time that I've been here. This is the office of my family doctor, but today, she becomes Felicity's pediatrician.

"Felicity?"

I look around. I wasn't expecting the nurse to call Felicity's name, but it makes sense. She is the patient, after all. We are officially acknowledging her personhood.

I slosh into the exam room and lower slowly into a chair, being careful not to sit down too hard. Doug handles all the parental responsibilities. He helps the nurse measure Felicity's height and head circumference and then he undresses Felicity for her official weigh-in.

"She's six pounds, thirteen ounces," the nurse pronounces.

Hm... Is that bad?

The doctor comes in and smiles. "Hey guys, how's it going?"

I want to tell her that I've never felt so horrible in my whole life, but what comes out is, "I'm exhausted. I'm just so exhausted. Last night, she nursed for three hours straight."

"Oh my God," her brow furrows, as she sits in a chair across from me. She looks me in the eyes. I hope she can see how desperate I am. "Does she do that often?"

"There's not really a pattern to her eating yet, but in the last few days, she'll just nurse and nurse. At a minimum, she'll nurse for an hour. On the day after she was born, she nursed for five hours straight. And last night it was three hours."

"Is she awake the whole time?"

"Well..." I think about it. "She'll start off really strong, and then she'll slow down into a groove. In the marathon feedings, she'll fall asleep after an hour. So I'd put her down to sleep, but then she'd be awake again, rooting around. So I'd pick her up and continue to nurse her. And that pattern just goes on and on until she passes out."

"It sounds like she's hungry."

"I mean, I thought so too, so I kept nursing and nursing her, but it didn't seem to help." I motion to Doug. "He thinks maybe we're holding her too much."

"No," she shakes her head. "She's hungry. She's eating and eating and not getting full, so she finally falls asleep after she's exhausted herself trying to eat." She pauses to look at the computer screen. "Let's see... she's six, thirteen. She left the hospital at seven pounds, five ounces?"

"Yes."

"And she was born seven pounds, eleven ounces?"

"Yes."

"So..." she looks at the computer screen before she turns back to me. "She's lost eleven percent of her body weight in four days. That's cause for concern," she nods as she says this.

I am so relieved. *I'm not crazy. I knew that she was hungry. I'm not crazy.*

"Do you have any idea how much milk you're producing?" she asks.

I shake my head. "We've just been trying to keep our heads above water, so I haven't even tried pumping."

"Okay... okay." She is quiet for a moment. "Have you tried hand expressing any milk?"

"The lactation consultant said that I have flat and inverted nipples, so that's why I wasn't able to do that."

"Okay... So I'd go ahead and try pumping just to get an idea of what you're producing. It's not going to be as much as what your baby can pull out, but it will do a few things. It will give you an idea of what you're producing. It will give you a break from these marathon nursing sessions. And it will keep stimulating milk production."

She stands up to examine Felicity. She looks into her eyes and feels her belly. "She's pretty jaundiced, too. We'll need to follow up on that."

"Can I ask a question about me?"

She turns to look at me. "I've gained eleven pounds of fluid, and it's all in my legs. And I can't sleep. I keep trying to go to sleep between feedings, and I just can't. I'm afraid that if this continues, it's going to affect my milk coming in."

"Okay, so that's something that I'd talk with your OB about."

Oh, wonderful, I think. *Her.*

"Great. She's in Italy," I say.

"Oh... She's in a practice by herself?"

"Yeah."

"Maybe the nurses there, then... But really your OB should be the one to consult about those kinds of issues."

It seems strange to me how we're talking about all of these issues: Felicity's weight loss, my lack of sleep and fluid retention, and my milk production. It's all related, but the pediatrician is responsible for addressing Felicity's weight loss, not any issues with me. But the issues with me are causing Felicity's weight loss. It seems to me that someone—I don't know who—should be treating this problem holistically. This is the time and place where I need someone to help *me* first so that *I* can help Felicity. I thought maybe this doctor—my family doctor—would be able to help. After all, she's also Felicity's pediatrician. But perhaps there are some legal issues here to consider? Who knows.

"So because of her rapid weight loss," the doctor explains, "she really needs to have formula as a supplement until your milk comes in."

There it is. All the on-line breastfeeding forums have cautioned me about this: the dreaded supplementation discussion at the first visit to the pediatrician. But I gather all of their dire warnings about supplementing in the first week and throw them to the wind. I'll do what I need to do in this moment—regardless of the shame that I know will befall me.

The doctor pulls a starter kit of formula from a cabinet and opens the box. She unscrews the cap of a premade bottle. For a moment, I cringe. But when my doctor hands it to me, I take it. I push aside all my thoughts about the most natural option being the best decision in this moment. Today, living off something synthetic is better than dying from the lack of something natural.

I nestle the nipple of the bottle between Felicity's lips and she starts guzzling. Her eyes flip open in surprise.

"You want to give her breaks, every half ounce or so," the doctor advises. "She needs some time for her stomach to realize how much she's eaten. If you let her eat too quickly, it could come straight back up."

"So... I should just take it away and check every now and then?"

"Yeah, until you get the hang of it."

The bottle has useful measurement marks to keep track of how much Felicity has eaten. I pull the bottle away after every half of an ounce. Then, I burp her, and we resume the feeding. Once Felicity has finished the bottle, she is fast asleep in my arms.

"Thank you," I say. "Just... um..." I shake my head, the heat of my tears stinging as they rise. "This means a lot." I wish there were stronger words than *thank you*, but I'm too emotional to find them.

"So what kind of schedule should we follow," Doug asks, "while her milk is coming in?"

"So I'd alternate nursing with pumping during feeding sessions," the doctor explains. "For one feeding, nurse her for thirty minutes, then supplement. These bottles have two ounces in them, but she doesn't need to finish them if she's full. In the next feeding, pump for thirty minutes while someone else feeds her the formula. That will help you keep your production going until your milk fully comes in. Then, you can drop the formula when she's able to get full from nursing."

"I mean... When can I expect my milk to come in?" I ask. "It's already been four days and I'm not really feeling anything."

"It can take longer for some women... Sometimes six or eight days."

When we get home, I take Felicity to our bedroom, take my shirt off, and put her skin-to-skin against my chest. I slowly lower to the bed and get comfortable. I breathe deeply and silence the internal voices shouting their advice from all sides. The doubts. The fear. The anxiety. The shame. The uncertainty of what comes next. And I allow myself to just *be*. For her to just *be*. I breathe and she rises. I breathe and she falls. I breathe. She breathes. And there, in just being, I find my peace.

I gently cover her back with the light sheet on our bed.

I let my hands rub her velvety back, her soft skin shifting over her tiny bones like a coat that is one size too big. She gives a tiny grunt. Her head nestles closer to my heart.

Time stops as I hold her like this. In this position, we are whole again. My mind is not searching for her. My heart opens. And opens. And opens.

I am open.

Now, I believe that I could do this again. I could do this eight more times if my body let me.

Doug cradles Felicity on the couch as she works on a new two-ounce bottle. I don't mind sharing the feeding bond. In fact, I'm happy to know that Felicity is definitely eating a certain amount of food. After she eats, she falls asleep right away and I feel like we've done something good for her.

"What can I do for you, baby girl?" Doug asks.

"I need... people. Like friends. Yeah, I need to see friends today."

"I can make that happen. Why don't you try to sleep?"

Okay... Here we go again.

Doug places Felicity in the bouncer and walks into the kitchen to make some lunch. It's just my Dad and Felicity in the living room now. He's watching a documentary about the Civil War. I watch from the corner of the living room to see if Dad will go pick her up. He doesn't. I walk through the living room, but his eyes are still fixed on the screen. I'm almost to the stairs, almost ready to take a nap.

"Hey, Dad?"

He turns to look at me. "Yeah."

"Do you want to hold Felicity?"

He looks at her in the bouncer.

"That's fine."

That's as close to *yes* as he gets these days. So I position his arms and hands and place Felicity's swaddled body into them. He lowers her to his leg to steady his grip and then he looks at her sleeping face. As he holds her, his hands stop shaking.

"Been a while since I've held a tiny baby," he says quietly.

"You're a natural, Dad."

He shakes his head so slowly. "Wasn't around much to help your mother when you all were this small."

I sit next to him as he holds her.

"They're not this small for long." He shakes his head again.

"I know." I swallow.

"They're just not this small for long," he repeats.

"I know, Dad." I give him a side hug and rest my hand on his. I stay downstairs to watch the documentary with him. I'll sleep later.

Later that afternoon, Jarod and Katy stop by to see us. Katy holds Felicity against her rounded pregnant belly, where her own daughter is growing. For Katy's sake, I try to focus on the positive. But then I find myself launching into a forty-five minute diatribe of how I thought the obstetricians had mistreated us. Katy listens and nods and then adds her own perspective as a pharmacist to help us understand the inner workings of hospitals.

When they leave, I feel badly that I spent almost all of our time complaining about the birth. Again, it's not what I wanted to do, but I just couldn't let the conversation go anywhere else.

That night, I set my mind to figuring out the new breast pump. Once I zip up the hands-free pumping bustier, I figure out how to position the nipple cups into the holes and attach the two-ounce vials to the cups. I start the pump.

"Ahhh!" I wince as the pump starts pulling at my nipples. "Wow... Oh God..." I search around the room for something to fix my eyes on. Then, I look at Doug, who is feeding Felicity. Her face is turned away from me. "This is going to sound strange," I say, "but can you aim her face at me? I feel like I need to see her."

As soon as I see her face, the pain subsides. I still feel the pulling sensation, but it has dulled. After two minutes, the pump ends the light *stimulation phase* and moves into the serious *expression phase*. Longer, harder pulls start to draw milk from my breasts. I don't want to see how much is being produced, so I cover my chest with a light swaddling blanket. My eyes follow the clear tubing that peeks out from underneath the blanket and connects to the pump. A digital timer ticks away on the face of the pump.

"How long are you going to pump?" Doug asks.

"Well, I'd like to do a long time to see how much I can get in just one go. So maybe an hour?"

As I look at Felicity's face, I remind myself that the odds are in my favor. My body is meant to do this. Ninety-five percent of women will make enough milk for their babies. It just takes a little extra time for some of us. Babies lose weight in the first week—she'll gain it back. If I stick with this, it will get easier. Breast milk is important. It will give her extra antibodies to keep her safe. It's the easiest thing for her to digest. Breastfed babies are healthier, not just now, but for years down the road.

Holly and my mom arrive and sit next to Doug on the couch. My mom takes out a blanket that she is crocheting for Felicity. While Holly cradles Felicity, Doug feeds me a sandwich. The pump drones on. I want to be the one holding Felicity, but I know that I have to do this in order to be able to nurse her by myself soon. I tap a button to increase the suction from level four to level five. I wince and turn it back down.

"How high does it go up?" he asks.

"Up to level nine."

"What are you on?"

"Level four."

"Wow."

"Yeah."

Around the forty-minute mark, I start to feel a little woozy. I ask for more water and I polish off sixteen ounces all at once. *How much water have I had today?* I can't even guess because I can't separate today from yesterday or the day before that. It all feels like one very, very long day.

"How long has she been doing this?" my mom asks Doug as she points to the pump.

I hold up the ticking pump: *43:07, 43:08*. She has a concerned look on her face, but she doesn't say anything.

At fifty-two minutes, I realize that I might pass out if I continue. The feeling is comparable to how I feel after having done one hour of intense cardio kickboxing. I turn it off and take a minute to catch my breath before looking at my production. I look beneath the blanket and see that the vials are not full. Not even close. I discreetly and carefully remove the left vial from the bustier. I feel some drops of milk land on my leg and I'm angry that I've spilled some of it. I realize that I should lean forward first so that any remaining milk can drain into the vials before I remove them.

There is a short layer of milk at the bottom of the vial. I can't believe how little there is. I don't even want to look at the measurement.

My mom sees me struggling with the vials and she comes over to help. She pours the contents of the right vial into the left one.

"How much is there?" I ask.

She scrutinizes the vial. "Looks like a little over half an ounce."

"How much does she need at every feeding?" I ask Doug.

"Two ounces."

Now, I feel the pain in my breasts. It's not the pain of engorgement, which is what I wish for. It's a sore, aching, tired pain. I ask Doug for some ice packs and he hands me two bags of frozen corn. I place them against my chest and lower my head. I can feel the eyes of my mother and sister on me.

And that is when I completely lose it.

It starts as silent sobs, but then the sound catches in my throat and becomes a short, high-pitched shriek. Doug is kneeling in front of me now as I'm sitting in the glider.

"What is it? What can I do?" he asks.

I just shake my head because there's nothing he can do. I have too many problems that he can't fix. That confident, prepared, attractive woman that I used to be? Gone. Completely and utterly obliterated.

My mom lowers her eyes and continues to crochet. But I know my mom—it's not that she doesn't care. She is giving us space. She is letting Doug help me. A moment passes as Doug continues to hug me.

My mom says quietly, "I know *exactly* how she feels..."

He helps me stand and as I do, I realize that urine is flooding out of me. It's soaking my disposable underwear. I'm peeing so much that I know it will leak. So now, I am sobbing and peeing uncontrollably, while covering my bare chest with frozen corn—all in front of my family.

I'm absolutely humiliated.

Doug guides me to the staircase and stands behind me, helping push my bloated body up the stairs. I clutch the rail and pull myself up each stair with all the strength that I have left. His chin rests on my shoulder and I start muttering.

"What is it, baby girl? What did you say?" he asks.

"I'm... so... broken."

We have the conversation of our lives while I'm naked, sitting on the toilet, a pool of urine puddled around my feet. Doug is sitting on the bathroom tile, looking up at me as hot tears pour from my dark ringed eyes and fall down my red face. My dirty hair is pulled back in a messy ponytail. My bloated legs crowd the toilet seat and when I look down at my left arm, I see the bruise from the IV during labor. A red mask of hives covers the back of my hands.

I tell him that I'm absolutely exhausted. That I have nothing left to give anyone. Then, I tell him about some of the things that I've been thinking as I try to sleep. That I never knew that I really loved him until all of this happened. That I believe in God now—even though I've been religious my whole life. And that she is the best thing that could have happened to us.

When it is over, we set to work on cleaning—Doug cleans the bathroom floor while I clean myself. It feels good to descend from an emotional summit and work on routine tasks. Maybe it helps us close a very long chapter of our relationship so we can move on to a new one. Whatever it is, we come out of that bathroom and tell my mom that we're going to take Felicity out in her stroller for a night walk. She joins us.

It looks like a full moon, but the calendar says we are two days away from that. As I walk, the fluid in my legs squishes around my feet. I feel like I'm wearing a wet suit that has been flooded with water. We take our time walking down the street. Identical small apartment lights line our path. I take a breath and listen to my mom and Doug talk about the weather and the plans for tomorrow.

The Shift

Birth brings an end to that strange oneness that I experienced in labor. But then I entered an even stranger space. I was expecting that the end of pregnancy would be the beginning of the "two" of us. Like cells dividing from each other, birth would pinch off that membrane between us. The baby would still need me, but we would finally be individual selves.

Not true.

In those first days and weeks, that membrane was still holding us together. I felt it every time she nursed and my body cramped in response. I felt it when I heard her cry and my breasts ached. I felt it when I'd close my eyes to sleep, only to see her face etched in golden relief against my eyelids. I felt it when I heard her move in the bassinet and my hand would lift to check her position. I felt it when I would wake up after a short stint of sleep and immediately think of her. In the midst of pumping, I would look at her face to dull the pain.

I couldn't fully articulate this feeling at the time. I was too caught up in taking care of Felicity to pause long enough to realize this paradox of being separate, yet still attached.

But now, I can see that my individual self was quickly swallowed by the constant demands of how to care for my baby. The demands dulled my ability to sense when *I* needed something, like a shower or food. They continued to teach me the lesson that pregnancy and labor had taught me: I was not in control. I could not find stability by leaning on my prior plans and expectations. And I could not find comfort by imagining the confident mother that I would someday become. That was simply too far away. I was in an unexpected limbo, and all I could do was embrace the present moment. In all of its ugliness. In all of its messiness. In all of its flux. Because it was the only truth that I had in that moment.

I see now that accepting my inability to maintain control over this whole process served a purpose. It made my identity flexible. It humbled my individual self over and over again. And this humbling was necessary to open the borders of my identity, so my new role as a mother could step in. I would not return to conversations with my close friends as simply a woman who now had a baby. I would return as a mother.

Perhaps one of the reasons that I was so desperate to see my close friends after the birth was because I didn't know who I was anymore. My individual self was suffocating underneath the weight of new motherhood. The baby saw me as a food source. My husband saw me as a tired, aching, recovering woman who was also trying to breastfeed. But how did I see myself? Sometimes, I felt like a formerly pregnant woman. Sometimes, I felt like a mother. But I felt that familiar piece of individuality disappear and I needed people who remembered that version of me. I needed them to revive her, so that I would know she was not gone forever—just waiting in the wings.

So they came to see me. And what happened? Was I able to slip back into the skin of my former self?

No.

My mind kept going back to memories of the birth. I knew that the feeling of oneness was over, that it was slowly fading away. And I didn't want it to end. I wasn't ready. So I replayed memories of the birth over and over in my head to keep it alive. To control it. It dominated my thoughts. And therefore, the birth was all I wanted to talk about. I wanted to find the right words to try to explain the experience. But when I would look at my friends, I would lose the words. How could an experience like that ever be explained in words?

So I found myself talking about the facts. And then the facts soon turned into complaints as all the hurtful memories burst forth, pushing aside all the gratitude that I felt. They couldn't exist together in the same conversation. So I talked about all of the things the obstetricians had said or done. I was so deeply hurt by their treatment of me that I could only see them as villains. They became my story's antagonists. When I was filling out Felicity's baby book to include the information about her birth, there was a blank for the name of the doctor who delivered her. I wrote "a nameless asshole." I hated the fact that he was the one who signed her keepsake birth certificate, which bore her footprints at birth. I didn't want to remember his name. At the time, I felt that he was inhumane.

Now, with some distance from the birth, I don't see this doctor as an antagonist, striving to disempower laboring mothers. Instead, I feel that he was just indifferent. I was just business, a twenty-minute slice of his day, the last task before he went home for dinner. He wouldn't remember my face because he never really saw it. He certainly wouldn't remember my daughter. He had no passion for what he did. And he will probably never know how much his lack of compassion affected me.

But in those first days after the birth, I couldn't see him so benignly. All I knew was that he presumed to know what would help me to have a satisfactory birth. Because he thought all women wanted the same thing. Because he thought there was one best way to give birth and I needed to be told what it was.

And he was wrong.

Although the negative memories of Felicity's birth dominated those initial conversations with friends and family, I think expressing how I felt about the experience helped me to process it. It helped me to build an identity as a mother. It helped me to see myself as a strong survivor. I didn't have anything else in my arsenal as a mother yet, so I leaned on the experience of giving birth to make meaning of what kind of mother I was becoming. I used the fact that I was in labor for thirty-four hours, that I had unsupportive obstetricians, and that I had labored without medication as evidence that I was a committed, competent mother who had proven the wisdom of trusting her body.

This new identity as "strong mother" fed into my internal dialogue and helped to reform my thoughts. If Felicity started crying just twenty minutes after I fed her, my previous self would have said, "Sorry, but I just fed you and I haven't slept in two days. Get over it." But instead, this new version of me picked her up and nursed her again. My daughter couldn't say, "Thank you for giving up more sleep to feed me." She couldn't even smile. But I did it. And I wasn't even angry about it. I could still hear those previous thoughts (*I'm so tired... Oh my God, go to sleep already. What's wrong with you?*), but they were a whisper compared to the new stream of consciousness that had begun to infuse my thoughts (*Are you hungry? Can I help you? It's okay. Let me help you.*)

Why did I do this? Some would quickly say that it was because I loved her, but I think this "love" started as something else. Love wasn't what I felt at midnight, 2:00, 4:00, and 6:00 when Felicity needed to eat. Beneath my heavy eyelids weighed down with exhaustion, what I felt was a sense of duty to help this tiny person who needed me so much. It was obligation. This person belonged to me. This person had come from me. So I had to care for her. Even though the excitement of birth had ended. Even though I was exhausted. Even though I was in pain. Even though I didn't know when I would sleep or shower next. Even though the nursing and pumping had winnowed me down to nothing but a food source.

Even though. Even though. Even though.

And so in those early, difficult days of new motherhood, I had to lean on something else in the absence of euphoria. I needed something to pull me through the darkness, the ardor, and the ceaseless hours. So I focused on the task of care—both caring for myself and caring for my daughter. I nursed until I couldn't nurse anymore. I cared for my swollen parts, my torn parts, my painful parts. I tried to sleep. I ate well. Every moment of those weeks was spent in the task of care.

And after all of that caring, I can say that the motivation to care for my daughter didn't truly begin with love.

I cared for her because she needed me.

Love didn't have a brilliant beginning. It didn't own a designated minute hand on the clock like birth did. Love grew like my child had during pregnancy: slowly and quietly. Like my daughter, love wasn't born fully developed or realized. It would grow. It would change. It would strengthen.

It makes me remember the words that the apostle Paul had written to the Corinthian congregation. They were words that I had once recited for Bible school. Ones that I had heard over and over again in wedding ceremonies. They had succumbed to the same fate as the Pledge of Allegiance—committed to my memory, but drained of power and meaning. So only now was I beginning to see their application in my life. Paul wrote, "Love is not self-seeking, it is not easily angered. It keeps no record of wrongs... It always protects, always trusts, always hopes, always perseveres."

But I don't think I could have felt the full power of those words without all the giving that mothering required of me. And this is where I think mothers and fathers differ. While both parents may sacrifice their time, energy, social lives, and careers, it is the mother who sacrifices her body—and I had no idea how much of my body I would give. I knew that pregnancy was going to change me and that birth would be painful, but nothing could have prepared me for the experience of giving and giving and giving myself until I was certain that there wasn't anything left to give. And then—only after reaching that point—did I find an untapped pool of strength way down in the bottom of my soul. And through that discovery, I can believe that—no matter how her life takes shape—she'll never be able to exhaust the love that I have for her.

There will always be more love.

Feeding

August 20 to August 24, 2013 (five to nine days postpartum)

Feeding doesn't get easier, but I take on a rally-the-troops mentality. Every time I hear Felicity cry, I gather whatever strength I have and prepare for a feeding.

We now alternate how we feed Felicity. For one feeding, I nurse her for thirty minutes and then Doug gives her a bottle to fill her up. During the next session, I pump for thirty minutes while Doug feeds her from a bottle. And back. And forth. I keep telling myself that what is important is that I keep nursing and pumping so that my milk production will increase.

But I am still not producing enough milk.

After thirty minutes of nursing, she can still suck down an ounce and a half of formula every time—which means she is getting a half ounce from both of my breasts in a feeding. On-line forums *tsk-tsk* the nipple shield and say that it can slow down the flow of milk, but I can't change the shape of my nipples.

I feel stuck.

What else can we do? Now that we're supplementing with formula and she's finally gaining weight, I don't want to see a lactation consultant or go to a La Leche League meeting because I feel that I will be chided for my decisions.

So Doug and I continue to try to solve the breastfeeding puzzle. We explore different options for how to increase my milk supply. I take an herbal supplement called fenugreek. I become militant about eating around the clock. I down pizza, loaded sandwiches, smoothies, peanut butter, sweet potatoes, chunks of chicken, macaroons, granola bars, milkshakes, ice cream, and more. After I eat, I feel almost full. Then, I nurse or pump and I feel like I've burned everything that I've just eaten.

We also attend to Felicity's latch. It was great when we left the hospital, but then we introduced the bottle. At her next feeding, she opened her mouth to my breast and did nothing.

So, we decide to trick her.

We use a syringe to drop formula around the nipple shield to keep her eating. This works, but it is time-consuming. We trick her with the syringe for thirty minutes and then Doug finishes feeding her with a bottle. I worry because her sucking is so slow during the process—it's like she's enjoying a gourmet meal at her leisure. She continually dozes off and I tap her feet and tickle her nose to wake her up.

Then, we have another idea. What if there is some kind of tube that we could use to continually feed her while she maintains her latch and nurses? We could use this until my milk supply increases. I find the answer in a breastfeeding book—it's called a lactation aid. Doug purchases one on Amazon and overnights it.

The next day, he jerry-rigs a clamp to the back of the glider and hangs a two-ounce vial of my pumped breast milk from it like an IV. The vial has four distinct frozen layers of milk, like a geological record of pumping sessions. A thin, flexible plastic tube extends down to my breast. Then, we take the additional painstaking step of threading the tube under the nipple shield.

When Felicity latches and starts sucking, the milk flows down from the vial, into the nipple guard, and then into her mouth. Her eyebrows lift as the flow begins. She closes her eyes and continues to eat, but this time at a faster pace.

For the first time, Felicity is drinking my breast milk in gulps—not just straining and straining to pull water from a rock. Her efforts are being rewarded.

I look up at Doug and thank him. A small trail of my tears lands on Felicity's shoulder and falls across her back. I wipe them with my hand. If this is what it takes to continue to breastfeed, I'm willing to do it. I will do whatever it takes. I will keep doing this until I can no longer do it.

I place Felicity in her co-sleeper, so tightly swaddled that she looks like a baby burrito. I climb onto the twin bed next to her and stare at her perfect, sleeping face.

Suddenly, it all makes sense. She is going to be the one to heal our families. She'll bring my parents back to Ohio. My estranged brothers will want to meet her, so she'll heal my relationships with them. Then, Doug's parents will want to reconcile with him because they'll want to meet Felicity. It's all coming together now. She'll mend all of our wounds. She is the one to make everything right.

Are you kidding me? You really think that's going to happen?

I look at her face again. Yes, it's possible.

Possible, sure. Likely? Come on. You know better. Everyone doesn't just drop their swords because a baby is born. You just feel this way because you just gave birth. You'll feel differently with time.

Yeah... Probably. But... what if?

Later that afternoon, I'm still lying in bed with my eyes closed. Still unable to sleep. Still putting pieces together.

Why do women have to go through so much pain to bring life into this world? It has to have a reason. Why?

Labor is suffering. And suffering humbles us. And humbling us makes us open. So we can be open to God. And God will do anything to reach us. Even allowing us to suffer. So maybe that's it. Maybe suffering is how God reaches us. Right! I mean, some people are more obstinate than others, so they need a big life event to break them down.

Wow. I get it now—why suffering exists in the world. I've figured it out.

Suffering exists because it brings us back to God.

But what about countries with widespread suffering, like famine? What about war?

Hm, well... maybe famine and war are caused by people... but God *uses* them to reach people. Yeah, that makes sense.

What about all the greedy people in the world that cause suffering, but don't suffer themselves?

Hmm... I don't know about that part, but the rest of it just makes so much sense.

Suddenly, terror seizes me.

If suffering is necessary to bring us back to God, what will happen to Felicity?

I turn in bed and look into the co-sleeper. Oh God, she's not moving. I put my finger underneath her nose. Soft puffs of air. Good, she's safe.

But for how long?

Calm down! Get a hold of yourself. What is wrong with you?

Nothing's wrong. I just want to make sure she's okay. Nothing wrong with that.

You're losing it. You've got to get control of yourself. You've got to get some sleep.

Okay, this time I will. I won't miss it this time.

When I tell people that I haven't been sleeping, I don't think they really understand. After all, that's what all new parents say. *I never sleep anymore.* I try to tell them how much sleep I've had, but it's just not registering with anyone besides Doug, who is witnessing my decline day after day.

Because the days have lost their conclusions, my body can't tell how many days have passed. Someone says that it's Tuesday, and I'm blown away. For me, it's just the fifteenth feeding since I've last had a shower. When a week has passed and the day hasn't concluded yet, I feel like I'm living in a separate world with nothing left in common with everyone around me. They are blissfully unaware of how healthy they are because they can sleep at night. I am so beyond exhausted that I'm tired-drunk. I shouldn't be allowed to take the stairs by myself, but I do. Thank God, I don't drive. When my eyes flip open at the sound of Felicity's cry, they are so dry that the air stings. I blink and blink, but it doesn't help. My eyelids feel like sandpaper.

I rest in bed, yes. But I can't fall asleep. Sometimes, I am able to doze off in my bed, but I'm not able to fully shut out the world. I'm still listening. I'm still making sense of what's happening to me.

All the blooming and expanding during pregnancy has changed direction once again and I feel that center of gravity make its dark home in my mind. It pulls everything toward me and then through me. Everything descends on me and whizzes by me at warp speed. I try to see it all, but I'm inundated beneath thoughts, plans, and the growing guilt of not being able to sleep. The carousel spins on and on, faster and faster, and my timing is off over and over again.

Maybe I need to see a doctor, but which one? My family doctor thinks I should see my OB, but she hasn't returned from Italy. And how would I ever fit in a trip to the OB's office between feedings? So far, my lack of experience with breastfeeding has made each feeding a huge production that requires me to be topless with a nursing pillow strapped to my midsection. Then I have to press a silicone nipple guard over my breast and maneuver Felicity's mouth into the right position. And then I have to stay like that for thirty minutes at least. I just don't feel like I can do all of that in public yet.

Maybe I could call the hospital? But this doesn't seem urgent enough to warrant a call to them. Or is it?

Doug buys me a sleep mask and earplugs. They help a little. But wine is more effective. It knocks me out for a delicious solid hour.

Great. Now, I'm a drunk mother.

But, I'm also a more rested mother.

I count the hours of sleep from the morning that I went to the hospital. Four hours of sleep in four days. Then, two hours of sleep in four days. That's six hours of sleep in 192 hours.

I cherish this tally of hours. They are sacred numbers. But they are also scary numbers. They tell me that I'm slipping from reality. In my mind, the day of Felicity's birth still hasn't concluded. Soon, I will be at an impasse because I know that no one can survive while staying awake ninety-seven percent of every day.

I'm kind of hanging in this space, untethered to the past or the future, where all my previous roles—wife, friend, teacher, daughter—are suspended, even forgotten. The baby doesn't care about how many times I failed in the past or how many accolades I've earned. The only role that holds any value anymore to her is my role as "nourisher."

And until now, I've never realized how much we rely on our connections to the past and the future to help us navigate the present. They are anchors to help us make reasonable decisions to move us from one point to another. But with the past and the future muted from consciousness, the anchors are ripped free and I think only about the here and now. All I can think about is what needs to be done right now in order to keep us alive and sane. And sometimes, I can't even do that well.

And then, I remember that day when I visited my father in the hospital. The day when he said that he couldn't believe that it was March. *It can't be much past February 15*, he had said.

Now, I know that my father couldn't imagine a future with a grandchild because he had lost his connections to the future. He was living only in the present. I think that, now, I understand a fraction of how he must have felt.

I am eight days postpartum and I feel like my breasts have some milk in them now. I'm excited to pump and see how much I'm producing. It has to be at least one ounce now.

But it's still only half of an ounce.

At my current pumping rate, I manage to fill a two-ounce vial of breast milk every day. The other twenty-two ounces of Felicity's daily diet come from formula. Less than ten percent of her nutrition is natural—but I'm still trying to make this work.

I'm still eating around the clock. The hours pass by so quickly and I'm constantly running to the refrigerator to try to figure out what has enough calories for the current three-hour block of time. I wish I could just sit down and eat a box of donuts, but then I remember how much fiber I need to consume in order to keep my hemorrhoids healing cleanly. If I didn't care about how it all felt coming out, I'd sit down and eat pizza after pizza. But I know I'll pay for it later.

I write the date on the dry-erase board in Felicity's room: August 23. It means nothing to me. I have no idea what day of the week it is. When I check my phone, I see that it's Friday.

Friday? Really?

I see a few new emails in the inbox for my work email and I go ahead and check the subject lines. *Reminder: Mandatory meeting, Placement test results, Leftover boxed lunches!* For all my colleagues, it is the end of a long first week of classes. There is a sense of accomplishment and closure. They can punctuate the week with a night out with friends or a quiet night with a good book. Even those who are parents will be spending time with their kids. There will be pizzas and movies and laughter. And then they will all go to bed and reset for the next day.

But for me, in this moment, there seems to be no end. I can't see accomplishment in all that I'm doing. At least not yet. When I look at Felicity, I see someone who needs me, but I can't see how my care is changing her. Yet I care for her. And care for her. And care for her.

And for someone who thrives in a life of productivity, this is hard. Really hard. I am someone who loves the sight of a crossed-off checklist or a computer screen now filled with words. I set goals and I work for them. Every day. And so I find myself lost in this life where the checklist is the same—over and over and over again. And as soon as an item is checked off, another three emerge.

August 25 (ten days postpartum)

It's about 4:00 p.m. A pile of dirty laundry sits on the end of the couch. I'm pretty sure there is a load of clean dishes in the dishwasher and a stack of dirty ones sitting in the sink. The breast pump moans away, *harrr... harrr... harrr...* I try to relax and think nourishing thoughts as I watch Doug feed Felicity a tiny two-ounce bottle of formula.

He sets the empty bottle on the couch and then cups his hand against her back. He pats her gently like this to burp her. Another feeding—complete.

And then, she vomits.

Everything. The whole feeding. The last thirty minutes of effort is now seeping through Doug's clothes.

He holds her away from him and looks to me for help.

"Ugh..." I look down at my breasts being pulled and pulled. I'm twenty minutes into this pumping session and I'm not ready to turn it off. "I don't think I can walk with these things on me."

He looks absolutely defeated.

"Here, hand her to me." I hold my hands out.

He drops her in my lap as the breast pump drones on. Then, he lies on the floor and rests his hands on his chest.

"It's grinding on me, baby girl." He is quiet for a moment. "I just don't know how much more of this I can take."

A cold wave of anxiety grips me. *What? What does he mean?*

"Um..." I mumble.

"Sorry, those are wrong words to use. I mean... Just..." he sighs.

"I know," I say. "It's okay. I got her."

"I haven't showered yet today."

Oh really? I haven't showered in three days, buddy. But this isn't what I say. Instead, I say, "Go take a shower. I got her."

"Did you get to shower today?" he props himself on his elbows.

"No," I admit.

He frowns. "Baby girl..."

Just the fact that he asked is enough to neutralize my sarcasm. I can wait. He needs it more than I do right now. "Really," I say. "It's okay. I'm almost done here, and then I'll feed her."

August 27, 2013 (twelve days postpartum)

Doug's parental leave will soon end and he won't be here during the day to preserve this process of alternating nursing, pumping, and syringe feeding. A thirty-minute pumping session is my limit—anything beyond that makes me feel woozy. And I'm still producing only a half of an ounce per session.

Doug knocks on the door and tells me that he's ready to feed her and that I need to pump. I slide out of bed carefully to avoid hurting my bottom. As I walk to the bathroom, I feel nauseous. When I pass the full-length mirror hanging in our room, I notice that my belly looks distended. I pause and examine my profile. *What is going on in there?*

And then I remember reading about the sensation of "hanging organs." After birth, the internal organs shift from their positions during pregnancy and return to their original positions. But I thought this was supposed to happen a lot sooner than it is. I wonder if all the recovery milestones that I read in postpartum books have been delayed because of my lack of sleep. Or maybe something weird is happening to me that no book would have anticipated.

After I pump, I lie in bed and Doug brings me a bowl of food: wild rice, a hamburger patty, and some potatoes. I can't even stomach the sight of the food, but I know I don't have a choice. I need to eat. I need to get ready for the next feeding. As I start chewing, I feel sick. I can feel gas forming in my stomach. I slow down and lower my head back to the pillow. The more I chew, the better I feel when I swallow. It takes me forty minutes for Doug to feed me the bowl of food. When I finish, Doug buries his head into the bed.

"Sweets, you can't keep this up. You're killing yourself."

I shrug my shoulders. "I know... but... what can I do?"

"Can we go see the lactation consultant?"

"What is she going to say? We already know that the problem is that I'm not making enough milk."

"Then will you call your OB's office? See if they can look into a hormone problem?"

This is something that we have talked about before. Doug thinks that I've had a lot of symptoms that line up with adrenal gland problems and those problems might be interfering with my hormone levels.

After a long conversation with the head nurse at my OB's office, she explains that they can't do any hormone analysis until my six-week checkup because my hormones are still in flux. I learn that I have three choices: 1) continue to nurse and pump as I'm doing now until the checkup, 2) start gradually weaning Felicity by pumping, or 3) wean Felicity cold turkey.

"And Sharon," the nurse adds, "please know that we are here for you. The doctor will be back in the office within the next few days, but know that you can always call the nurses here. We are here to help."

When I hang up the phone, I already know what I have to do.

I will wean her cold turkey.

I can't continue the pattern that we've been doing for another four weeks. It's unsustainable. Another day of sleep deprivation feels like it might send me to the hospital. My mind-body relationship is completely off-kilter. I don't feel attached to my body much anymore, let alone the physical world. When something happens now, my first inclination is not to think of a logical cause-effect relationship. Instead, my first inclination is to find a purpose or reason linked to the spiritual world. Or to destiny. For a time, I feel that I have been awakened to a new way of looking at the world, but I'm still too self-conscious to share any of these thoughts with others. But now, I realize that I'm moving into a state of being where I don't understand the physical world anymore.

It scares me. And the only way that I see out of it is to start to sleep again.

So I can't gradually wean Felicity because it means I would still be awake every three hours and every pumping session would continue the adrenaline rush that keeps me from sleeping. I read on-line forums and so many mothers talk about feeling sleepy after nursing. No one talks about the alertness that I experience. I feel more and more alone in my experience.

"Is this what you want to do for sure? We can't go back after this," Doug says.

The finality of it breaks my heart. I remember one specific moment, sitting on the edge of the bed, nursing Felicity. I looked down to see her thin, tender neck. Then, her tiny jaw lifting and lowering as she nursed with her eyes closed. Music played. Sunlight spilled across my shoulders. I chomped away on a granola bar as I slowly swayed her back and forth to the music. She wore a yellow striped onesie that swallowed her tiny limbs. The short hairs on the back of her neck stood out and I rubbed them against her velvet head.

Once I did this, we would never be this close again. I would feed her, yes. But our bodies wouldn't cry out for each other anymore. This symbiosis would end.

I point to my heart and nod. I know I have to do this, no matter how hard it is. I have reached the end of what I have to give. I have nothing left.

I surrender.

"I can't nurse her if I'm dead."

Doug curls up beside me and holds me. This time, *he* is crying. "I'm just so worried about you. I can't *stand* seeing you like this."

A long time passes while we hold each other and assure each other that this is the right decision.

Doug comes home with an Ace bandage and then tenderly helps me wrap my breasts to prepare for the weaning. He tells me that he will stay with

Felicity for the night while I finally sleep for a whole night. I'm skeptical if this is how it will actually work out.

But it does.

I sleep and sleep and sleep. I wake up several times during the night because my breasts ache and milk is slowly leaking from my left breast, but I go back to sleep. When I finally wake for good, it's 7:00 a.m. and I've gotten seven hours of uninterrupted sleep.

I feel magnificent.

The only drawback is the pain. I rate it as a four on a scale of ten, but it's a five when Felicity cries. When I update my doula during our postnatal visit, she tells me to use cabbage leaves instead. I take her advice and the relief is unbelievable. I feel almost nothing once the cool leaves are pressed against my breasts. I change them throughout the day and into the next day. By the end of the second day, my breasts have stopped leaking and I feel like a new person.

The Conflict

Why did my inability to breastfeed cause me so much devastation? Was it perhaps because I still felt so connected to Felicity? Certainly, this presented a paradox: How could our needs be in such conflict while we were still so attached? She needed food, and I couldn't provide it. It seemed impossible.

But there was another, deeper layer to my devastation—the devastation of a wounded identity, one that was still a newborn itself. That fresh identity as a competent mother—hero of my own story, defender of my newborn baby—was now at risk. I was becoming some breed of mother who didn't neatly fall into one category or another. How could I have had an unmedicated childbirth and now be formula feeding my baby? What kind of mother was that?

Mothers like me didn't seem to exist in mommy blogs or on-line forums. Mothers who gave birth without medication always breastfed their babies! They endured the pain so their babies would be alert after birth and latch with no problems. If they could stand the pain of childbirth, the pain of nursing cramps and chomped nipples and mastitis would be child's play.

This is what I thought.

But again, these thoughts emerge from living in a society that emphasizes choice. When our concerns are not simply feeding our children, we can refocus our concerns on *how* we are feeding them. And when those feeding choices are presented on a continuum of "good, better, and best", it's fairly easy to jump to the conclusion of "good, better, and best mother."

Even after I reassured myself that I was a competent mother, I knew the stereotypes that follow mothers who formula feed today. Our identities are not solely composed of what we think about ourselves. They also include—whether we like it or not—what *others* think about us. We may not care what some people think about our parenting, but we want those whom we respect to see us at least as good parents, if not great parents. And so this was a major psychological blow at a time when I was already bottoming out because of the fluctuations in my postpartum hormones.

So when I was unable to breastfeed, I had to reconcile many truths. I had to surrender my commitment to breastfeed. I had to accept that my baby wouldn't be eating what everyone was calling "the best." I had to reconcile what this decision said about my new identity as a mother. And I had to accept a very definite separation from my baby at a time when I wasn't ready to let go.

Until I decided to wean Felicity, I had relied on evidence-based research to make decisions about labor, birth, and feeding. And while all of this knowledge helped me to avoid an unnecessary labor induction, it was not the definitive authority that I had imagined it to be during pregnancy. Because I lacked confidence in my own instincts as a woman and a mother, I placed all of my trust in this research, believing that it would provide me the best counsel about how to solve any problem that I could encounter as a new mother.

In fact, Davis-Floyd (2003) explored this tendency of American mothers to grant more authority to scientific knowledge than their own intuitive and bodily knowledge. She asserts that this tendency arises from American cultural beliefs that possessing, "scientific knowledge about medical birth" gives mothers power and control in a culture where, "knowledge... is respected... (and) enables one to be a competent player of our cultural game" (p. 31). Not only does her cultural observation explain my intense desire to read and research during pregnancy, but it helps me understand my own distrust in my body's signals.

But if I had been able to listen to my body and trust my instincts more, I would have probably stopped breastfeeding around eight days postpartum. It was at this time that I knew my milk supply was not going to increase. My daughter was already eating mostly formula despite my constant pumping and nursing. I had done all of the interventions that I could try and the outcome was the same—one to two ounces of breast milk per day. At this point, I had to start denying what was happening to me in order to keep going. Every time I nursed her, I reminded myself that breastfeeding was best and that I was doing the right thing. I refused to let myself focus on the fact that she could only draw half an ounce of breast milk during a feeding. Instead, I allowed statistics and the results of scientific studies to overshadow my own personal experience.

But it wasn't just research that fueled my self-denial.

It was also my own pride.

I shared in today's breastfeeding enthusiasm to the point of sacrificing my own health. I had read about the dangers of infant formula. I didn't want processed food going into my baby's body. Unlike women of my mother's and grandmother's generations, I live in a time when breastfeeding is now heralded as the best decision that mothers can make for the health of their babies. It supports their immune systems. Breast milk is more easily digested, so babies have fewer cases of constipation and diarrhea. It makes them smarter? It decreases their chances of developing obesity? Okay, those findings seemed like a stretch, but I was willing to believe them— since I was going to breastfeed.

But ultimately, it was my own pride that kept me nursing and pumping until I literally had nothing left to give.

I didn't want to be criticized. But I also didn't want to be wrong.

I realize now that in those early months of her life, whenever nursing came up as a topic, I found myself trying to convince people that I didn't *choose* to formula feed. Instead, I was *forced* to formula feed. I thought about all the assumptions that someone might have about me if they thought that I had chosen to formula feed. Assumptions that I had gathered from the hospital's breastfeeding class, from popular breastfeeding books, and from on-line forums about breastfeeding. Through the postpartum fog, I could almost hear their thoughts.

Maybe you should have pumped more. Nipple shields slow the stream of milk. You should have taken more herbal supplements or tried this medication that I took. If you slept more, your milk would have come in. Are you sure her latch was good?

For the first few months of Felicity's life, nearly every conversation with another mother started with the presumptive "So how's the nursing going?" or the kinder "Are you nursing?" I never started these feeding conversations, but they came up in every conversation with a visitor who came to our home in those early months.

"I'm not breastfeeding anymore," I would say.

The long pause. The nod. The silence, as if waiting for more.

Every time, I tried to figure out how to get out of the conversation without breaking into tears. I found myself answering questions that they hadn't even asked. I launched into explanations of how hard I tried, how often I nursed her, and the types of interventions we used. The two weeks of devastating insomnia, the miniscule yield from pumping sessions, her weight loss, my descent into hell.

And then I would end with, "But really, medically there's a problem with me. My milk never really came in. Really, I didn't have any engorgement. I have thyroid issues, so that's probably what caused it."

But no matter how convincing I thought I was, I was embarrassed to even talk about the issue because of an oft-repeated statistic about how nearly every healthy woman can produce enough milk for her baby. *Only one to five percent of women are not able to produce enough milk for their babies*, I had read over and over again in breastfeeding literature.

And that was how I was *asking* others to view me—as a person as uncommon as someone who grows scales instead of skin.

Me. The person who believed in the power of her own body. Who had just given birth without medication. Who believed that if she just listened to her body, that it would do what it needed to do.

Me. The person who was convinced that all problems with breastfeeding could be solved with knowledgeable interventions and perseverance.

Me. The person who was disciplined and persistent enough to kickbox and portion-control her way to a size six.

Me. That person.

Suddenly, it seemed that all of those qualities that I had spent a lifetime practicing were not true anymore. That freshly crafted identity as a strong, capable mother was now unraveling fast.

So underneath my explanations for why I wasn't breastfeeding, my tone was desperate. It screamed: *Please, please, everyone! Please just believe that I'm a medical anomaly, defective on the inside. I'm not stupid, or uninformed, or lazy, or selfish. I'm just broken, everyone. That's why I'm formula feeding, not because I chose it!*

When we made the switch, I prepared myself for the worst. A sick baby. A colicky baby. Diarrhea. Constipation. Blood in the stool. But none of that happened.

What *did* happen was much more positive. Formula feeding helped me expand my understanding of what it means to be a mother. Before I stopped nursing Felicity, almost all of my interactions with her revolved around marathon feedings and pumping sessions. My sole role was nourishment. There was no room in my mind to be anything else to her. When I wasn't nursing, I just wanted to be alone. I just wanted to sleep. I just wanted to feel better. But I couldn't sleep and I didn't feel better. Near the end of my time breastfeeding her, I would tear up at the sound of her hungry cry and think, *Not again. I can't.* But then, I would get up and do it.

But once the pumping sessions and the marathon feedings were gone, once the sleep returned in increments of two hours, I started to look at her. Just look and look at her. Listen to her. Talk to her. Play with her. Here was this person whom I felt that I already knew, and yet I still had everything to learn about—what her voice would sound like some day, what activities she would like to do, and how it would feel for her to hug me. For the first time, I started to look into the future a bit and get excited about helping her pack her bag for her first day of kindergarten or helping her learn to tie her shoes. I was finally able to imagine what kind of mother I wanted to be.

And then I started to wonder, *Why does it matter how I feed her? And why is this topic open for public discussion?*

And finally: *So what if I did choose to feed her formula? Does that make me a bad mother? Don't we value choice in our culture anymore?*

All those breastfeeding books had presented formula as a choice for mothers who weren't dedicated to the sacrifices and challenges of breastfeeding. Was I dedicated? Did I care about the health of my child?

Why, yes, I did. So that meant that I would breastfeed.

The decision to breastfeed wasn't framed around the starting point of what was healthiest for me. Instead, the decision was framed around what was healthiest for my baby. And breastfeeding can be incredibly healthy for many mothers. But breastfeeding literature never mentions that it can be unhealthy—either physically or emotionally—for others. So the message is clear. I should be more concerned about what is healthiest for my baby because I'm a mother now. And mothers sacrifice. Everything, if need be.

And I did.

But when the herculean attempts to eat enough, pump enough, and nurse enough had worn me down into a sliver of a human being—no longer able to make rational decisions, no longer able to feed myself, no longer able to walk to the bathroom without assistance, no longer able to recognize my own face in the mirror—I started to wonder, *How much more do I really have to give before I'm dead?*

Still, it was tiring and it hurt to feel the need to defend how I fed Felicity. Feeding is part of the public sphere, a topic suitable for conversation with others. Everyone could figure out how I fed her and, with that knowledge, a host of assumptions were already in place about why I fed her this way. Maybe I thought breastfeeding was repulsive. Maybe I lacked confidence that I could do it. Maybe I had fallen victim to the hospital procedures that often interfere with the breastfeeding relationship. Maybe I didn't know all the medical studies about the benefits of breastfeeding. Or maybe I was misinformed and thought that breastfeeding would ruin my boobs. Or maybe I was just selfish and wanted someone else to feed her while I got some decent sleep.

How did I know about these assumptions? They belonged to me. They were my thoughts before I gave birth.

In fact, I can attest to the fact that as a first-time mother, I greatly appreciated the cultural divide over breastfeeding because it made my choice much easier. I read books about breastfeeding. Then, I looked within my own educated, upper-middle class, white community and I saw that breastfeeding was valued and widely practiced, and that—as far as I could tell—everyone had been successful at it. I wasn't looking for a reason to be different from everyone else.

But perhaps the most convincing evidence for my decision to breastfeed was the testimony of the nurse who taught the hospital's breastfeeding class. As I reflect on that class, I can now see how the nurse's own personal experiences regarding breastfeeding shaped her response to that question about the possibility of not producing enough milk. From her position as a medical professional, she advised, "Feed your baby." From her position as a lactation consultant, she stated that, "Ninety-five percent of women can breastfeed their babies." From her position as an experienced breastfeeding mother, she claimed, "If you stick with it, it will get easier."

She had given me exactly what I wanted to hear—a positive view of breastfeeding, approved by both a medical professional (to meet my husband's criteria for credibility) and a mother of four (to meet my criteria).

As a new mother, advice based on personal experience was often compelling to me, even if it varied so much from person to person. I simply listened to the voices whose advice matched what I wanted to hear and ignored or discounted the voices that I didn't. I didn't want to hear about women who had epidurals, or C-sections, or formula fed their babies. That wasn't going to be me. They had made bad decisions that had put them in those positions, so I didn't want to listen to their stories.

This way of viewing the world didn't pose a problem until I found myself on the other side of the line that I had drawn. Instead of a breastfeeding mother, I was a formula feeding mother. And all those silent judgments that I had once pronounced in my thoughts—never once out loud—were now heaped upon me. I hadn't even realized how harshly I had judged formula feeding mothers until I had become one. The pressure was more than I could bear. I was forced to mentally confront each stereotype that I had about formula feeding. I was not lazy. I was not selfish. I was not a quitter. I was not stupid or uninformed. I was not pro-corporate America.

It helped to talk with friends about how difficult breastfeeding had been for me and to read stories of women who had traveled this road before me. It took months of reflection to create a mental space where I could be confident in how I fed Felicity.

I remember the day that I realized that I had this confidence. Felicity was six months old and one of Doug's cousins was visiting. She was a single woman in her mid-twenties. She had never met Felicity before. When I started mixing a bottle of formula, she asked if I had ever breastfed Felicity. It didn't sound like an accusation. I doubt she realized how emotional that question could be for a new mother.

I said, "I did. For twelve days. And then we had to switch to formula. I wasn't making enough milk, so that's what we had to do." She didn't push the issue, and finally I didn't feel compelled to explain myself further.

The First Weeks

August 30, 2013

168 pounds, size "pajama pants"

I'm so amazed at the changes that are now happening in my body. Doug notices it too. I start melting like an ice cream cone. The weight and puffiness first drain from my face, my neck, my arms, and my chest. Every day, I lose another pound or more. The hives disappear. The fluid retention recedes. I drop my daily intake of calories from 2500 to 1600 and this sheds even more weight. My body starts to feel the rhythms of eating and sleeping again. Soon, hunger returns. My mind is more alert and my rational internal voice is louder than my emotional one. Cause-effect relationships make more sense to me. I'm returning to my physical self and finding comfort in the mundane and the routine. My memory improves. The healing in my pelvic floor speeds and I soon retire the sitz bath. I can now walk a twenty-minute loop at a decent pace without feeling exhausted. I am able to shower without holding onto a rail.

Around 8:00 p.m., my mom stops by our place for one last visit before she and my dad begin their long drive home to Minnesota. They are planning to leave early the next morning. Dad has already fallen asleep for the night, so he hasn't come to say good-bye. My mom holds Felicity for a while and talks to her. I take a video to remember it.

When my mom hugs me good-bye, it hurts. While she has been here, I've felt comforted to know that there was a mother in the house or just a phone call away. Someone whom I could call for advice. Someone who could help me if we couldn't calm Felicity. Who would I call now?

Doug rubs my arm as I pull away from her. I dab the corners of my eyes.

"It's just hard," I say. I look at my mom. "You know? I mean, I'm just thinking, what should I do if she starts crying and I don't know what to do? Or what if she gets sick?"

"That's why you have a good pediatrician!" she says cheerily.

I laugh. "It's not the same."

"I know…" she casts her eyes to the side before looking back at me. "But it's going to be okay. She's a great baby. And you're a great mom already."

I nod my head, eyes fixed on the carpet. I bite back the tears. "Okay… Okay." I hug her again. "I guess I'll see you when I see you… Sooner than later, I hope."

"I'll try to come back soon," she says.

Once the door closes behind her, I let myself cry.

Now, *I* have to be the mother.

Doug needs a few things at Target and I'm feeling strong enough and rested enough to drive a car. I even decide to take Felicity. I wait until after I've just fed her and then we leave. With my hand on the car seat, I realize that I need the diaper bag.

Oh… That's going to take some getting used to.

I think about what goes in it. Diapers, wipes, packets of formula. Maybe some burp clothes. That should be good.

I maneuver slowly through the store with the car seat in the cart. I've covered the car seat with a light swaddling blanket to block accidental sneezes from strangers. I drop the items into the cart, one by one, wondering when she'll be hungry next.

A realization seizes me—I don't have any bottles in the bag.

Oh my God. Oh my God. What if she wakes up hungry? I won't be able to do anything about it. People are going to hear this tiny baby crying to be fed and they're going to wonder why I'm not responding to her. Should I buy bottles here? That seems like a waste of money. Wait, that won't even work because I have to boil them first! Maybe I should just get home as soon as I can.

I hurry through the rest of the shopping trip and drive home. I don't miss anything on the list, Felicity doesn't wake up, and I still get home without her waking to be fed.

I feel like Superwoman.

While we've figured out a good routine with feeding Felicity, sleep is pretty unstructured. It's not so bad at the beginning of the day, but between 8:00 p.m. and 2:00 a.m., she needs someone to hold her all the time. She'll fall asleep on me and then when I put her down to sleep, she wakes up. We swaddle her, but her arms break free and then she wakes herself up when they spasm.

One night, Doug says we should just let her "cry it out."

I don't think this is a good idea. She seems too young. She's only two weeks old. She still finds comfort in my heartbeat, so I think she's crying because the world apart from me is still a very confusing place. But I don't want to argue with Doug either. We're a team.

The witching hour approaches. I feed her at 8:00 p.m. and she falls asleep at 8:30. Around 8:45, she is crying again.

"Okay, let's give her twenty minutes. If she can't calm down, we'll help her," he says.

Ah...Aaaa... Aha.... Aaaaaa! Aha... Ah... Aaaaa! Aaaaa! Aaaaaaaa!

The sides of my heart pinch together.

Ah...

Silence.

"See? She's asleep," he points out.

A few minutes pass.

Ah.. AAAaaaa! Aha.... AAAA! Aaaaaaaa...

I look at him and purse my lips. His eyebrows arch.

AAAA! Ah... AAAAAAaaaaaaa.... AAAAAAAAAAAAAAaaaaaaaa.....

I grip the sides of my head.

"She's fine, Sweets."

"No," I shake my head. "She's not!"

"We just fed her. She's fine."

I rub my temples and sink my hands into my hair. Her cries are hands around my heart. They squeeze and squeeze and squeeze.

Aa... AAAAAAAAaaaaa! Aha... AAAAAAAAAAAAAAAAaaaaaaaaa!

"Oh my God, I can't take this," I say.

"Sweets, she's fine."

"Well, I'm not fine," I admit. "I'm not ready to do this and I don't think she is either."

He sighs, clearly frustrated, but I go in and pick her up. I sit down with her, and place her on my chest. She calms.

"We've got to let her cry it out," he says. "Or she's going to learn that she can get whatever she wants like this."

"She's two weeks old."

"Fine," he tosses his hands in the air.

I feel like we are speaking different languages. Was he hearing the same cry that I was? Where was this intense desire to control this baby coming from? Did he really think that she had the mental capacity to manipulate?

You're both exhausted. Give yourselves a break, I remind myself.

When Doug gets home from work the next day, I'm washing dishes while Felicity is sleeping in the bouncer. He closes the door.

"Hey," I say.

"How's Kermit?" he asks.

The nickname is sticking. I kind of love it.

"She's good."

"So..." he sighs. "I was talking to my co-workers today... And I'm sorry."

"Huh?" I turn off the faucet.

"I was talking to them more about the sleeping thing. And... she's too young to let her cry it out."

I nod and button up the *I-told-you-so*. "What did they say?"

"Just that newborns don't really respond to sleep training. You have to wait until they're about four months old before anything you do has a real effect."

"It's called the *fourth trimester*," I tell him. "Babies are just trying to get used to being in the outside world."

He nods and surrenders his hands. "I'm sorry, Sweets. You were right. I was wrong. I should have listened to you. Every single time that I've doubted your intuition on dealing with her... I've been wrong."

"Thanks, Dougie."

He kneels down next to the bouncer where she is sleeping. Then he says, "You got something with her. I don't know what it is, but you understand her. I promise I'll start listening to you more."

This guy, I think. *God... this guy.*

September 9, 2013

160 pounds, size fourteen

After my tearful phone call to the head nurse that concluded with my decision to wean Felicity, my obstetrician wants to see me for a checkup at three weeks postpartum. It will be the first time that I've seen her since I was thirty-nine weeks pregnant.

I want to rage at her for leaving me with doctors that didn't give a shit about me. I want to tell her how horrible it was to have Dr. M break my water. I want to rail on and on about how the doctor who delivered Felicity should have kept his mouth shut about my second-degree tear.

But what I need to talk about is breastfeeding. That is the focus of this conversation for me.

"How are you doing this week? Any better?" The head nurse asks sympathetically.

"Yes, this week is a lot better, now that I'm finally getting some sleep. I'm just still very bothered by the fact that I wasn't able to breastfeed."

"But you *did* breastfeed," she assures me.

"Well, not really," I think about how to respond. "I mean, I wasn't able to continue... I mean, I didn't breastfeed as long as I wanted to. She wasn't even really getting any of my milk."

"But you *did* breastfeed," she repeats, looking me in the eye. "You should be proud of that. It's not an easy thing to do and any breastfeeding that you do is great."

I know that we are approaching this issue with two different lenses and with two different objectives. Hers is to care for me. Mine is to care for my baby. I get that—but I just want her to sympathize with me and help me find an answer. I understand that she's trying to make sure that I see the positive side of all of this, but... it also seems to underestimate the importance of solving this problem.

"I just want to know what's wrong with me," I say. "Like why couldn't I make enough breast milk? I want to know what to do the next time that I have a child."

When the head nurse leaves the room, I stare at the medical equipment that has never been used on me. I see that there is a light attached to the examination table. The stirrups have covers on them that advertise a brand of birth control. Great. I hear the nurse talking with the doctor in a low voice, but I can't hear them. It sounds like they are plotting their moves.

That's okay. Because I am, too.

When the doctor comes in a few minutes later, she is beaming. "Is this the baby girl? Can I see her?"

At first, I'm surprised. But then, I think, *Smooth move, Doc. I should have known you'd drag Felicity into this.*

She washes her hands at the sink before she lifts the cover on Felicity's car seat. "Oh... Look at her... May I?" she coos.

I crumble. "Sure," I say.

My doctor sits with Felicity on her lap, and I know now that I won't be able to make it out of this appointment without crying.

"So how are you doing this week?" she asks. "We were just really concerned about you after you called our office. We wanted to make sure that you are doing better."

"I *am* doing better," I say. "But I'm really concerned about how difficult it was for me to breastfeed. I was just not making enough milk, so I want to find out what's wrong with me. Maybe my hormones are off. Like my thyroid. I haven't had my thyroid checked in a long time. But I know something's really wrong because I didn't respond to breastfeeding the way most women do. I didn't lose weight when I breastfed. And every time I nursed, I was so amped up afterward that I couldn't sleep. I literally did not sleep for the first two weeks that she was alive and I really thought I was going to die," I say desperately.

"Okay," she nods knowingly. "I can put your mind at ease a little here. First, breastfeeding is different for everyone. And it's different for every baby. I had three children and I had different breastfeeding experiences with each of them."

Did she not hear how little I was sleeping? My breastfeeding wasn't "different." It was abnormal!

"But you could at least make enough milk, right?" I asked.

"Well, let me explain. I breastfed my first child for three months. My second child had a terrible time latching on, so we stopped breastfeeding earlier than I wanted. And my third child, I couldn't let down enough because of all the stress of the first two kids running around. My supply was greatly affected by that."

What "let down?" You had a "supply?" I wish I could use those words. I never had any let down, let alone anything that I would call a supply. I wouldn't know the let down reflex if it bit me in the ass!

"But I had really optimal conditions for breastfeeding," I argue. "And I followed all the advice for establishing good breastfeeding and it still didn't work. I really wanted to do this. And it's just... all of the books say that almost every woman can make enough milk and I feel like... *Really?* Am I that strange? It just makes me feel..."

I'm crying now. My doctor hands me a tissue with her free hand.

"Look," she levels with me. "There are all kinds of reasons that women choose not to breastfeed. It's not a death sentence to feed your baby formula. My kids grew up fine on it. And I bet your daughter will be fine too."

There's that word again. Choose. Did she not hear me? I wasn't choosing not to breastfeed! I was being forced to stop.

"Okay," I dab my eyes. I still feel misunderstood, but why share my tears with her? "But what about next time?"

"Next time, we can try out some medications that can help increase your milk supply before there is a problem. That's my recommendation. But the proof is right here," she nods at Felicity. "If she's fed and she's growing, that should be your main concern right now. She's beautiful and you've done a great job. And you'll keep doing a great job. You're *not* a bad mother. No one thinks that. You're doing a *wonderful* job."

And the tears are back.

There. That was it. That was exactly what I needed to hear. I didn't even know that I needed to hear it until she had said it. I needed to know that someone else could look at me from the outside and tell me that I was doing a good job. I needed to hear those words from someone with some authority.

"Thank you," I whisper.

As the days pass, we start to establish a bit of routine.

Formula feeding helps us know exactly how much Felicity needs to eat to be full. Soon, we are able to make good estimates on when she'll wake up to eat. *If she eats X ounces, she'll wake up in three hours.* Soon, we see the number of ounces per feeding change. She moves from two ounces per feeding to two and a half ounces. A few weeks later, she's eating three ounces per feeding.

I start to see that there are rhythms to Felicity's eating and sleeping. At times, the rhythms make the days monotonous. But after what I've been through in the first weeks of her life, I *love* monotonous.

I use these rhythms to help make plans for optimal times to leave the house. One afternoon, I'm able to take Felicity to the library while she naps in the car seat. As I browse the parenting books, a title jumps out at me: *The 90-Minute Baby Sleep Program.*

It seems like a joke. So I check it out for a laugh.

The book claims that starting around four weeks of age, babies start to stay awake in ninety-minute intervals, which follows the body's internal clock. Once a baby wakes up from a nap, he will probably be ready to fall back asleep after ninety minutes. The lengths of naps can vary—and it takes some babies longer to establish a regular ninety-minute rhythm—but it's a good rule to follow to make sure a baby sleeps enough throughout the day. The more a baby naps during the day, the easier it is for him to extend the hours that he sleeps at night.

I think these are strong claims. But I wonder, *How long does Felicity stay awake?*

So I track her naps for a few days and record the time that she is awake between naps.

I'm shocked. It's ninety minutes. Every. Freaking. Time.

Wow.

I tell Doug about the book. He tracks her awake periods.

He is a believer, too.

September 25, 2013

161 pounds, size fourteen

When Felicity is almost six weeks old, we decide to try to put her to sleep without swaddling her. It seems like a good idea. She's already able to break her arms out of the swaddle and kick through the wrapped blanket after thirty minutes. Then, it's all over. Her arms and legs flinch and then she's awake. And angry about it. And then we have to try to put her to sleep again.

It's not that we're bad at swaddling her. If Doug is nothing else, he is an optimizer. He spends his life experimenting his way to the most effective and efficient methods of doing everything. And he has mastered swaddling.

So we commit to helping her stay asleep without the swaddle.

It is tough.

It is exhausting.

From 9:00 p.m. to 5:00 a.m., we listen to her cries and determine whether she really needs help. Sometimes, she makes sounds in her sleep, but she's not fully awake. We don't want to wake her up accidentally. If her cries persist, we figure that she is awake and hungry. At other times, we take turns calming her by shushing. We try to keep her in her bassinet. Sometimes, we pick her up to calm her, but then we struggle to transfer her to the bassinet without her waking. She doesn't really have meltdowns when she wakes. She usually whimpers, grunts, and gives a tiny cry, as if trying to figure out how to stay asleep.

After two days of the constant turn-taking, we decide to split the night into shifts. One person would sleep in her room on the twin bed, and the other would sleep in the bedroom. Doug takes the 9:00 p.m. to 1:00 a.m. shift and I take 1:00 a.m. until 5:00 a.m. shift. Then, Doug takes over so I can shower and eat breakfast. Then, he gets ready for work.

This schedule works well. It ensures that both of us get at least four hours of solid sleep.

I can't believe that I'm at a point in my life where I'm grateful for four hours of sleep. But four hours of sleep helps me function at half-capacity on most days. I know that I'm not thinking very clearly, so it's good that the most challenging part of my day is keeping track of the next feeding.

And then a thought occurs: Most women in my position would need to return to work next week.

Oh. My. God.

How?

Really, how would that work? How could you physically stay awake the whole day? Wouldn't you struggle all day to put thoughts together? And what about the emotional toll of being apart from your newborn? And what if I were still breastfeeding? What if my baby refused to take a bottle?

Holy cow.

Who started this tradition? My guess is men who didn't have to get up at 6:00 a.m. after a 1:00 a.m. and 4:00 a.m. feeding. That's who.

So thank you, Faculty Maternity Leave.

Even though I'm not getting my full salary, I'm getting time. And having that time off lowers my stress. I don't think constantly about returning to work. January might as well be five years from now. And so I'm able to do this new kind of work, which is arguably much harder, but also much more beneficial for society as a whole.

One night, my eyes flip open at 3:00 a.m. I listen for her. *Did she cry for me?*

I don't hear anything. I haven't heard anything since I fell asleep around 10:00.

I walk into Felicity's room. Doug is still lying there on the twin bed, fast asleep. I come closer to the bassinet. Her arms are resting next to her. Her legs are splayed heavily on either side of her hips. She is completely out of it. I lean closer to hear her breathing. And she is.

I think we have done it.

September 30, 2013
159 pounds, size twelve

I don't see my doctor again until my six-week checkup. Doug wants to solve the mystery behind my lack of milk production. Combined with some of my other symptoms, he wants to get some bloodwork ordered to rule out several hormonal imbalances. I tell him that if he's serious, he needs to come to my appointment because I'm sure my doctor will tell me that I'm fine and that I don't need any tests. And, let's face it, I'm struggle with being assertive with doctors.

The examination is not as painful as I thought it was going to be. She is gentle and takes her time when doing the pelvic exam. I am grateful.

"I thought about you while I was at this year's ACOG conference," my doctor says. "In Hawaii! Who says work can't have some play in it?" She chuckles.

I chuckle too.

"So yeah, I went to a presentation about this increasing rise of homebirths in the United States—which by the way, is a *very* dangerous trend—and, well, I can't remember how we got on the topic, but someone mentioned that she's been seeing more and more patients who come into their postpartum checkups with just *tremendous* feelings of guilt and shame about not breastfeeding. She's never had so many patients like this. And I think we're really doing a disservice to women by telling them that they *have to* breastfeed. I mean, there's no doubt that breast milk is more natural, but it's just not for everyone and that should be okay. But now there are just so many of these La Leche League *nazis* that women are developing really crushing depression at not being able to breastfeed."

I nod as she tells this story, and I feel a little comforted that others are having similar experiences. I haven't met any of these people yet, but I hope that I do in time.

"But, like I said," she says, "next time, we can try out some medications to help increase your milk supply."

"What about tests for her hormones?" Doug asks.

"We can order some tests, but I can pretty much tell you that they'll all be normal."

"I still want to do them," he says.

"Okay, no problem." She taps on her computer screen with a stylus. "And we'll check your thyroid again while we're at it."

Until now, I've been using a snug fabric wrap that secures Felicity to my chest for babywearing. She could fall asleep like that and I could do other things. But now, she is realizing that there is an outside world to look at. She pushes away from my chest and looks around. She doesn't want to spend hours cuddling close to my heart anymore. I try different positions with the wrap, but she squirms and protests in each position. I buy a nicer sling, one with top reviews, *the one* that everyone wants to have. I put her in it, find a good position, and wait for her assessment.

She cries. And cries. And cries.

No more babywearing, I decide.

But maybe this is fine. We have taken a path toward helping her fall asleep on her own, to not need the heat and contours of my body to calm down. She is starting to sleep through the night. I'm not breastfeeding anymore, so it wouldn't be more convenient to nurse her while wearing her. And I have to say, the weight of her pulling forward on me was starting to hurt my back.

I chuckle when I remember how much I was looking forward to not carrying around extra weight after pregnancy—and yet I still wanted to do babywearing. Ah well. It didn't seem contradictory at the time.

My blood tests have come back.

For the first time in my life, my thyroid is overactive. Way overactive. When I read about hyperthyroidism symptoms, I mentally highlight the ones that apply to me: rapid weight loss, anxiety, nervousness, difficulty sleeping, fatigue, and muscle weakness. I wonder how this may have affected my milk production, too.

All the other tests to check for other hormonal abnormalities have come back normal.

October 2013
159 pounds, size twelve
"How much has she eaten so far today?" I ask Doug.

He looks at the dry erase board that hangs on the wall in her room. We're still keeping track of the time and amounts of her feedings. We also keep a motivational count of cloth diapers that we've used. We're up to almost 200.

"Let's see... She's had twenty-three ounces so far."

I look at my watch. 9:45 p.m. We just fed her a little over an hour ago. "I think she's hungry again."

He shrugs. "Hey, if she eats more now, maybe she'll skip that middle of the night feeding."

We feed her another four ounces, and she falls asleep.

That night, she sleeps through the night for the first time. From 10:00 p.m. to 5:00 a.m. Solid. Not a peep.

We are victorious.

Days with Felicity are low key now. Twenty-seven ounces of formula is her magic number for getting her to sleep through the night. Some days, she makes it. Other days, we're a little short and she wakes up for a night feeding.

Whenever she wakes up from a nap, I calculate the ninety-minute mark so I know when she'll fall asleep next. Getting her to nap throughout the day is my top priority. It takes precedence over meals, showering, and getting out of the house. When I take her somewhere, I come prepared with a white-noise maker and watch for the time when I should put her in her car seat to nap. When I'm out having breakfast with some other young moms, they see me slip her into her car seat and cover it with a light swaddle blanket.

"Are you leaving?"

"No, it's time for her nap."

"Really? She didn't look tired."

But five minutes later, I lift the blanket to reveal her sleeping face.

"Whoa! Neat trick!"

I'm so excited to tell them about the book. As I'm explaining it, I see their nods turn into furrowed brows. I feel a little silly. I feel a little like I did when I was a child, asking my friends from school to come to church with me—self-conscious, timid. They seem a little interested, but then they find reasons that it won't work for them. I back down. I shrug it off.

I had been hoping to share some helpful motherly wisdom, especially since I knew how useful this advice could be. I had hoped that I could be that wise mom who had figured out a small piece of the puzzle.

But I guess not today.

Today, I'll go back home and let her finish her nap in her car seat. I'll take her out, feed her, change her, play a little bit with her, look for her sleepy signals, take her to her room, and rock her to help her body understand that she's tired. Then, I'll resist the urge to keep her on me while I watch her eyes get heavy, that drunk-with-sleep-and-love look. I'll put her in her crib and let her fall asleep there. I'll take the baby monitor, walk away, and wait for her happy babbling when she's ready to do it again.

When I'm not feeding, changing, or putting Felicity to sleep, I read and write. And lose myself in Facebook and the Internet.

This is how I discover just how much more difficult and complicated becoming a mother is today. Not only do you have the advice of family and friends weighing you down, but also thousands of websites, blogs, and forums, blaring their own advice for giving your baby the best— and therefore, becoming the best mother.

I learn a new term that confuses me: "The Mommy Wars."

A few bloggers mention this term as if it is common knowledge, but it takes me a few more examples with context to understand that it is a reference to mothers criticizing each other for their parenting choices. I instantly think about my trouble breastfeeding and what some mothers have written about formula feeding. *How could you feed your baby that garbage? Low milk supply is just an excuse for not wanting to breastfeed. Formula-fed babies are so much chunkier than breastfed babies. No wonder they are more likely to be obese!*

Yeah, I know what the Mommy Wars means.

I acquire the language of these discussion boards. Abbreviations like DH, DD, and DS become part of my vocabulary ("dear husband/daughter/son"). Women include their style of mothering in their signature that punctuates each of their posts (breastfeeding/co-sleeping/babywearing/natural parenting and proud of it!) A lot of them include the ages and genders of all their children, like those stick figure bumper stickers that show just how many people and pets are in the car.

It feels so shallow—summarizing who I am in a signature like this. I read a lot of these discussions, but I hardly ever join one. I don't see the point. These women don't have any reason to care about me or to give me solid advice.

Aaaa... Ahhh... AAaaaAAAaaa...

I roll over and look at the clock. 2:15 a.m. And it's her hungry cry. After that victorious night of uninterrupted sleep, Felicity's ability to sleep through the night has been spotty. A few nights were great. And then we're back to night feedings. I tell myself that we haven't failed and that this transition takes time.

"Doug?" I nudge him.

"... Wha?"

"She's awake."

".... Wha?"

I think about it. He has to work in the morning. I'll try to get a nap later.

"Nothing," I tell him. "I got it."

Our friend, Josh, organizes a beer tasting and asks me to come. How long? The whole day. He has rented a van for the excursion. I say I'll think about it.

"She's going," Doug tells Josh.

"Well, maybe just half of the day," I say.

"She's going for the whole day." He looks at me. "Sweets, it will be good for you to get out of the house. When was the last time that you got to just hang out with friends?"

So I go.

That day, I have breakfast at home and then leave for the trip.

On the way to the first brewery, Josh hands out a creative scavenger hunt to complete as we travel from brewery to brewery. As I read through the paper, I pause at a few words.

"A selfie?" I ask.

"Yeah, one point for a selfie with the bartender."

"Okay, not sure what a selfie is," I admit.

"Really?" My sister, Holly, says. "It's a picture that you take of yourself."

"Oh. I didn't realize it had a name now."

A song comes on the radio, AC/DC's "Thunderstruck." The van erupts into cheers and shouts. I didn't realize this was such a popular song now.

"God, I always get stuck at the one part," someone exclaims.

"Oh yeah, wait for it... There it is!" Everyone claps and cheers. I have no idea what's going on.

"What are you talking about?" I ask.

Someone turns around and says, "It's a drinking game. You drink every time the word *thunder* comes up."

God, I feel so old.

The song goes on and they are all singing it. I feel about ten thousand miles away. I swallow a growing knot in my throat and try to figure out why I'm so bothered by this. I tell myself that I'm not old just because I don't know about this drinking game. True, most people in the van are a few years younger than me, but at least three of them are the same age as me. *What's the big deal?*

At the first brewery, the mood is still light. One guy asks if I want to read the beer list.

"No, I don't want to read about beer."

"Okay, well, the first one is a chocolate stout with smooth notes of—"

"I don't want to hear about them either," I interrupt him. "I just want to drink."

A few seconds go by and then I realize how rude I must have just sounded. *What's wrong with me?* Something is off. I'm on edge.

The beer is delicious, but it's also strong. Before I know it, I'm very drunk. I know that I should stop drinking for the rest of the day, even though there are four more breweries to go.

As we travel from brewery to brewery, I tell myself to enjoy hanging out with other people and not having to feed Felicity all day. It's a treat to get out, right?

But after four hours, I'm done. I'm ready to go home. But there are still two more breweries to go and I don't want to inconvenience the group or disrupt the organization of the tour. I decide to continue to tough it out in favor of the tour continuing without interruption.

At the last brewery, I glance at my watch. It's 6:00. Some people are getting food at a food truck outside of the last brewery, and I think that we'll be leaving soon. I decline food, saying that I'm going to be eating with Doug at home. I plan to make it home by 7:15. But at 7:00, I see that my friends have ordered additional pizzas and they break them out at the brewery and start another round of eating. They plunge carefree hands into the boxes, pull slices apart, and pinch off dangling strings of cheese. They don't have babies at home waiting for them. They won't be stumbling in the darkness if the baby decides to wake up in the middle of the night. They won't have bottles to clean or diapers to wash tomorrow.

I decline food again, but I realize that I'm on the verge of tears.

"Oh, I know that face," Holly says. "She misses Felicity."

Her comment stings. Because it's true. I wanted to be that mother who isn't tethered to her baby all the time. It's the stereotype that I fear the most—the mother who needs to be attached to her kids all the time. Who can't help but live through her children. And I don't want to be like that. I want to be free to continue to live my own life.

But I'm not ready for that yet. I haven't wanted to admit this—that I need Felicity as much as she needs me.

"You've been such a trooper," another guy comments.

I can't take it anymore and I leave the table to cry in the bathroom. Once I'm in a stall, I let myself cry into my hands. As I rub my eyes, I realize that I've lost a contact lens and now I can't see well out of my right eye.

That does it.

I walk out of the bathroom, out of the brewery, and call Doug. He tells me that he can't leave because I took the car seat base and he can't transport Felicity without it.

"Baby girl, what is wrong?" he asks.

My voice is shaking. I can't even put the feeling into words. "I don't know, but something is... very wrong." I pause before I say, "I feel like maybe it's my hormones."

The moment that I say it, I realize that it's true. This is close to how I felt at four days postpartum. I feel like I'm falling apart again.

After driving home with one-eyed vision, I sit on the couch while Doug rocks Felicity in the glider and I cry more.

"Talk to me, Sweets. What's going on?"

"I just realized today that I don't know what to talk about with anyone anymore. I'm just so far away... from everyone... even our friends."

"You can talk to them. There are lots of things you can talk about."

I shake my head. "What can I talk about anymore? My whole life all day long is feeding her, changing her, feeding her, putting her to sleep, changing her. No one wants to hear about that. I have nothing in common with anyone anymore. I have nothing to talk about." I cry harder.

I used to be so close to all of our friends. We would talk about education, politics, careers, and technology. Now, I feel that slipping away. When I'm with them, I'm not with them. I open my mouth to say something and I realize that it's about cloth diapering or putting Felicity to sleep or something cute that she did. I haven't watched, read, or listened to the news in so long. It's been months since I've read anything besides baby-related websites and books. I don't want to talk about babies all the time, but I don't have anything else in my repertoire right now. The monotonous—at one time my savior—has now become my demise.

This is the pain of knowing that motherhood has swallowed me. There is no room in me right now to be anything else besides a mother. I can't be a friend. I can't be a teacher. I can't even really be a wife. I'm alienating everyone. *Will this ever end? And will anyone stick around long enough to see if I come out on the other side?*

"Why don't you read a book?" Doug suggests. "But not one that's about babies or pregnancy or any of that. You need to get your mind off the whole thing."

I shake my head again. "That's not going to help."

Who have I become? Is this what I wanted? Who am I anymore?

"Sweets, I'm trying to help here," he says.

"I just want you to listen to me. Can you do that? I don't want any advice right now."

"I'll listen to you. I've *been* listening to you. But when you keep coming to me with the same problem over and over again, I'm going to start giving you advice. You know that."

I cry more.

"Sweets, I'm sorry. Hey, Sweets? I'm sorry."

"I think I'm having a hard time figuring out who I am right now."

"You're her mom. But you're still a friend, and you're still my baby girl. You're just one more thing."

In the next few days, I realize what has made everything so much harder. I've started my first cycle since the birth. I think.

It's hard to tell at first. I'm spotting. And then nothing. Then spotting. And then nothing. I go ahead and start taking my birth control when I start spotting. As the spotting starts and stops, my mood flies high and low, over and over again.

One morning, it takes a dive. After Felicity wakes for a 3:00 a.m. feeding, I decide to exercise rather than go back to sleep. My mood needs it. But then I'm not able to go back to sleep because Felicity decides to nap for only thirty or forty-five minute bursts. Around noon, I put her in her crib, tears running down my face, I crank the baby mobile, shut the door, and just sit down on the floor and cry.

For a good ten minutes, I just cry and allow myself to start the inner dialogue.

You're a terrible mother. Be grateful you have a child. Some people have trouble getting pregnant. Terrible mother, why aren't you happy you have a baby? These days don't last forever. What kind of an example are you setting for her? Terrible mother.

After I've let myself go to the dark places, my emotions start to calm and I start hearing my rational side again. *You're tired. You can't think straight when you're tired. Felicity is safe. She doesn't even know you're having a rough time. You're a good mother. You're just tired. You're exhausted. Look at how far you've come! You have been through hell and back and you are still going! You are fierce! So get up!*

And I do.

For a week, the spotting drags on, so I call my OB's office. The nurse says, "Oh, yeah, the first cycle after birth... it can be a doozy."

"Yeah, but all I'm having is spotting. Nothing besides that."

"Oh... well... it can take a few cycles for things to level out. And your thyroid is still correcting itself... So... Another thing to keep in mind is that when you *do* get that first cycle, it could be very long and intense since you started breastfeeding and then stopped. Did you keeping pumping after you stopped nursing?"

"No, I just weaned her cold turkey."

"Okay, so yeah, your first cycle is going to be... maybe a little rough. You should call us back if you have more than five days of heavy bleeding."

The doctor's determination is that I continue with the birth control until further notice.

And then the bleeding picks up. Really picks up. Six more light days, three heavy days, three medium days, two light days, a day of nothing, another light day, three more medium days and then it's over. In total, I bleed for almost a full month.

It is experiences like these that show me the difference between postpartum depression, baby blues, and typical mother guilt. Throughout these mood swings, I am able to balance that inner voice of doom with another inner voice of positivity. If I had postpartum depression, that inner voice of doom would lack an equally rational voice. And it would last for a long period of time.

I conclude that what I'm experiencing is a hormone crash as the result of my first cycle after giving birth. Maybe it's even complicated by the fact that my thyroid is still adjusting to new levels. The hormone fluctuations are so wild that it takes a week for me to not break down into tears while thinking about Felicity or worrying that I'm a terrible mother.

But the mood swings eventually end. They are not long-lasting. But in the moments when I'm having these thoughts and feeling these emotions, I don't know what they mean. I don't know how long they will last. I don't have the foresight or the hindsight to be able to tell myself that everything is okay and that I'm going through a rough spot in my first cycle. All I have are thoughts, feelings, and blank pages on which I write what I'm going through.

The Reconciliation

After all of this identity crisis brought on by feeding, I needed to reconcile my past expectations with my current reality in order to see the way forward. I was not going to be able to breastfeed. I was not going to lose the weight easily in the first few months. I was not going to be able to leave my baby at home without feeling emotional. I was not going to be able to return to all my friendships without skipping a beat. So I had to step back and take a good look at what kind of mother I really was—and then be proud of that.

I had to start accepting the mother who I was becoming even if I didn't fit neatly into one box or another.

I started to feel this disconnect acutely during the early postpartum period. During pregnancy, I cavalierly believed that the postpartum period was going to be a cinch for me. It seemed to me that the biggest obstacle in the postpartum period would be losing the pregnancy weight. And mood swings? I handled those for years, so I was pretty sure I could handle them well enough.

But my greatest fear was that I would become that weepy mother who couldn't look at her baby without crying. These women had completely lost themselves. But that wasn't going to be me. I didn't see myself as a typical woman. I wasn't going to feel that way. I was going to return to exercise ASAP and lose all the baby weight within six months. People would look at me and say, "Wow! You look awesome!" And I would credit it all to my commitment to fitness and good nutrition, as a kind of backhanded comment that women who couldn't drop the weight weren't taking care of themselves. They worshipped their babies to the point of sacrificing their own happiness and health. And I wasn't like those mothers. I was different. I had retained and nourished my individual self despite the challenges of motherhood. I wasn't going to turn off my own personhood in order to be a mother. I was going to rise above. I wouldn't just be a mother. I would be Superwoman.

Oh, how much it hurt when I couldn't live up to my own expectations.

Oh, how much it hurt when I had to accept that this fantasy of becoming Superwoman was void of all that was womanly.

I had to acknowledge that being a mother isn't an identity full of weaknesses that I had to overcome. Instead, motherhood is an identity that requires continuous strength and perseverance that largely remains unheralded.

But I didn't realize any of this until after I had fallen into the thick mud of the postpartum period. All I knew was that I *had to* pull myself up—for my daughter, for my husband—even though my feet were caught in the mud. Even though I couldn't see the way forward. I had to keep walking, no matter what was holding me back.

Because they needed me.

And so I learned a new kind of strength—one that emerges not from vanity to prove my own strength, but from a desire to serve my fragile family, still in its infancy. After a lifetime of being strong only for my own benefit (and occasionally for the benefit of my husband), I had to learn how to be strong for the benefit of my family—even when the payoff to me wasn't immediate.

As hard as it was to reconcile my postpartum expectations with reality, it was even harder to occupy a mind disengaged from the past or the future, to exist as a fluid self, and to practice surrender to whatever challenges the day presented. I was trying so hard to be a mother. To determine what was a priority. To accept when things didn't go according to plan. To soothe a crying baby. To defend my intuition. To make sense of a baby's sleep patterns. To not just bring the diaper bag, but to stock it well.

To an outsider, it may sound easy. *What is so hard about all of that?*

What is hard is that you're doing it all day, every day, for weeks on end. And you can't recharge with a good night's sleep. You have to just keep going.

What is hard is that mastering these necessary moves of motherhood pushes aside all those other dances that you already know. The ones that defined you. The ones that earned you trophies. But they become irrelevant, no matter how well-choreographed they once were. Because the audience that appreciated them is gone. The only spectators left are those that live with you. And the only judge is your baby.

So that was how I spent those weeks—living in humility of the weight of motherhood, building my resilience and strength to do these moves well, and stretching myself beyond my previous limits. I couldn't just stretch to my previous capacity. That wouldn't have been enough. I had to break—because I needed to accept that my role as a mother was coming forward, pushing aside other roles, and reshaping who I was.

So it pounded me. It prodded me. Sometimes, it beat me senseless.

And what it changed was my respect for motherhood. This was not an easy path to follow in case my career didn't pan out. This was not a hobby that I could abandon to a box in the closet or a job that I could quit if I didn't like the workload or the lack of recognition. Through my previous lens of life, seeing enjoyment in motherhood would have been impossible. It is only through a new lens, acquired by taking on a new identity, that the joy of motherhood makes sense.

I would be remiss if I didn't acknowledge the other physical effects of the postpartum period—and how they shaped my early weeks of motherhood.

First, the insomnia. Great sleep deprivation has been found to mimic psychosis—the dreaded "losing touch with reality." As the days passed while I remained awake, I felt myself becoming lost in time. I felt isolated, as if I had nothing left in common with people who could sleep. I started to see connections between things that other people couldn't see— like how my daughter would heal all the wounds in our families. And how I had discovered the purpose of human suffering. The voice of my emotional brain ruled my thoughts. It trumpeted over my rational stream of consciousness. I still had a voice of reason, but it had to fight its way through the sea of emotion and struggle to the surface, just to be heard.

In addition to insomnia, a postpartum hormone crash added fuel to the fire of my emotional brain running amok. Within five days of giving birth, I was submerged in a mental fog. At first, I thought that it was brought on simply by my severe insomnia. But looking back now with a clear head, I see that when I told my husband that "I was coming apart inside," what I was feeling were symptoms of the least severe form of postpartum depression—the baby blues. I had skimmed through the sections about the baby blues in my pregnancy books because they were so vague and unhelpful. Mood swings, weepiness, and anxiety? It sounded a lot like pregnancy. How different could the baby blues be?

For me, the difference was that these symptoms erupted suddenly after the first few blissful days of new motherhood, at exactly the time that I was discharged from the hospital. As I lay next to my daughter in her bassinet, I remember trying to sing her a song through my tears. Why was I crying? I was imagining myself fifty years from then, hearing that same song in a store while I would be Christmas shopping, and then longing to be back with my newborn daughter, and then realizing that I was there right then and that I should enjoy the present moment. At other times, I would think about a time when I told a friend that I didn't want kids. Then, I would look at my daughter's face and apologize for all the times that I thought I didn't want her. Or I would think about how her tiny feet looked just like her father's feet and then I would remember a conversation with Doug about what we imagined our child would look like. It was like every present thought was connected to infinite moments in the past and the future and I could not separate them from what was going on in the present. And I could not turn off the associations. They just kept coming and coming.

During this time, I felt a fraction of what people who live with depression experience every day. Those weeks helped me realize how dependent we are on our hormones to help us manage our emotional brain.

Hormones are the laces that hold us together and keep the body and mind in balance. When I think about my lowest moments, I remember feeling like the laces had all come undone and every part of me was just spilling out in all directions. I felt completely detached from those invisible anchors that keep us steady. This was my emotional brain unchecked. This was me without the voice of reason. I remember that feeling of being everywhere and nowhere, and it makes me grateful that I am now aware of this unspoken, invisible balance.

It gave me a window into how my father may have felt in his darkest days of depression.

But I didn't have postpartum depression, which was all that my pregnancy books had prepared me for. I remember sifting through the mound of paperwork that I brought home from the hospital and finding the brochure on postpartum depression. I read through the symptom questionnaire. *Did I blame myself when things went wrong?* No. *Was I unable to laugh and see the funny side of things?* No. *Did I feel anxious or worried for no reason?* No. *Did I feel so unhappy that I had trouble sleeping?* Well, I wasn't sleeping, but not because I was unhappy. *Had I ever thought about harming myself?* Hell no.

And this is what pregnancy books didn't prepare me for—how to navigate a postpartum experience that was not marked with postpartum depression, but was littered with other debilitating, albeit common, symptoms.

In fact, what was a typical postpartum experience?

The truth is there is no typical postpartum experience. Not every mother suffers from severe insomnia or the baby blues. Some mothers skate through relatively unscathed. Others battle the pain of incision sites from Cesarean deliveries. Still others tearfully cling to plastic incubators that hold their too tiny babies, their minds consumed with unwarranted guilt and valid worries. We all travel these individual paths of loneliness and isolation, and we wonder if anyone else has felt this way. And we wonder where we went wrong.

We wonder this because pregnancy and childbirth were so different. Pregnancy and childbirth tend to follow defined narrative arcs, with a beginning, middle, and end with the woman positioned as the heroine. There are recognizable milestones that women can use as guideposts on their journey. During pregnancy, there is the ultrasound, the announcement, the baby shower, the nursery preparations, and the prenatal appointments. People ask for updates and share congratulations. During labor, cervical checks and timing of contractions indicate a woman's progression in the process. People send flowers and cards and balloons and coo over this beautiful baby that your body produced.

But the postpartum experience is much more nebulous. There are few guideposts that women follow to track their physical recovery. Women don't openly share when their cycles return, or when they resumed sex, or when they finally stopped peeing when they sneezed.

But the public tracking of milestones doesn't disappear altogether—it is just transferred to the baby. *How is the baby growing? Does he sleep through the night yet?* With this shift, the baby becomes the protagonist and the woman becomes a supporting character. And therefore, her experiences become less noteworthy. And maybe this is why a lot of our stories about becoming mothers end once we leave the delivery room. But in leaving the story there, we implicitly neglect to acknowledge the entire experience of how women become mothers.

I will never be able to parse out all the connections to determine what caused what in those early weeks. I'll never know whether insomnia exacerbated my postpartum hormone crash. Or whether it was postpartum thyroiditis that primarily caused my insomnia or whether part of the blame should be attributed to the stress of caring for a newborn. My doctors certainly didn't care to figure it all out. They knew my body was in so much flux that whatever symptoms I was experiencing on one day might have disappeared in a few weeks—so they limited their concern to whether or not I had postpartum depression.

What I do know for sure is that first-time mothers need to hear more postpartum stories. And not just stories of dealing with postpartum depression. Certainly first-time mothers need to be familiar with the signs and symptoms of PPD, but it shouldn't comprise all of their information about the postpartum period. New mothers need to hear the other voices of the postpartum period—ones that talk about the scary, the unpleasant, the embarrassing, and the downright soul-testing. We need to tell these stories because there is comfort in seeing that we are not forging an entirely new path. In fact, we are walking in the footprints that other mothers have left behind.

The First Year

November 2013

159 pounds, size ten

I start the DVD. Excited people appear, hopping in place, ready to get this workout going. They are pumped up. I am pumped up.

Let's do this!

I've given myself the last month to slowly ramp up my ability to sustain a long cardio workout. I started with easy weight lifting. Then, I moved to heavier weights. I did long sessions of yoga. Then, some short cardio workouts: twenty to thirty minutes. Lunges got easier. I could hold the Warrior One and Warrior Two poses longer. I could almost do a tricep push-up to the floor.

Today is the day of a full forty-five minute cardio workout.

Five minutes in: *Okay... doing good.*

Ten minutes: *Breathe... Breathe... You're strong.*

Twenty minutes: *You're great. You can do this. You're not tired.*

Thirty minutes: *Oh man... Breathe... Breathe...*

Thirty-five minutes: *Holy shit... Okay... This is worth it. You've been through worse. You gave birth!*

Forty minutes: *You are strong!*

When I've finished the workout, I'm thrilled. Exhausted, but thrilled.

"Good workout?" Doug asks, as he passes by the living room with Felicity's morning bottle.

"Yeah... just..." I gulp the air. "I don't remember getting so tired like this."

"You need time to get back into it."

"Yeah, maybe... I don't know. I just feel... sluggish. I mean, it was really hard to finish that."

"Give it time."

I have finally found a community of mothers who formula feed their babies. It's Fearless Formula Feeder.com.

I spend hours reading other women's stories about infant feeding. I am surprised and comforted by how many other women have first suffered through breastfeeding challenges and then later suffered shame after switching to formula. The reasons they stopped breastfeeding are many: low milk supply, constant mastitis, latching issues, inability to maintain pumping with work, and on and on. The majority of these women tried breastfeeding, but because of the challenges, they found that method of feeding unsustainable.

I feel so much relief. Relief that problems with milk supply are much more common than I had been led to believe. Relief that there are other women—many other women—who felt that breastfeeding was not in their best interests. I know now that others share my story. I am not as alone as I once thought.

Following Felicity's sleep schedule is still my top priority. She wakes, I check the clock. As the ninety-minute mark approaches, I hold her and rock her. I put her down, she falls asleep. Her naps are usually forty-five minutes long. A good nap is an hour and a half. On a great day, she has a two-hour nap.

And the payoff is finally here. She's sleeping through the night regularly now. From 10:00 p.m. to 6:00 a.m.

People are still amazed that we know when she's going to fall asleep. We take her to restaurants, watch the clock, put her in the car seat when it's time, and she's out. We tell other people about the book that we're following. Every now and then, someone is really interested in the idea. But usually, people raise eyebrows. They tell us that their children never went down for naps. They tell us that every baby is different and that we got lucky.

It's hard not to get upset that we are dismissed so easily, but really, as long as she's a great sleeper, who cares?

And she's growing. Quickly. She has been following the ninety-fifth percentile curve since eight weeks. And God, she's happy. Almost all the time. She smiles at strangers in the grocery store, the UPS delivery guy, church members, and anyone at a party. She is content to sit and watch what's going on. She studies people's faces and looks to see who is talking. She holds objects in her hands and examines them from all angles. I can put her on the floor, walk into another room to make a cup of coffee, and when I come back, she's still looking at a toy or her hands. She only cries when she's hungry, too wet, or tired.

I feel infinitely lucky.

"When's that baby coming out already?" Ben jokes with Katy as she lowers her eight-month pregnant self to a chair. It's Monday Night Dinner chez Ben and Sarah tonight.

She rolls her eyes and rests her hand on her belly. "You know, I've been hearing that for like two months. Total strangers say shit like, '*Oh it must be any day now!*' Ugh! I just want to kill people sometimes," she vents. "Not you," she motions to Ben.

"I mean, I deserve it," Ben shrugs. "I know I just stepped on a minefield."

I sit next to Katy. She rubs the side of her belly and I remember how that felt—those little nudges and kicks. And for a moment, I swear that I feel phantom kicks where Felicity used to nudge my sides.

"So, I'm probably going to regret saying this later," Katy whispers to me, "but I'm sooo ready for this to be over."

I laugh at the word, *over*. I could break out an *oh-you-think-you're-not-sleeping-now* comment. But come on. I like Katy and I want to be supportive of her. So what I say is, "Hey, that's a completely reasonable feeling at this point. I just wanted it to be over, too."

I'm going to turn thirty-two this year.

Before the birth, I had mentally charted a reasonable weight loss goal for my birthday. When I lost weight in the past, one pound per week was reasonable. So I thought 145 pounds was a reasonable goal to reach by my birthday, November 24.

Despite five days a week of cardio and weightlifting and sticking to about 1500 calories per day, I haven't lost one pound since September. Not one. I'm still 159 pounds. I look at my floppy midsection and I acknowledge that my waist is slowly returning. I don't see any stretch marks—thanks to the flap. I take my measurements, and happily, I see that I've dropped half of an inch in my waist and hips, but I keep staring at the number on the scale. I hate that I'm obsessing about this. It makes me feel vain and whiny. Part of me screams, *Who cares? You have a beautiful, healthy baby! She sleeps through the night!* Another part of me screams back, *Why the hell haven't I been losing more!*

I get it now—the feeling of *Oh whatever. I'm a mom now. I've got better things to do now. Like getting some sleep.*

But I don't stop working out. I keep going. The pounds aren't coming off, but damn it, exercising helps. It empties all that emotional turmoil that builds in my brain. I feel happier to take care of Felicity after I've taken care of myself. I intended to portion my meals and work out as a permanent lifestyle before I got pregnant. It makes me feel more balanced.

So I stick with it.

My hair is falling out. In clumps.

I find out that this is common at three months postpartum. When I wash my hair, it takes a while for my hands to leave my scalp without loose pieces trailing behind. I haven't noticed any bald patches, but maybe that's because I have so much hair.

As I'm drying my hair, I notice how much gray has spread across the hairs around the center of my head. I haven't cut my hair since the beginning of my pregnancy. And this gray... I just can't have it anymore. I'm not ready to be gray yet. I think it's finally time to dye my hair.

"Would you like a new mom makeover?" Doug asks when I say that I need to get my hair cut.

I hate the sound of that. *New mom makeover*. It feels like code for *covering up all the damage the baby has done to you*. But as soon as I think that, I silence that voice. That's not what he meant.

I don't really know anything about makeup. In middle school, I learned what to call the different tubes and compacts: mascara, eye shadow, and foundation. Sometimes, I tried out some blue and purple eye shadow, but I always thought it looked weird on me. But no one ever taught me how to put it on properly. In college, I bought a shade of Cover Girl blush and tried it on. My roommate asked me why I put on so much. That was the end of makeup for me.

Doug never cared that I didn't wear makeup. In fact, he loved that I had strong features even without makeup. The only time that he remembers me wearing makeup was our wedding day. *It made you look even more beautiful*, he said.

"How would I do that? Get a makeover?" I ask.

"You can go to the mall and get one at a makeup counter."

"How much does it cost?"

He chuckles. "They're free, Sweets."

"Really?"

"Yeah. They kind of assume you'll buy something, but they're free. If you go on a weekend, you should make an appointment though."

"I don't want to go alone..."

"Well, take your sister with you."

I shrug. "Eh, I mean, I don't want to pick a look that you don't like."

"All right... so we'll get your sister to watch Felicity and I'll go with you."

When we approach the makeup counter on a Thursday night, the nearby junior's section is blasting some new pop song that I can't place. Who is the new Britney Spears now? Is it Hilary Duff? Miley Cyrus? What's the difference?

I already feel way out of my realm.

"Can I help you?" a tall, blonde woman with a Russian accent asks.

"I need... makeup," I say.

"Okay, what are you looking for?"

"Um... I guess all of it?"

She nods slowly with a puzzled look.

"Okay," I confess, "I really don't know what I'm doing."

Doug laughs. "Maybe, just start us from the beginning."

December 2013

158 pounds, size ten

At four months old, Felicity is still growing rapidly. She outgrew her six-month clothing in two weeks and now she's sporting nine-month clothing. She's not very mobile yet. She just rolls from side to side. She hasn't rolled from her back to stomach yet, which I guess is a big milestone.

I'm starting to feel okay in my body again, at least emotionally. My mood isn't plummeting like it was in October, and I feel more in control of myself again. I'm also starting to talk about other things besides babies, so it's getting easier to talk with my friends who aren't parents.

But then there's my physical health. My digestion is at a crawl. I look in the mirror and my face is puffy, even bloated. My weight still hasn't budged. I feel tired and I don't think I should be. Felicity has been sleeping well and napping during the day. But I still feel sluggish during workouts.

And then I wonder... *What if my thyroid is underactive now?*

I have my blood checked.

It *is* underactive. Way underactive. It is functioning at about half its normal levels. It's practically a miracle that I've lost any weight. If I had just been eating normally without exercising, I would have been packing on the pounds.

And so my family doctor arrives at a diagnosis: postpartum thyroiditis. The swing from hyper- to hypothyroidism after birth is a telltale sign. I google *postpartum thyroiditis* and find that women who have it are more likely to experience low milk supply, weight loss followed by weight gain, extreme fatigue, and constipation.

As Doug and I are clearing the table of mugs and plates from Saturday Morning Breakfast, something tragic happens.

He breaks my favorite ceramic mug. Into at least ten pieces.

He is apologetic—the kind of apologetic that makes me feel badly that I'm angry.

I tell him that it's okay. But I feel the tears rising. I don't want to be emotional about something small like this. It's just a mug.

From our honeymoon.

From a time before we were pregnant.

That I cradled in my hands during hundreds of breakfasts with friends.

That I rested beside me as I wrote and wrote and wrote—essays, journal articles, novels, short stories.

I always joked with Doug that it was going to be one of our kids who broke it. And that I'd have to hide my sadness that it was broken. I didn't think it was going to be Doug or that it would happen so unceremoniously.

One moment it was whole. The next moment—shattered.

After our friends are gone, I cry into his shoulder until the feelings pass. He wraps the pieces in dishtowels and says that he's going to find a place that will glue it back together.

It's about one month before Felicity is due to start daycare and I haven't heard from the university's daycare center about whether or not she can start in January. I call. I leave a message.

Four days later, I get a call. *Sorry, but we don't have room in January.*

I call back and make sure that Felicity is on the waiting list for the next enrollment period, which is May. And then I start daycare hunting.

After some research, some calls, and a tour, I enroll Felicity in a daycare about ten minutes from our house. And I feel good about it.

I check my phone and I see that Jarod has called. *Yes!* I finally have a reason to call them and see how the baby is doing. Katy just gave birth two days ago to her baby girl, Adelyn. I've been watching the clock since then, wondering how she is doing. Did she need someone to talk to? Was she feeling okay? How did the delivery go?

Jarod picks up.

"Hey, Jarod! Congratulations! How's everything going?" I ask.

He sighs and chuckles. "So, right..." he pauses. "I mean... Yeah, I think you know how it's going."

I laugh. "Yeah... I do. I *really* do."

"Katy was nursing for like six hours last night. Continuously."

"Yeah..." I nod, wondering what I should say. I don't want to say it's going to get easier, but I also want to be encouraging. What I decide to say is, "That's so hard. I know how hard that is. Is she sleeping now?"

"Who? Katy?" he asks.

"Yeah."

"Oh, yeah, she's out. They've both been asleep for a while."

"That's really good. So she's getting sleep when she can?"

"Yeah. Not much. You know that. But she's getting sleep here and there."

When I hang up, I say a prayer for Katy. Because I know. Boy, do I know. And then I smile because we are both on the other side of birth now.

We're listening to Christmas music in the nursery. Felicity is lying on the floor underneath an activity gym that dangles a flower with a bell in it and a bird sitting on a ring over her head. She tries to connect her hand with the objects, but her movements are random and choppy. When she succeeds in hitting one, her eyes fixate in wonder.

This is nice. This is simple. The laundry is done for now. There are enough diapers until tomorrow. Doug won't be home for another three hours, but Felicity is only thirty minutes away from a nap.

But it has been two days since I've talked to anyone besides Doug. I'm actually looking forward to going to the dentist while a friend from church watches Felicity. I'd like to go Christmas shopping, but it's just easier to stay home and order everything on Amazon.

I miss my days of morning classes and small talk at the coffee maker. I miss the headache of students with excuses and poor email etiquette. I miss those do-or-die advising sessions with students who are straddling the line between passing and failing.

There was always something to complain about—not enough resources, not enough time, not enough motivated students, not enough responsive administrators.

Now, I just miss it. All of it.

Three days before Christmas, Felicity starts waking up in the middle of the night. Every forty-five minutes. Crying and crying. Inconsolable. We try feeding her and changing her. Rocking her helps a little. We wonder if she's sick, but there's no fever. No congestion.

Doug suggests we let her cry it out, but I'm still not ready for that. She cries and cries. Then, she pushes away from me. She arches her back and flails her arms. She doesn't want me to hold her. She doesn't want Doug to hold her. We put her in her crib and she screams. I pick her up, and she wiggles away. I put her down and she screams louder.

"What should we do?" Doug defers to me.

"I don't know... I really don't know," I admit.

"Okay," he pauses. "Just go in the other room. I got this."

I leave and she screams louder. I swear I can hear the tears hitting the sheets. My heart breaks. I sit at my desk and I google, *four-month sleep regression* and find comfort in other parents complaining that their babies—once champion sleepers—had a setback at four months. But no one has advice on how to fix it.

She cries and screams for another forty-five minutes.

And then she's silent.

Doug walks in and says, "Well, that was fun."

The next night is a repeat performance.

The next night is Christmas Eve, and she's at it again. Waking up, crying. I think she's in pain, so we give her Tylenol. She falls back asleep eventually, but I'm exhausted.

Christmas Day, we see it. A tooth has broken through her lower gums.

Four months old—teething has begun.

January 2014

154 pounds, size ten

I start thinking about what Felicity needs for daycare every day. At first, I think I'm going to be carting a huge bag of supplies every day—burp cloths, bibs, blankets, sheets, bottles, diapers, toys, and on and on. But when I review the list of items that she needs, I see that the only things that I need to bring every day are her bottles and food and her diapers. Every week, I need to provide a sheet and a blanket, but I don't need to send anything else.

I wonder if she'll be okay.

I wonder if her teachers will hear her hungry cry and respond quickly enough. Or if they will know how to hold Felicity to help her realize that she's tired. Or if she'll even be able to fall asleep with the noise.

I wonder if her teachers will think we're neurotic new parents when we tell them about the ninety-minute rule. But then, Felicity is changing. She's almost six months old and she's beginning to extend her awake periods to three or four hours.

I wonder a lot of things. I don't doubt—I just wonder. And hope.

I take out a permanent marker and write *Felicity* on each bottle. When I'm finished, I think, *Hm. I like writing that.*

Winter has brought record-breaking wind chills, hazardous ice, and sizable snow accumulations. Felicity's first day of daycare is slated for January 6 and my first day back at work is January 7.

When we wake up on January 6, we realize that a lot of businesses are closing because the forecasted high is -14° F. My university is closed. Doug's office is closed.

But the daycare is open.

So what do we do? We take her.

I think it's a good decision because we can try out a shorter day and see how she does. I've already met her teachers during the tour, but we still spend about twenty minutes talking to them about Felicity's feedings, naps, and cloth diapers. When it's time to leave, I give Felicity a hug, hand her to the head teacher and then unceremoniously leave the room.

I don't hear her crying. When I turn to look back through the classroom window, she's looking around the room, checking out her new surroundings. Part of me wants her to fuss a little bit about me not being there. But a greater part of me feels relief that she looks like she's going to be okay.

The house is too quiet when we return. We kind of wander around the rooms, looking for something to do, amazed that we don't have to think about the next feeding or the next diaper change. I make coffee. Doug watches a TV show. I go upstairs and I write for a long time. My mind follows a train of thought for a whole hour, and I write without any interruptions. I pick up a book for research. I read it. I write notes. I think.

When we return around 3:30, Felicity is sitting in the lap of one of her teachers, who is helping her clap her hands to a song as the babies sit in a circle. When she notices us, she smiles, as if saying, "Oh, hey guys! Good to see you again."

I'm a believer. Daycare is amazing.

It isn't until the next day, my first official day back at work, when I start to let the transition really sink in. I leave Felicity at daycare at 7:20 and I won't be back until 5:20. As I'm heading north on the interstate toward work, I realize that I'm letting go. I'm allowing us to become two separate people.

She is at daycare by herself. And I will be at work by myself. We will have separate days. She will have experiences that I won't witness and may not even hear about. I will resume work and manage to go an hour or so without thinking about her.

I'm weaning myself from her. I'm finally at a place in my mind where I can handle hours of separation during the day. I just needed time to arrive at this place.

By Thursday afternoon, Felicity has acquired her first cold virus. We learn how to use the nasal bulb to suck snot out of her nose. We learn how to administer Tylenol via medicine dropper to a squirming baby. The cold has aggravated her blocked tear duct in her right eye, which she has had since birth. Green goopy mucus builds in the corner of her right eye. We wipe it away all the time now. Doug massages the duct with his pinky and green pus flies out when he hits it just right. All weekend, we tend to her needs. We buckle her into her bouncer to keep her inclined while she sleeps at night.

By Monday, we are sick. And we are back at work.

On the Friday of her second week at daycare, Felicity brings home a stomach virus. She slowly pushes away her evening bottle as I rock her in the glider. She pauses, furrows her brow, looks up at me, and then vomits all over me. As I move her to the floor, she vomits all over my shoulder. I don't even flinch. I gently rub her back and help her. She continues to wretch and wretch against the carpet as I pat her back. She finally stops, completely dazed.

We spend the rest of the weekend doing loads of laundry and administering Pedialyte.

By Monday, she is ready for daycare. And then Doug is sick.

In her third week of daycare, I start to feel woozy on Tuesday. By Wednesday, I can't get out of bed because my muscles hurt too much. Doug comes in to tell me the good news that the university is closed because it's too cold again. I can't even muster excitement. I'm just thrilled I don't have to make the decision to get out of bed.

I have the flu. I'm sure of it.

The muscle aches continue until Friday, and then the congestion starts. When we pick up Felicity, we realize she's starting to get sick again.

That weekend, Felicity starts crying around 2:00 a.m. We give her some Tylenol. She continues to cry. I hold her and she calms down. I put her back in her crib. Fifteen minutes later, she's crying again. Doug tells me to give her time to calm down. Ten minutes pass.

"What do you want to do?" Doug asks me.

"I don't know... Maybe she's stuffed up."

We both get back up. She has scooted across her crib and her head is bumping the opposite side. She cries every time she smacks her head against the crib. *Why is she doing that?* We suction her nose and then put her back in the middle of her crib.

We climb back in bed. Another fifteen minutes pass. She is crying again.

"Oh my God," I rub my face.

"What now?" Doug asks.

"I don't know... Maybe put her at an incline? Maybe that will help her?"

Doug brings the bouncer to her room. She is at the other end of her crib again. I pick her up. She's wearing a sleep sack, so we can't buckle her legs into the bouncer. I don't want to change her clothes either. We set her in the bouncer, and she seems snug. But she is still crying.

I lie on the floor and gently bounce the seat of the bouncer to calm her. Doug shuffles back to bed. In a few minutes, she is asleep.

An hour passes. And then she's crying again.

"Oh my God..." I moan. Doug doesn't stir.

I get back up and check her. Her legs are rigid in the bouncer. I lie back down on the floor of her room and bounce her in the seat. She falls asleep.

I repeat this for another three hours. And then I decide we should all get up.

Doug helps me change her diaper. And that's when we see that she's been sitting in poop for hours. She had been trying to get away from poop all night long. A bright red rash lines her butt. I just assumed that her problem was the virus.

I feel terrible.

February 2014

151 pounds, size ten

By the time Monday comes around again, I'm still not feeling well, but I can move. I take a bag of cough drops, a bottle of cough syrup, and a box of tissues. I power through. I come home after teaching and drop into effortless sleep. I don't do any extra work beyond my teaching duties. I barely even grade the things that I need to grade.

On Tuesday evening, Felicity wakes up from a nap screaming. As soon as I walk in the room, I smell something like rancid cheese. When I look into her crib, I do a double-take. Milk-vomit surrounds her head, neck, and shoulders. At some point during her nap, she threw up and fell back asleep in it. That night, I hear her crying at 2:00 a.m. I bring her some Pedialyte and she manages to keep it down.

Doug stays home from work on Wednesday. We take her back to daycare on Thursday.

On Thursday afternoon, I hear my cell phone ringing while I'm passed out at home after a half-day of teaching. It's Felicity's daycare teacher. Felicity has a fever. I drag myself out of bed. I wonder how I'm going to be able to carry her in her car seat. *Do I have enough strength for that?* I call Doug and tell him that I'm going to pick her up.

By the time I return home with Felicity, Doug has come home. I have never been so happy to see him in my whole life. Never. Not even on our wedding day.

He takes Felicity and tells me to go to bed.

I do.

At first, we think Felicity is getting over this new virus. She seems to be doing better. We are diligent about suctioning snot from her nose, day after day. We spray her nasal passages with saline and suction, suction, suction. She is getting good at knocking the bulb from our hands and dodging it. She coughs, but nothing comes out. She must be almost over the virus.

But during the next week at daycare, she starts to expel chunks of mucus after coughing fits. For most of the day, she's very happy and she doesn't have a fever, so I continue to take her to daycare. But then Felicity starts waking up in the middle of the night again. Doug tells me to let her cry it out.

"I don't know... I think something's wrong," I say.

"Sweets, she's six months old now. When are we going to start making her cry it out?"

"I just think... I think she needs help."

"She's fine."

He turns over to go to sleep. Felicity is screaming now.

I get out of bed and go to her room.

"Sweets! Where are you going?"

I hear him, but I'm not in the mood to explain myself. I pick her up and hold her. She continues to cry as I hold her. I feel her head. She's warm, but not hot. I suction her nose and then rock her some more. She calms down a little.

But as soon as she's back in the crib, she's wailing again.

I sigh. And walk away.

"What did you do?" he asks.

"I held her, cleaned her nose, and put her back down."

"You're just teaching her to rely on us. We've got to be on the same page here. She's just manipulating us now."

Felicity continues to scream.

"That's her manipulating us," he says.

I'm so furious I can't even find the words. I don't think she's manipulating us at all. I think there's something wrong, but I don't know what it is. I thought she was getting better. I feel like I'm having to choose between my husband and my child. I hate that choice. It's unnecessary and unfair.

"Sweets?"

"Fine." I don't say anything else. I just want to go back to sleep.

She cries for another forty minutes. And then it's silent. I creep into her room to hear her breathe. Her breathing rattles her chest, but she's asleep.

I'm angry with Doug, but I'm even angrier at myself for having given up on the argument. I look at the clock. 4:15 a.m.

I decide to do some light yoga that won't cause me to cough. Then, I start to get ready for work.

The next day is Felicity's six-month checkup with her pediatrician. I pick her up from daycare early, feed her, give her some Tylenol at home, and then drive to the doctor's office. As we are sitting in the waiting room, Felicity starts to cough. And cough. And cough.

I pat her back and tell her, "It's okay... Take it easy." She keeps coughing. And coughing. And that is when she vomits an entire bottle of formula—pink with cherry Tylenol—all over me. I catch some of it in a burp cloth—the rest of it drips into the diaper bag and down my pants.

A few concerned mothers in the room rush over to me, carrying tissues and towels from the bathroom.

"Poor girl! Here, let me help you," they coo. One of them holds Felicity while I try to wipe off my pants.

All I can say is, "Thank you. We've been going through this all week..."

But what I want to say is, *Bless you for being so kind. Thank you, fellow mother, for not making me feel worse about this.* I feel that they have all been there before, wearing their children's vomit in public because they needed to be the strong one. A nurse tells me that I can wait with Felicity in an exam room. I'm so grateful.

Doug arrives within a few minutes. I'm holding Felicity as she stares at the wall.

"She's sick," I say.

He pauses and kneels down to look into her eyes. He shoulders go lax and he sighs.

Then he says, "You're right. I'm wrong. You knew something was wrong, and I didn't listen to you."

"Look," I say, "I think we'll be able to tell if she's trying to manipulate us. Wouldn't we start to see that kind of behavior during the day? Look at her. She doesn't do that during the day."

He nods. "Sweets, I'm sorry. I've doubted you in the past, and I've been wrong every time. So I'm just deferring to you now."

The pediatrician doesn't take long to reach a diagnosis. Felicity has RSV—Respiratory Syncytial Virus. It's a common virus, but it's worse for young babies who aren't capable of expelling all of the mucus that builds up in the lungs. Felicity doesn't need to be hospitalized, but she needs nebulizer treatments.

Doug takes Felicity home and I stop at the pharmacy to buy a nebulizer and fill her prescription.

I hear her coughing through my earplugs, which I'm now wearing regularly at night. They help drown out the sound of her sporadic coughing. If I don't wear them, I wake up constantly every time she coughs.

I look at the clock. 2:40 a.m. I wait, listen.

Ah-huh... Ah-huh... Huh... Ah-huh-huh-huh... Ah-huh... Huh...

"Doug?" I shake him. He's sound asleep.

Ah-huh... Ah-huh-huh-huh-huh... blech...

I get up, walk to her room, and open the door. She's nestled in the bouncer instead of her crib. The incline helps the mucus drain through her throat.

I assemble the parts of the aspirator, open a vial of nebulizer solution, pinch the vial in half, and squeeze a half-dose into the chamber. I pick her up, sit in the glider, and cradle her in my arms. I flip on the power button of the nebulizer with my big toe and a rumbling and hissing starts. I lower the smiling fish mask to her face. She struggles, flails her head from side to side. Her eyes open and she searches wildly around the room. She cries. I rock her.

"It's okay," I say. "Shhh... It's okay."

I hum—a hymn from childhood.

She stops struggling, breathes in the mist.

"It's okay... There you go..."

A few minutes later, she's asleep, but we're not finished yet. I grip her head in the crook of my arm and then take the nasal bulb from the side table. When I start suctioning out the mucus, her arms flail and knock at my hands. I empty the snot into a burp cloth. Over and over again.

Then I rock her back to sleep. I listen to her breath. The rattling has lessened.

I finally walk back to bed. 3:15.

What day is it? Oh, Monday.

I feel that I've just fallen asleep when the alarm screams. 5:15. I think about it. *Did I wash my hair yesterday? Yes.* I pick up my phone to check the weather. It has snowed overnight—about three inches. The university is still open. Her daycare is still open. I should probably leave early to be safe. I feel the soreness in my throat again—I've picked up another virus from her daycare. I'm still coughing up mucus from the last one. *Do I have cough syrup left at work? Should I bring another box of tissues?* I run through the day in my head. *That... that... that... and that... Do I need that? Oh, and that.*

She's crying now. It's her hungry cry.

You've had less sleep. You've felt worse. You are fierce. So get up.

And I do.

When we walk through the door that morning, I tell her daycare teacher that Felicity caught RSV.

"Oh no! That's what two of the other babies got and they're in the hospital now. Both of them were having trouble breathing. One stopped eating. Poor Felicity..." she rubs Felicity's head. "Is she eating okay?"

"Yeah, actually, she is. And we've been giving her nebulizer treatments and that's really helping. She's breathing better now. But, anyway, yes, she's eating well."

"What a little trooper..."

A few more days pass and Friday approaches. It's a joke now that every Friday, we expect Felicity to bring home a new virus for us to enjoy all weekend. I keep my fingers crossed.

On Friday morning, we start to load the car so I can take Felicity to daycare. I arrange my work bag, her daycare bag, and my lunch bag in the front seat and Doug buckles Felicity into her car seat. Every morning, he waits for her to smile back at him before he shuts the door. Sometimes, they make a game out of it.

"She's not smiling, Sweets."

I see Felicity's reflection in the car seat mirror. She's gazing listlessly to the side.

"Does she have a fever?"

He feels her head. "No."

"Well, then we're going."

He shakes his head. "Something's not right."

"Do you want to stay home with her?"

"I've got an 8:00 meeting," he says.

"So I'll see you tonight."

By 10:30, I get a call from daycare.

"Well... I know her eye gets goopy but..." her teacher says diplomatically.

I brace myself. "Do you think it's pinkeye?"

"...Yes."

I sigh. "I'll be right there."

Later that afternoon, I call to congratulate Doug on his paternal intuition.

"You were right," I tell him. "I was wrong."

"I just *knew* something was wrong! I could feel it!" The happiness in his voice is palpable. I feel good for him.

March 2014

150 pounds, size ten

After eight weeks of constant viruses, I think I'm finally getting better. When parents said, *Be prepared to be sick all of the time*, I didn't realize that this could go on for so long. And that they wouldn't just be consecutive illnesses—they would also be *concurrent* illnesses. The flu *and* bronchitis. A stomach bug *and* a cold.

For weeks, I haven't been able to talk without coughing. Or my voice was inaudible—which makes teaching a challenge.

My co-workers would sometimes ask, "Why are you here? You look terrible!"

I was there because if I stayed home every day that I wasn't feeling well, I wouldn't have been at work for two months. And on the days when I did stay home, it was because I needed to take care of Felicity or because I couldn't move. If I could move and Felicity was at daycare, I was working. I'm not proud of that—but those were the decisions that I had to make in order to keep my job.

However, it's important to be honest about this care-taking—it wasn't solely my responsibility. My husband and I shared the responsibilities of taking off work to care for Felicity when she was sick. We coordinated a schedule, depending on the day of the week that she was ill. We agreed that he would stay with her on Mondays or Wednesdays. On Tuesdays or Thursdays, I would stay with her. And on Fridays, I would work a half day in the morning, and he would work a half day in the afternoon. As a full-time instructor at a university, missing a day of work just pushed all my work to the next day. However, for my husband, missing a day of work required him to use vacation days.

But, hey, we still got paid.

Being sick for two months puts my exercise program at a standstill. My muscles have lost their tone, and I have once again plateaued in weight loss. The good news is that my thyroid has finally kicked back into gear. My levels are normal and the next time I start to exercise, I should start seeing some real results.

I wait for the day when I can take a deep breath without coughing. And then I give it two more days.

And then I resume exercise.

We have a fairly stable schedule in the morning now.

5:15 a.m.: I wake up and exercise.

6:00 a.m.: I wake up Doug. He feeds Felicity. I shower.

6:20 a.m.: I blow dry my hair. Doug dresses Felicity and starts preparing her bottles and food for the day.

6:30 a.m.: I eat breakfast and make my lunch.

6:45 a.m.: We start loading the car.

6:50 a.m.: I leave for daycare.

7:00 a.m.: I drop Felicity off at daycare and update her teachers.

7:15 a.m.: I leave for work.

7:40 a.m.: I arrive at work.

8:00 a.m.: I teach.

The evenings also have their rhythms. Felicity goes to bed at 8:00 p.m. and there's a magical hour from 8:00 to 9:00 when it's just Doug and me. It's nice.

Work has a different rhythm, too, now that I'm coming home to a baby. During the day, I'm functioning at maximum efficiency whenever possible. I eat lunch at my desk while answering emails. I make a lesson plan and move on. There are no additional frills. I limit small talk. I wear headphones to block out conversations in neighboring cubicles so I can forge ahead and finish all that I can before I leave the office. Grading and planning almost never come home with me now. Not only will I not finish this work at home, but it's not fair to Felicity for me to spend the evening with work when I haven't seen her all day. When it was just me and Doug, I didn't think twice about catching up on work at night or on the weekends.

But now I realize that there are only four weekends to spend time with my seven-month-old daughter. And only four weekends to spend with my eight-month-old daughter. She is growing up right now. Did I really want to spend my free time planning and grading a course for students that I might not remember a year from now?

I know that I'm still an effective teacher, but I also know that I'm not winning any popularity contests any time soon. Anyway, I don't feel like I need to be a stellar teacher at this moment. Good enough is okay for me. It's much more important to me to be a good mom.

That modern day *can-women-have-it-all* conversation is hitting home now. And for me, I have determined that I can't be one hundred percent of every role that I have to fill. Sometimes, fifty percent has to be enough. I know it isn't my usual standard, but I feel that as long as I'm meeting the requirements of my job, I'm still succeeding.

"Is that Felicity?" Cate asks.

We're sitting around the dinner table, plates scraped clean of food. It's our turn to host our twelve friends in the weekly rotation of Monday Night Dinner.

aaaaaaaaa.... aaa.... aaaaaaAAAAAAAA!!!!

I look at the clock. It's 9:00 p.m. Felicity fell asleep exactly one hour ago. I look at Doug and I can tell that we have already arrived at the same conclusion—*the dreaded one-hour mark.* For the past week, she's been going to sleep for the night, but then waking up at the one-hour mark. She wasn't hungry. She wasn't lying in poop. And she would calm if one of us held her. Then, another hour later, she'd wake up again. During the day, she has been napping well, so we know she's getting enough sleep. She has a long nap from 10:00 a.m. to 1:00 p.m. and then she has a short nap from 3:00 p.m. to 4:00 p.m.

"Let her go," I say.

"Yeah?" Doug asks.

"If she can't calm down in five minutes, let's check her out."

Felicity continues to cry as the conversations resume. I can't join a conversation yet—I'm still listening to her cry. *Did I do the right thing? She's probably fine... She's not sick... She's eight months old. That's old enough right?*

"Hey, Sharon, where are the dishtowels?" someone asks from the kitchen.

"Oh..." I stand up. "I'll get one for you."

Once I've found a towel, I find myself cleaning dishes. *Just a few to make space*, I reason.

I rinse a few plates underneath the water and load them into the dishwasher. If I had to explain to another mother what I'm doing, I would say that I'm teaching. A child can't grow unless she steps a bit beyond her current abilities. But it takes good judgment to know when that moment has arrived. You have to observe, experiment, and make mental notes. It's much easier to pick up the child and take her where she needs to go. It's harder to restrain yourself so you can see what she can do by herself.

But this is exactly how we learn: by reaching beyond, by taking a risk, by failing, and trying again. Learning is most meaningful and long-lasting when it emerges from a struggle.

But you can't teach a child how to do something that is not within her reach. It was not within Felicity's ability to learn to soothe herself to sleep at two weeks old. However, she's eight months old now. And I think it's time to let her truly attempt that struggle. Cautiously. Being mindful that she may need me to respond.

It's a different kind of compassion than unconditional comfort. This compassion looks beyond this present moment and considers the future. It knows that a reaction that can seem uncompassionate now can be seen months and years from now as the most compassionate response.

"Sweets?" Doug calls.

"Yeah?"

"Do you hear that?"

I listen—no more crying. I pump my fist in the air. "Oh yeah!"

"And that," Doug points to the stairs, "is how you cry-it-out!"

Felicity stays asleep for the rest of the night.

April 2014

151 pounds, size eight

After a month of exercise and portion control, the scale still hasn't budged. I reason with myself that it takes time for numbers to change as the body regains heavier muscle while losing lighter fat. I watch my measurements and they continue to shrink. I know that I'm at a turning point in this weight loss journey, so I resist the urge to grab a cookie or brownie or whatever dessert someone has brought into work. I tell myself it makes a difference. I tell myself that I'm strong and that I've done this before. I'll do it again. I enjoy the food that I eat—sandwiches, soup, rice, salads, beans, chicken, and pork. And once a week I give myself a break and have a treat.

We take Felicity to a friend's housewarming party, and she is the belle of the ball.

How old is she? Wow! She's huge! Are you still nursing her? I couldn't take it anymore either—once they had teeth. Does she have any teeth? Whoa! No kidding! Look at those chompers!

I can't believe she's smiling at me. Does she have any stranger anxiety? Huh. She probably will.

Is she crawling? No? Well, she will soon.

Is she eating solids? Maybe she can have some cake today!

Are you getting any sleep? Really? My kids were terrible sleepers. I should tell you stories. Well, you're lucky that you got a baby that sleeps. You know what they say. You get an easy one first and then that convinces you to have the second one—which is a monster! Ha!

I haven't heard from the daycare center at my university yet. When I call, I'm told—once again—that there isn't a spot for Felicity to begin in May. At first, I can't believe it. We've been on the waiting list since I was five months pregnant. Then, I start to wonder if I would even want to move her to a new daycare right now. I like her teachers. I feel that Felicity is well taken care of. And how will Felicity adjust to a new environment at eight months old?

I ask to be put on the August waiting list for the one- to two-year old classroom, but I also don't believe that there will be a spot for me in

August either. I guess I'm doing it to have the option, but I'm not sure I really even want it.

The day after Easter, I see a text message from my mom to call her.

I know that it's bad news.

And it is.

Dad has fallen and broken his neck. My mom tells me that he fell outside of their apartment when he took the dogs out for a walk. It's an injury at the C2 vertebra. It doesn't take me long to realize how serious the break is. If he lives, he won't walk again. He may not be able to breathe on his own.

A few days later, an orthopedic surgeon manages to stabilize Dad's neck, but now he is bedridden, his neck frozen in a stabilizing collar.

And then, in a cruel twist of fate, my mother falls and breaks *her* arm—in three places on the ball of her shoulder joint. Exactly one week after my father fell.

I don't know what to do. I could buy a plane ticket now, but I'd only get a few days off and I may only get to see my dad in a very medicated state. Or I could wait and see.

My mom thinks it would be best for me to wait. So I do.

May 2014

148 pounds, size eight

At nine months, Felicity starts to crawl.

Until this point, she's been rolling and rocking on her hands and knees. And I have loved that. I could still walk into another room and know that she's still in generally the same spot where I left her. Within days, she has learned to stand up in her crib. And now, she's cruising around the house by using the couch and chairs as props.

Suddenly, she's a standing person. Suddenly, I remember that she is growing. That she couldn't stay a huge, lumbering, rolling baby. And now I have the distinct feeling—after all these months of struggle to give life—

that she is starting to move away from me. There is no more gravity between the two of us. We are no longer pulled together by the weight of how much we need each other. Now, we are just two objects, ever so slowly beginning to drift apart. Time pushes us forward, whether we want it to or not.

Stranger anxiety has started. Now, a new version of Felicity emerges.

It starts with her protesting as soon as I leave the room. When the babysitter comes, she immediately bursts into tears and crawls toward me. She cries at daycare when a new person enters the room. The saving grace is that she still doesn't cry when I leave her at daycare with her teachers.

One night, we have dinner with some friends at a Thai restaurant. On the way out, I glance at a stack of magazines. On the cover of a magazine, a headline screams, "Phillip Seymour Hoffman's Final Days."

I turn to Doug, "Whoa! Did you know that Phillip Seymour Hoffman died?"

He laughs.

"I'm serious!"

"Wait, are *you* serious?" he asks.

"Yes!" I turn to my friends. "Did you know about this?"

They are all laughing now. "Sharon, he died like three months ago."

"What!"

"Yeah, it was all over the news. How did you miss it?"

I count backward in my head. *April, March, February...*

"Oh..."

"What?" Doug asks.

"That was when I catatonic under a sea of mucus."

"Oh, come on, Sweets," he chides. "You probably heard it at some point."

I shake my head. "I'm pretty sure I would have remembered that. It was all I could do to make it to work and home every day during that time."

"Wow…" he shakes his head. "Pretty bad, Sweets."

I call my mom every other day to get updates about my dad. His neck is stabilized, but he suffered a bad bout of constipation, which sent him into renal failure until the nurses helped relieve the blockage. Since the fall, he has been bouncing back and forth between the emergency room, the ICU, and nursing homes. Medicare will only pay for twenty days in a nursing home.

"What do we do after that?" I ask my mother.

"We'll figure that out once we get there," she says. "In the meantime, he's doing better."

June 2014

146 pounds, size eight

I flip through the mail on the counter as Doug starts rinsing Felicity's bottles and food containers from daycare. Felicity stands by my legs, holding onto the knobs of the cabinet doors. She opens a door. Closes it. Opens it. Closes it.

There's a thick letter in the stack of mail. I turn it over.

It's from my obstetrician's office.

Dear Patients,

After much consideration, I have made the difficult decision to close my practice. Many factors contributed to this decision, both personal and financial…

"What is it?" Doug asks.

"My OB is closing her practice."

"Really?"

I hand him the letter. He dries his hands on a towel and reviews it.

"Wonder what happened," he says.

I shrug. "It's not easy being an OB. Malpractice insurance is high… And she was shouldering all of the costs of the practice by herself. Or at least it seemed that way."

The rest of the letter offers to send my medical records to a different doctor. Or to have them sent to me.

I have them sent to me.

My father goes back to the emergency room with pneumonia. They place him on antibiotics. When I call to check on him, my mom tells me that the antibiotics are helping, but that Dad is giving the nurses a hard time. She tells me that he doesn't want to support himself. That he keeps curling up and wanting to go to sleep.

My heart sinks.

"Mom... Do you want me to come home?"

She sighs. "Well... no, I don't think so. Not yet. He just needs to try to get better. And then he will. I told him that he has to try."

When I hang up, I check on the prices of flights. A round-trip ticket is about $900. It's a Tuesday. How many days of work will I miss? I need to make lesson plans for someone if I'm going to fly there. What about Doug and Felicity? She has eye surgery tomorrow to unblock her right tear duct. I can't just leave Doug to take care of everything by himself. I don't want to put all of that responsibility on him. That's not fair to either of them.

I decide to wait until the weekend and check on how dad is doing then.

The eye surgery is, thankfully, uneventful. The hardest part was consoling Felicity while she cried in hunger from the pre-surgery fast. She was only in surgery for fifteen minutes. After the surgery, the ophthalmologist commented that there was more pus than usual built up behind her eye because of the tear duct blockage.

"It's a good thing we did the surgery now instead of waiting until she turns one!" he says.

June 13, 2014

It's Friday. I exercise, shower, and get ready for work. Doug feeds Felicity and dresses her for daycare. I stop by my desk to pick up my phone where it has been charging all night. My mom has sent me a text.

Sharon, call me as soon as you can.

My heart bottoms out.

I already know.

I sit on the top of the stairs and call my mother. I barely hear her voice over my own thoughts as they scream, *Just say it! Just say it!*

She says it.

I feel relief. *It's over. Thank God.*

I don't really know how the conversation ends. I make it downstairs and I'm not sure of the words to use.

"What's wrong, Sweets?" Doug asks. He's standing in the kitchen, putting Felicity's solid foods into containers. Felicity is looking underneath the refrigerator, her new obsession.

I shake my head, my mouth open. All I can do is shake my head.

He comes over to me quickly. "Sweets! What's wrong? Is it your dad?"

I nod.

"What's going on?" he hugs me.

"He died." My voice is so small, but the words are so big.

"He died!" He pulls away to look at me. "Baby girl! I'm so sorry..." Now, he's crying. "What happened?"

I shrug. "The nurses just called my mom... said he had trouble breathing... then they called back and said he..."

Doug tries to hug me again. I push him away and hold back my tears. "I can't do this right now. I have to teach today."

"You're going to work?"

"If I'm going to be gone for a funeral, I need to make lesson plans," I reason.

He's still crying.

"Stop it!" I yell. "I can't go there right now."

"Okay, I'm sorry, I'm sorry." He straightens himself. "What can I do?"

"Take Felicity to daycare... and I'll figure the rest out later."

I soldier through the day. My boss helps me secure substitute teachers for the following week. I make lesson plans. I teach for two hours. It's not my greatest lesson, but I manage to get through it without my students asking if I'm okay.

I decide that I'm going to hold it in until I get home.

But as soon as I'm in my car, sitting at a stoplight just outside of the university, I see a police officer on motorcycle pull into the intersection. He sits there. I can hardly believe it.

A funeral procession starts to go by.

And then I start sobbing.

I feel guilt.

I wasn't there when he passed. I didn't get to say good-bye. I should have flown there when I had the chance.

I feel anger.

Why didn't any of the nursing staff tell my mom how close to death he was?

I feel more guilt.

My dad was alone when he died. No one was there to hold his hand, to tell him they loved him.

I feel more anger.

Why couldn't my mom see how badly he was doing?

I feel sadness.

I'll never hear his voice again. I'll never see him laugh again.

But then, I haven't heard his laugh in years.

That night, I sit with Felicity in the glider for our nighttime routine. I read her a few books. I let her turn the pages. When she yawns, I put the books away and turn her towards me. Her head rests on the inside of my left elbow, my right arm holds her body in place. She stares over my shoulder at the leaf pattern on the curtain. It's a faraway stare that I love. It is peace. Even trust. She doesn't look at me. She just stares over my shoulder until her eyelids get heavy.

This is the best moment of motherhood so far. I wish there were a word for it. She is in that space between worlds of consciousness. She trusts me to hold her as she relinquishes her grasp of this world for a while. How many people in her life will be able to say that they've seen her drift off like this?

As her eyelids close and her breathing deepens, I feel a deep pull at my heart.

I remember an afternoon that I spent with my father when I was visiting my parents in Minnesota in 2009. We were in my grandmother's kitchen, sitting next to the oven, waiting for some cookies to finish baking. His medication for bipolar depression had not taken full effect yet, so he oscillated between endless chattering and bursting into tears. He told me about his aunt Hilda, who was a master knitter. *Oh, you'd like her. Man, she can knit! She makes sweaters!* He told me in which house she still lived in Fergus Falls. He told me about the games that he and his brothers used to play. Then, he paused.

"Sharon," his voice cracked. "Don't make the same mistakes that I did." His eyes welled with tears.

"What mistakes?" I asked.

"Don't miss those times with your family." He lifted a finger and pointed it at me. "Work is *work*. They won't *ever* care about you the way your family will."

He started to cry. This big, broad man. This guiding star in the universe of my past—slowly folding into itself.

"It's okay, Dad."

"No, it's *not* okay," his voice quavered. "I missed *so* much."

I close my eyes, and tears spill out. My heart squeezes and squeezes.

You will never be more important to anyone else in your life as you are to your husband and kids. Do you hear me?

I look at Felicity's sleeping face. Someday, she will see my imperfections. And I hope in those moments, she can find the grace to forgive me, as I am now forgiving my father—for all those hours that he spent hunched over a green and white spreadsheet at a park picnic table, its accordion pages flapping in the breeze, just a few feet from the swings where I wanted to fly off into his arms.

It stings—that someday, somehow I will also be too distracted to catch her. That there will be times when she will fly out into the open, trusting me to be there, and I will fail her. There is no way around it. There is just imperfect me, loving imperfect her.

I cry.

Your family is never an inconvenience. Do you hear me?

I nod. "I hear you, Dad."

And this will be my life's newest and greatest challenge—to see those moments when she needs me to catch her.

The tug loosens. And then loosens more. And then it is gone.

And that is when I know that he has left me.

It takes two days to drive to Minnesota with Felicity in tow. The car rides low, loaded with baby gear and luggage. When Felicity naps, I work on a draft of my father's eulogy. I write a lot about how I feel. Then, I trash it. People don't want to hear about how I feel about losing my father. They're coming to remember my dad. I try to write it the way that he would want to be remembered.

On the day of the funeral, our family walks into the church and fills the front pews. There are flower arrangements adorning the front of the church and the altar, the exact spot where my parents pronounced their marriage vows thirty-eight years earlier. Ribbons hang from a floral arrangement, *Husband, Father, Brother, Son, Grandfather.* My eyes fixate on that word, *Grandfather.* It takes me a while to look away.

My older brothers, Phil and Nate, sit in the pew behind me. Once the jokesters and schemers of the family, now silent, tearful men. Holly locks her arm around my mom's free arm, her broken arm now resting in a black sling. My youngest sister, DeAnna, sits quietly beside me.

My mother is the first person to speak.

This is amazing to me. I don't ever remember a widow speaking at her own husband's funeral. She told me that she was nervous about it. She hadn't spoken in public since middle school. I had offered to stand with her, but she said, *No. I can do this myself.*

She stands there alone, flanked by funeral flowers, a piece of lined notebook paper with a bulleted list of what she wants to say, *He was my date's brother. Then, my date. Then, my dad's buddy. Then, my one true love in life... When he died, he took a piece of me with him. But I keep a piece of him with me, too.*

I am awed.

How can she stand there, so upright? Her left arm is still in a sling from the fall. She is not sobbing, but her emotions are real, emerging in wavering tones over the most heartfelt phrases.

But she has been tempered for this. Marriage and motherhood have done that. Five children. Incessant working, juggling, cleaning, stretching, and prioritizing. Weathering all of the typical family stressors along with some atypical ones—a devastating house fire, cancer, and bankruptcy. She hasn't had the luxury of the time and space to wallow after each disappointment or setback. But I also know that she chooses to move forward rather than stay chained to the past.

This is beauty. It's not beautiful, an adjective to describe something else. This is it. Beauty. This is the strength of the human spirit—the decision to keep living, even though part of you is dying. Even though you are not sure that you'll make it another day. It is irrational. And courageous.

When it's time for me to speak, I take a breath and tell myself that if my mother can do this, so can I. I'm going to do this right. I'm going to give the speech of my life.

And I do.

I tell everyone about who my father really was—a vivid, animated storyteller. I retell some of his stories. I acknowledge some of his weaknesses. I explain how he showed his love for us. Then, I talk to him.

Dad, I don't know if the space between us is unimaginably vast, or if you're closer to me than you've ever been. But I hope you can hear this. I hope my voice carries to wherever you are. I hope that it makes you proud. I hope it makes you feel like your life was well-lived. Because, Dad, it was a well-lived life.

When the funeral is over, I wonder what I want people to say about me at my funeral. I wonder who will speak. I wonder who will try to commemorate who I really was. But then, I wonder if who I think I am is actually how others see me.

Because in the end, after we have gone on past this life, what remains here are other people's memories of us. And maybe some words on a page. But even words won't matter if they are not powerful enough or meaningful enough for people to keep reading them.

And so I think that is why I write—in the hope that other people find these experiences comforting and meaningful. That some people— years and years from now—understand that they are not so singular and unusual in their experiences. And that they ultimately feel less alone in a world where we push for more and more independence from each other even though what we really crave is connection.

I know that it's going to be tough when I say good-bye to my mother. I can't stand the thought of leaving her here in Minnesota, without my father. But

I have to return to work. I've gotten my classes covered for a whole week—no small feat in the week before final exams. Even if work weren't an issue, I still need to get Felicity back to her daily routine.

I don't know what my mother's plans are, whether she will stay in Minnesota or not. I want her to come back to Ohio to be close to Felicity.

But I don't say any of this to my mother yet. She hasn't had enough time to think about all of it. So with tears spilling onto her shirtsleeves, what I say as I hug her is, "I just want you to be happy. I don't want you to feel anything but joy for the rest of your days."

She hugs me right back and she says, "It's okay. You already have. Really. It's okay now."

How can she say that? I marvel. *How can she say that it's okay?*

But then, how many mothers have comforted their grieving children before attending to their own grief? And certainly, there must be comfort in shifting your focus to your role as a mother even as your role as a wife fades away.

July 2014

145 pounds, size six

Doug's family—all five of his siblings and their families—are going to be in town for the Fourth of July. They are coming from Michigan, Florida, and Finland. It is one of the last times that all fourteen cousins will be able to get together before the oldest ones go away to college.

And they want to celebrate Felicity's birthday while they are in town.

And they want to see Felicity as much as possible.

So we plan to spend all day with his family on the Fourth of July and Felicity's party will be on July 5.

After two days of family festivities, I have a new respect for all the times that my own mother "put on the happy face" during vacations and holidays. It's exhausting caring for an infant on foreign turf. We cart around diapers, bottles, little containers of baby food, bibs, toys, and a portable playpen for naps. Then there are all the things that Felicity needs in order to swim in a pool: a bathing suit, swim diapers, baby sunscreen, and a hat. We follow her while she crawls and cruises around new territory. I help her through stranger anxiety over and over again. I stay positive.

On the day of her birthday party, Felicity's naps are cut short by noise. She is crabby throughout the party and bursts into tears during the tradition of smashing her first birthday cake. The last thing that I want to do is get her ready to go swimming again.

But I do.

I keep hearing my father's voice. *Your family is not an inconvenience. Don't miss those moments with your family.*

When I look back over the pictures and videos from those two days, I see Felicity laughing as Doug takes her underwater. I see Felicity's uncles, aunts, and cousins holding her and smiling. I see a video of Felicity and me in the pool, that moment where my niece accidentally kicks water all over my ponytail, which I was trying to keep dry. I was annoyed. But you can't tell from watching me. I'm smiling, taking Felicity around the pool.

Putting on the happy face for those two days was the right choice.

On the day Felicity turns eleven months old, she says her first word.

When I pick her up from daycare, one of her teachers tells me that Felicity has developed a bad diaper rash because she's been pooping all day. Perhaps a new stomach virus? When I get home, I check her. She is dry. I stand her upright in the kitchen and she leans against the cabinets, happy to play with the doors. She kneels down and lowers her head to check beneath the refrigerator again. Then, she stands back up and handles the knobs of the cabinets.

She squeals. It's a squeal of pain.

I turn and check her fingers to see if she has pinched them. They are fine. Then, I smell her. Bingo.

I take her into the living room and start changing her. There is the tiniest liquid poop in her diaper. It must really sting for her to squeal like that. I gingerly clean her bottom, trying to wipe carefully. Her legs go rigid and she does a full plank in midair while my hand holds her feet together. Tears shoot from her eyes. And that's when I hear it.

"*Maaaaammmmaaaaa!!!*"

It breaks my heart. I bring her to her feet, still diaperless, and I hug her. She hugs me back.

"It's okay," I tell her. "I got you. Mama's got you."

"Mamamamama..." she whines.

"I got you," I tell her.

"Has Felicity shown you her new trick?" her daycare teacher asks.

"What new trick?"

She bites her lip and looks at Felicity. "You haven't seen her do anything at home yet?"

I laugh. "Is she walking around here?"

She grimaces and says, "Oh! I was hoping that she would do it for you at home! I didn't want to tell you!"

"Well, I've seen her take a few steps, but I thought it was mostly momentum."

"Let's see if she can do it for you."

She pulls Felicity into a standing position, her hands underneath her armpits. "Come on, baby! Show Mama what you can do!"

Felicity takes a step and falls.

We try again. "Come on, baby! Come on, baby!" This time, she tempts her with a toy at an arm's distance.

Felicity goes for it. She reaches out for the toy. One step. Two steps. She's grinning now. Three, four, and five steps. She falls just before she gets to me.

I give her a huge hug. I thought that I would be teary at this moment, but I'm too happy for her to want to cry yet. Later, I'm sure I will. But right now, it's overwhelming to see how happy she is to discover her own power and ability.

"That was great!" I tell her. It's all I can think to say.

I'm scrolling through the PDF of my medical records, feeling excited to be privy to this information. I've just received a CD of two hundred pages of medical records that cover ten years of annual visits to my OB/GYN and all of my prenatal and postnatal care. I've gotten copies of lab results before, but never memos between my doctor and the nurses, a running history of my check-ups and complaints, complete with weight and height measurements and vitals. I feel like I'm spying, but then I feel ridiculous. I already know all of this information. I lived it.

My eyes land on a fax from Hospital A to my obstetrician. It reports Felicity's birth.

Underneath the name of the obstetrician who delivered Felicity is what looks like a description of the birth.

Term preg. del

Spont vag del

Female

Local anes

300 cc ebl

Cord and plac normal

Sulcus tears, 2nd tear, repaired.

It's a little easier to see now what I meant to the doctor who delivered Felicity. Seven bulleted points. Not even whole words.

"How much of her bottles did she eat?" I ask Felicity's new daycare teacher. Felicity has fully transitioned out of the Infant classroom. This is her first week in the First Steps classroom.

"Only about half of each."

"Hm... She's been doing that a lot lately," I say.

Her teacher nods. "Yeah, I tried, but she didn't want more than that."

"Do you think she's weaning herself?"

"Probably. She's about that age when they start weaning."

August 2014

144 pounds, size six

Since Felicity took those first few steps, her walking has improved exponentially each week.

She pivots on one foot, raises to her tip toes, and grabs at the baby monitor on her bookshelf. She slowly lowers into a squat, grabs a ball in each hand, stands, and then waddles ten steps before losing her balance. Then, she pushes her occupied hands into the carpet, stands up and continues. When she reaches a new toy, she pauses, considers, and tries to add the third toy to her hands. She fails. She drops one of the balls, squats to pick up the new toy, stands, and continues.

Oh my God, I think. *She's not a baby anymore.*

She's a little girl.

August 15, 2014

I pick her up from daycare early today.

It's her first birthday.

All day, I've been sentimental. *A year ago right now, I was in the worst pain of my life. A year ago right now, I was ready to give up. A year ago right now, I was pushing.*

When I get there, I spot Felicity through the window of her classroom. She is holding a block, shaking it in the air, her head tilted up. She uses her whole body in what I call the "King Kong" pose—fists pounding in the air, accompanied by *ah, ah, ah!*

"Hey, Kermit!" I call to her as I open the door.

She sees me, smiles, and takes clunky, uninterrupted steps toward me. I squat down and she opens her arms for me to hug her and pick her up. I kiss her cheek and look at the clock. It's 4:10.

"Happy birthday, baby girl," I say to her.

The Separation

A nd then comes the separation. Not just Felicity's separation from me, but also my separation from Felicity, and my separation from my previous self. And after all of this separation, the surprising discovery that I was also joining—the community of mothers.

Separation: Felicity from Me

Daycare didn't begin this separation. It just reinforced what I already knew was happening—that I wasn't in charge of Felicity. I was just caring for her.

She was in charge of herself.

The separation of daycare helped me see that she didn't need my presence to sleep or eat or grow. By the time she started daycare, she had been governing all of those areas for a few months. But we didn't realize it because the process was so gradual.

When Felicity was almost one month old, we started to feel like we had control over the feedings and changings. We would become accustomed to a particular routine, and then nod at each other, as if to say, *All right. We got this.* We loved the *90-Minute Baby Sleep Program* because it offered some structure for understanding what to expect in baby sleep patterns. Having that knowledge helped us feel that we were clued in to the mystery of baby sleep. We still couldn't control her sleeping, but we could understand it. Once again, having knowledge helped me to feel at peace in surrendering to the uncertain.

But then, Felicity would go through a growth spurt, and her naps would suffer. She would be cranky and clingy. Her sleep patterns would shift. And we would briefly wonder if we had done something wrong. Maybe the ninety-minute rule was bullshit and we had been stupid enough to fall for it. But then, we would see her perform some new skill, and with it, a new pattern of sleeping would emerge. Then we'd realize, *Oh. She was growing.*

The same shifting happened with her feedings. As she grew, she would regroup her feedings into larger feedings at different times. She would stay awake longer and move her naps together into longer chunks of time. She pushed her bedtime earlier. She started to wean herself. All of this, she did by herself. I didn't control it—and I was constantly amazed that all I had to do was pay attention to her rhythms and follow along.

Separation: Me from Felicity

Once I accepted that Felicity was separating from me, I was ready to redirect my attention back to myself. Daycare helped me do that. It gave me two priceless commodities to new parents: space and time. And having space and time to be creative makes me feel fulfilled, like I'm living life well. This is the tension in which artistic mothers—in all of their various forms—live. We can choose not to feed that side of ourselves, but it continues to hunger. It eats at us and we loathe the emptiness of the vision left unpursued. The one to which we still haven't had the time to give birth. Creativity doesn't die. It might slow or go stagnant as life reaches a stasis. But any time there is change—and a new child is massive change—the creative self hungers. It needs to make meaning of the change.

Nevertheless, I gave myself some time to make the true decision— the one that I had to make in my heart—about whether or not I would go back to work.

By the time Felicity was four months old, I had decided. In order for both of us to be happy, I needed that time. I needed that space. Sure, the cost of daycare consumed the majority of my earnings, but I was thinking of the future me, the one who would someday find herself in a marriage, in a house, in a life *without* her kids. I'm looking out for her, for the pain that she is going to feel when her kids grab their independence and go. Another identity crisis is coming down the line—mother with grown children—and I want that future me to have an outlet for finding her new purpose and path in life. I want her to feel that she still has other roles to fill. So for me, the benefit of giving me this time and space is worth the cost.

Even as I write these words, I feel that I have to acknowledge the privilege that underlies my ability to use the word "decision." In America, it is truly a privilege to have a choice about whether to stay at home or return to work. For many women, it's not a choice. It's a matter of finances. It's either, "I have to work to earn money" or "I have to stay home because daycare is too damn expensive." Our government does not pick up the tab for daycare. (And by the way, you're welcome, U.S. government—for raising your future taxpayers with little financial help from you.) And so, for this generation of American mothers, who have been raised their whole lives believing that they can "be whatever they want to be"—this sudden inability to choose a path in life can be especially frustrating.

I wish that all mothers were truly able to choose whether or not to work while raising children—no matter what they would decide. Just as I believe that women should have choices in labor. And choices in feeding. And choices in parenting. Those choices grant us the freedom to become the best versions of ourselves, which in turn, helps our children to do the same.

Separation: My Current and Previous Selves

Becoming a mother is like moving out of your house—and then moving back into it with more stuff. You know that everything can't fit back into the same rooms, so you need to decide what to keep and what to leave behind. Even then, you need to rearrange the furniture in order for life to be smooth and efficient. The more things you hang on to, the harder it is for you to navigate the crowded spaces.

To be clear, I don't think that you have to give up everything that you once loved in order to become a mother. But I do think that you should be prepared to let go of any part of your previous self that no longer fits with your new life. Once you understand how your life now looks as a mother, you can slowly start adding pieces of the old furniture as they fit alongside the new pieces.

This proved to be the hardest part of the transformation into mother for me—letting go of who I once was. At the beginning of my pregnancy, I had set a goal to not fall down "the hole of parenthood" and relinquish everything that I loved about my life until that point. But in those first months of motherhood, I realized that complete and total surrender to the priorities of mothering was the only way I could survive. I had to kick all of my furniture out into the street. And I understand now that kicking everything out made the process so much easier to accept. Trying to fit everything into the same space caused chaos and so starting over with a clean slate helped me to chart the boundaries of this new identity.

And so at the beginning, I became a mother—totally and completely. I was an expert in Felicity. But I lost my expertise in everything else. For months, I wasn't a great friend. I think Doug would say that I wasn't a great wife at this time. When I returned to work, I realized that my panache for teaching had suffered, too. The more I tried to just go back to the way that I was, the more lost I felt. I couldn't find that destination. It had disappeared.

Maybe that was why I cried when my mug broke. I knew that my body and mind would never really be able to return to the way that they once were. The breaking of motherhood makes it impossible for them to ever go completely back to their original states. They couldn't hold together in the same arrangement. They weren't big enough to hold all that I am now.

And so underneath the exciting and joyful narrative of giving life, I realized that there is an equally present—yet widely unspoken—narrative of death and destruction throughout my transition into a mother.

Death surrounds new life, but it largely goes unnoticed. It starts in a womb where the death, birth, and growth of cells happens every month. A tiny fertilized egg trusts its fate to this volatile environment. Sometimes, it works out. Sometimes, it doesn't. Thousands of other eggs mature, spring forth, and die unannounced. It is in this fertile soil of death that the roots of the placenta take hold. The placenta grows and grows. For weeks and weeks, the placenta's growth trumps the baby's. It isn't the baby that is doubling and tripling in size—it's the placenta. As it grows, it breathes for the baby more. It feeds the baby more. When the placenta reaches its prime, the roles start to reverse. The baby doubles. And triples. And quadruples. And after the baby has run out of space, the placenta starts feeling its age. Then, labor. Then, birth.

The baby breathes. And then the placenta dies.

And so, life cannot be without death. But the narrative of giving life that dominates our thoughts is much more sanitized. It focuses on the victors, not the victims. We show no gratitude for the dying placenta. Instead, we either ignore it or degrade it by treating it like conquered prey. And then we turn our attention to the living: the strong mother and the delivered baby. Death has not overtaken them. How could they be touched by death? They are alive! But the truth is much more balanced—they are alive because something else died.

Through the lens of this balance of life and death, I can better cope with the changes in my identity. It helps me understand that the death of my previous self was necessary. However, motherhood isn't solely the subtractive force that I had once expected it to be. Now, I am able to see the larger truth. Motherhood *does* take away. But it also replaces. Sometimes our hands are empty and sometimes they are full. And accepting this truth helps me find contentment and joy.

But I wouldn't call it *happiness.*

If there's one thing that this journey from woman to mother, from single to double, from "take-care-of-myself" to "take-care-of-someone-else," has taught me is that I don't want happiness.

Happiness has a ceiling and a floor. And finding it is elusive.

What I want is joy—dependable, limitless, and eternal. But joy is only felt in the context of great contrast. You can't know joy until you've known pain.

I think we often confuse happiness with joy, so let me explain. Looking out at the view from a mountain summit might make us feel happy, but that happiness is short-lived unless we climbed the mountain to get there. If a ski-lift drops us at the top of the mountain, the excitement of standing on the summit soon fades. There is no context to cement that feeling into our memories. We only see the present moment. We don't think of the past or the future. But how different would it be if we could only look out from the summit after having spent millions of years watching the mountains form?

That is joy—it is a deep, meaningful context that surrounds a moment of happiness and keeps it anchored in our memories. It means that we look all around a beautiful moment and appreciate all that it took to arrive at that point in time and space.

The ticking rhythms of motherhood build this context. For me, those happy moments were couched in days and days of clouds. In fact, for me, the first year of motherhood has felt like a mostly cloudy summer day. At first, there were just thunderstorms after soul-testing thunderstorms. But in time, I started to experience them differently. Within a few months, I didn't even need an umbrella to weather the same storm that months before had drenched me to the core and left me reeling. I developed those mental and emotional muscles of parenthood that helped me to not recoil when my child vomited, but rather lean in and check her mouth for stuck food.

Then came the everyday clouds: the routine and the mundane. But joy broke through those clouds at unexpected moments, casting rays of sunlight that I would commit to memory. Her first real smile. Her first laugh. The first time she recognized me. And when the clouds rolled back in, I was happy to carry on. These moments were short, but their light illuminated the truth that joy doesn't leave me. It's always there, underneath it all, supporting everything that I do, shining through the holes that motherhood makes in my soul. It is forged into the fabric of my identity. It has helped me to find contentment in simplicity. Clean laundry. A quiet moment. Health. Laughter. The gentle sound of rain on the windows, a baby now asleep in my arms. These things didn't make me nearly as happy before I became a mother.

Becoming a mother is different from all the other transformations that I've experienced in life. Unlike weight loss. Unlike education. Unlike falling in love or getting married. Unlike growing into my own individual identity, apart from my family. I could make those transformations at my own pace. I could pause to reflect or think about what the changes meant to me. I could even put limitations on the changes that I wouldn't consider. I had time to debrief life's events and reframe myself as the hero or the helpful sidekick in each situation.

But in parenthood, there is no time for all of these revisions of history. You just do. You just move forward. It all happens so fast that after a situation ends, you see that you play all roles in life—even the parts that you don't like. You see that sometimes you are the villain. Or the passive bystander.

So I think that parenthood holds the mirror up to you with no flattering angles and it forces you to see who you really are. Not just your strengths, but also your weaknesses. You can look away and deny what you see. Lots of parents do.

But what happens if you look back into that reflection and say, "Okay... So I have problems. What should I do about them?"

You grow.

Joining the Community of Mothers
It took me most of the first year to accept that I was joining this community of mothers. During pregnancy, I was ambivalent about what becoming a mother meant for my life. Once I started to interact more with other mothers, I realized that my hesitation to embrace motherhood is partly because mothers compose a schizophrenic community. At times, they are whole-heartedly welcoming. At other times, they are blindly judgmental. I have never occupied another role in my life where I have felt as much scrutiny and as much guilt over my performance—not as a teacher, not as a writer or presenter or employee, and definitely not as a friend, daughter, sister, or wife. Entering the sphere of motherhood places me on a stage in

front of an expansive, much more experienced, and foreign audience, always ready to praise or pounce on my moves.

I venture to guess that part of the reason that mothers are so likely to pass out advice and judgment is because we feel that we have become experts in mothering. After years of mothering day in and day out, we feel that we have acquired a tried-and-true arsenal of knowledge. But we forget that our expertise is specialized in one area—our children. We know them inside and out, but we can't make the same claim about other children. And so, we confuse depth of knowledge for breadth of knowledge.

But when new mothers stand on the border of motherhood, they are looking for approval from those who have already crossed over. So they seek out pieces of an identity as a mother in order to announce what kind of mothers they are. We can't control so many things about motherhood, so we grab on to an identity to gain some bearings and clout. In that process, we gravitate toward these debates over infant feeding, babywearing, diapering, sleeping, and on and on. We choose a side and then arm ourselves against opposing criticism with knowledge and advice and parenting ideologies. They bolster us. They give us credibility.

We do this because we are so hungry to take on an identity. And when there are only two options for each issue, it's easy to select which one you like and more quickly settle into your own particular brand of motherhood.

We do this because we want everyone else to know what kind of mothers we are at a time when we're not even sure what kind of mothers we are.

We do this because assuming the identity of *mother* is so big and unwieldy that we focus on carving an identity out of smaller practices over which we have more immediate control. Then, we find mothers that think like us. And then we become judgmental—or worse, blind—to the other faces of motherhood.

In the end, we disrespect the identity of *mother* by reducing it to a checklist of black and white choices: breastfeeding or formula feeding, disposables or cloth, co-sleeping or crib, daycare or staying at home, Attachment Parent or Tiger Mom. All of these labels speak to one facet of motherhood, and not even a facet to which we always hold true. These labels can't possibly show the whole picture. This is the error that we make in these debates—we measure the quality of our mothering by the narrow manner of care-taking rather than the whole health and happiness of the child.

I am not so naïve as to believe that the way that I experience motherhood right now is how it will always feel. Right now on most days, I wear motherhood lightly, in the mornings, evenings, and weekends. The bulk of my days are spent in my other roles.

But as time passes, I feel my daughter burrowing and tunneling deeper into my identity. But this time, it's a different kind of connection. What we had during pregnancy and after birth was a biological need for each other, a physical connection. But now we have a connection of the mind—of shared memories and trust. And yes, love.

Like so many other women, I wish that I could go back in time and talk to my pregnant self. That thirty-nine-week-pregnant woman, waiting for labor to begin, wanting to know what she could do to prepare.

What would I say to her?

I would say...

Your worries are valid. I'm not going to belittle your concerns or tell you that things will be wonderful. You don't need to "grow up" or "get over it." But on the landscape of your life, your worries right now are small, a mere blip.

A child could ruin your marriage. I've seen how easy it could have been for you to become the martyr and insist that you were the only one who could take care of your baby. I've seen how difficult—but important—it is to strike the balance between communicating directly, yet patiently with your husband. But you'll find it. Because you'll discover—after eight years of marriage—that you care more about your husband and your child than you do about yourself. So this child isn't going to drive you apart—this child will actually push you both forward.

You will see your career differently. I won't say that you'll find out that your career isn't as fulfilling as raising a child or that the work-family balance is impossible. But those evening and weekend hours will become sacred to you. And the last thing that you'll want to do is sacrifice those hours to finish what you couldn't get done in the office.

Babies are expensive. You'll spend hundreds of dollars on car seats. Thousands on daycare. But you'll also be glad to spend the money to know that your child is safe and in good care.

Childbirth. Is. Hard. But it's not important to know how long your labor will last or how much pain you're going to feel. What *is* important is that you'll never doubt the depths of your strength again. Ever.

The postpartum period is even harder. But you are normal. Those crazy hormone shifts that detach you from reality—they happen to so many new mothers. You're not broken. You're not defective. And you *will* be able to take care of your baby.

You will lose many hours of sleep. It will alter your mood, your health, and your ability to connect with others. And even though it feels like forever, I assure you, it will end.

You will have a hard time losing the weight. Breastfeeding will not magically melt it away for you as it does for some women. But you have already made that forty-pound journey down the scale two times before. It will take a whole year, but you will do it again.

You'll learn that some women hunker down into brands of motherhood. But rest assured, you are not required—nor is it even possible—to fit into one particular category all the time. And how you feed, clothe, diaper, and carry your child is not an indication of how much you love your child. Or how good your mothering is.

Read and research, but don't let what you read speak louder than your own intuition and personal experience. And yes, you do have intuition. Trust it.

Approach the first year of motherhood like you approach labor: one small piece at a time. Don't think about the whole year. It's too dynamic. Every single week has its own flavor, its own rhythms, its own challenges, and triumphs. Focus on one day at a time. Carve the good days and weeks into your memory. Then, remember them to give you strength to pull through the bad ones.

It's not possible to enjoy every single minute of this first year. It's an unrealistic, romantic standard that no mother can achieve. So, for God's sake, sob and vent when the time calls for it. And don't you dare feel guilty about it. Because those moments of sadness are a brilliant contrast to those moments of happiness. And without them, you don't experience the full weight of joy.

And your vagina will be fine. Different. But fine.

But you're not truly concerned about all of these things.

What you're really concerned about is whether or not you'll be a good mother.

So let me wholeheartedly assure you that it's not about being a "good mother," as if I could pull a picture from Google Images to show you what that looks like. As if there is an approved checklist of criteria to meet in order to earn that title. As if following this mythical checklist is best for all babies.

So it's not about being a good mother.

It's about being the right mother. For this child. In this moment.

So what I'm telling you, pre-pregnant self, is to seek to be the right mother. Every day. And if you can do that, you can find peace in the chaos of motherhood.

Dear, dear first-time mother, who is reading this in those last months, weeks, and days before birth, who has been traveling with me on this journey throughout all of these pages...

If you take away nothing else from this time we've spent together, please remember this:

You can do this.

Pregnancy. Labor. Birth. Recovery. Feeding. Care-taking. Mothering. All of it.

You. Can. Do. This.

One night, you'll be changing a diaper with your eyes half-pasted shut. You will wonder if you are still wearing your contacts, or if you took them out. You will not have any idea what day of the week it is or what time of night it is. You will just do what needs to be done and not care about what needs to be done in the morning. You will go back to bed and soon be drifting back to sleep.

And then ten minutes later, you will hear the baby cry.

And then *you* will cry, feeling like you have nothing left.

And in that moment—filled with guilt that you resent your baby's cry—I want you to remember that you are strong. So freaking strong. Mothers have been doing this from time immemorial. It will be hard to believe that anyone could have possibly felt as worn out as you do in that moment—but know that so, so many women know *exactly* how you feel, especially in that very moment when frustration rings in your ears and tears blur your vision.

Give yourself a good ten seconds. And then get back up.

You got this.

And when you are ready, find your community of mothers. They are everywhere: gyms, daycares, the doctor's office, playgrounds, churches, grocery stores, Starbucks, and libraries. But there is one place you won't find them—your house.

So you need to get out.

You don't have to be friends with all of them. And some of them you will find downright annoying. But find a few who share your humor, who listen well, and with whom you feel comfortable sharing this path. Make time to talk to each other—sometimes with your kids and sometimes without your kids. A journey is always easier to take when you have companions to help carry your bags every now and then.

I have been continually touched by this community of mothers—and you will too. You'll notice it when a mother stops to help you as you struggle to get your squirming baby into a shopping cart while the diaper bag pulls at your shoulder. She'll offer to hold your bag while you get the baby situated. She'll ask how old your child is and then she'll say he's beautiful. At parties, you'll swap stories with other women who are holding babies or running after toddlers. Soon, you'll start holding elevator doors open for other mothers pushing strollers. You'll say hi to their children and tell the mothers how much you loved whatever age their children are. There will still be annoying questions passed back and forth like handshakes (*Is she sleeping through the night yet? Getting any teeth? Did you breastfeed?*), but find your way to take them in stride and guide the conversation back to the fact that what you are both doing is so wonderfully hard and amazing. And only truly understood by those who go through it.

And soon, you'll be the one giving encouragement to another first-time mother.

So, first-time mother, I say to you, welcome.

You are so welcome.

Afterword

I remember those lazy afternoons in July 2013. I was nine months pregnant. Nothing to do.

My favorite part of the day was right after lunch, around 1:00 p.m. I would lie on the couch on my side, my knees bent, feeling the baby settling once I found a good position. Some unknown body part would nudge my side and dig against the sofa. A hand? A foot?

We would nap like that, together—me curled around her while she was curled up inside of me. Before I knew she was a she. We cuddled like that after she was born, too—me curled around her, her curled up next to me. And I would think of her as if she were the center of a rose, still closed, curled up tight. And I was the petal around her. And then there was my mother around me. And around her was my grandmother. And after her, my great-grandmother, and on and on.

There was a lesson to be learned somewhere in that metaphor, but I couldn't see it at the time. I just knew that it made me respect and honor the women who had come before me. My grandmother and great-grandmother had experienced the same pains and joys that I had, but on the isolated plains of Iowa, without supportive husbands to share the responsibilities of caring for the household—*and* with many other children depending on them. And for all the women who had come before them, whose hardships and trials I would never know and can only imagine. It makes me feel honored to wear this badge of motherhood. I add it to my other badges, but I wear this one over my heart, where everyone can see it. It is my gateway to a bit of immortality. The world may continue to read my words, but my blood lives on in my children.

And someday, I will be the one tugging at my daughter's heart, shouting the lessons that I didn't learn across the planes between us. Someone will send flowers to my funeral. And they will have satin ribbons proclaiming the ways that people want to remember me—*Wife, Sister, Daughter. Mother.* And if I'm lucky, *Grandmother.* None of those ribbons will read *Teacher* or *Writer* or *Faithful Employee.*

I hope that I cross that plane before my daughter, although of course, there are no guarantees. I wish this because there is a pain on the other side of the joy of having a child. Because you begin to understand that if you watched death overtake that tender body, you wouldn't just resume the life that you lived before the child ever came into being. The identity of mother would stay with me. And so I would become a living paradox. A mother without someone to mother.

And I would be forever homesick for her.

Parenthood remodels your identity in every facet. Once those renovations are complete, the process is permanent. It cannot be undone. And so parenthood becomes an exercise of faith. Faith that—despite the risk of pain and suffering, be it emotional or physical—it is worth it.

All of it.

The nausea. The sound of a heartbeat. The weight gain. The little kicks. The swelling. The congratulations. The contractions. The euphoria. The sleeplessness. The tiny cry. The anxiety. The new confidence. The doubt. The contentment. The loss of old self. The gain of new self. The illnesses. The strength.

Through all of it, I see my daughter.

And I realize that I had it all wrong. I *couldn't* lose myself.

I am not a static self. I am fluid. I am dynamic. Motherhood would change me, but everything that I experience in life—in some way—would cause me to change. My marriage wasn't ruined. We grew closer together. I didn't lose my friends—we just now have a new set of topics to talk about. And I've gained a new circle of friends.

And I have a new confidence that I've never had before. I have seen how much pain I can take, how long I can go without sleep, how much I can accomplish in one hour, and how much I can change in one year. I think that the stretching of the body that happens during pregnancy is a living metaphor for what it means to be a mother. Becoming a mother is all about stretching. When you enter motherhood, you enter it with one version of your body, your mind, your habits, your routines, your personality, your behavior, and so on. When you become a mother, all of those facets of your being are pulled in all directions. Everything becomes thinned out. You need to do more with less. More work with less sleep. More patience with less time. And somehow, you manage to do it. And when you look back, you see that all of this stretching has helped you grow. And when a challenge arises, you can look at it and say, "This is *nothing* compared to what I've just been through."

At the beginning of this journey, I opened my hand to the unknown. I expected to one day look down and see a child's hand in mine. I expected to comfort it, to soothe it, and to guard it.

But I didn't expect that hand to lead *me*. To teach *me*. To refine *me*.

She taught me that you cannot be truly strong until you have nothing left.

That you cannot be wise until you have been humbled.

And that you cannot be loved until you have no vanity.

I am grateful for this new journey. For all the doors we have yet to open. And for all the lessons she'll continue to teach me.

I am grateful for her.

Appendix:
On Labor and Belief in God

I n Christianity, God is light.

But that was not my experience.

I felt the presence of God for the first time in the darkness of a shower, hours past sleep deprivation, and in the hardest hours of labor. In those sacred moments, punctuated with pain, I was finally truly aware of a portion of the self that is beyond the body and beyond the mind. My spirit soared into the foreground. And there, in the quiet darkness, as water spilled over me, I was connected to the Divine. Its energy flowed into me, took control, and pushed me forward. It stayed with me for days. It caused me to glow.

It was the ultimate reversal of religious symbolism for me. There was no fear, or punishment, or death, or hell in these moments. The boundaries between me and the Divine were gone. There was just love. Wholeness. Openness. Existence.

Before this moment, I had hoped, wanted, even needed God to exist. But it wasn't until labor had eroded the filters of my body and mind that I actually felt God's presence.

Only then did I believe.

Despite a lifetime of attending Sunday School, Bible studies, and sermons. Despite a memory full of Bible verses and hymns. Despite all the mission trips where I had presumed to bring God to other people. None of this truly made me a believer. Because belief doesn't come from the mind. The best argument and the strongest logic can't construct true belief. And it doesn't come from the heart. Simply being overwhelmed with emotion about your need for forgiveness and redemption doesn't create belief. It just showcases your guilt. Instead, belief comes from your soul, from that innermost fire of self that remains when everything else is taken away.

In the hardest hours of labor, I couldn't turn anywhere for comfort. Not my thoughts. Not my body. Only then did I realize that I had surrounded myself with so many safety nets to catch me in tough times. I had relied on reason to make sense of difficult situations. I had relied on my body to pull me through illness. I had relied on others to comfort me in sadness. I never truly relied on God for anything—even though I'm sure I had pronounced those very words when I talked about coping with tough times.

But I had never truly looked all the way down into my soul for that last bit of me that remained after the body and mind were torn away. I had never completely surrendered. I would like to say that I *trusted* or *had faith*, but that sounds like I had something to give. The truth is that I had nothing left. Not even faith. I felt completely empty—but not in a hopeless way. It was the feeling of emptiness that only comes when you are completely detached from the past or the future.

It was the emptiness of the present moment—and that present moment was either a moment full of pain or a moment free of pain. I can't even call those moments *good* or *bad*. They didn't oppose each other. One wasn't even more desirable than the other. Because the moments when the pain was gone were also moments when my labor wasn't progressing. In that sense, both moments were simply *true*.

After experiencing labor, the story of Job makes sense to me. Only after Job had lost everything—his wife, children, friends, wealth, home, health, social status, and pride—did God speak to Job. It was only after everything else had been removed that Job could be open enough to hear God's voice. And then he believed. And that belief opened his eyes to the insignificance of everything that surrounds us. *Surely I spoke of things I didn't understand, things too wonderful for me to know*, Job said.

Happy is not the word that describes Job's encounter with the Divine. Instead, he is ready to surrender everything, even his own life. He is finally ready to die. *Therefore, I despise myself and repent in dust and ashes*. And only through death can you be reborn.

I know that I am not alone in my experience. I know that others have felt something similar. I know that all around the world, people have a way of experiencing this same peeling away of mind and body.

I remember that when I was in college, I read a few books by Mircea Eliade about common coming of age initiation rites for boys in traditional societies in South America and Australia. He reported that for many boys in these societies, when it was time to become men, they were torn from their homes, thrown into dark huts, told they were now dead, and went without food or water for days. At the end of it, the elders of the tribe pulled them from these huts and shared with them the story of how the world began and how their ancestors came to be.

But why stories about creation?

Before these men could move forward into adulthood, they needed to return all the way to the beginning. Confining them in that dark hut symbolized returning to their mothers' wombs. It was a return to the very beginning, a return to the Source of Life, a return to the Divine.

And they could only return to the very beginning if every shred of their previous selves was taken away.

Only if every understanding that they had about the world was turned on its head.

Only if they could not depend on any of their previous ideas about the way things were.

Once everything from their previous life was removed, they were ready to be reborn. Armed with these new understandings of life and their roles in society, they could fully embrace their new positions in it—where their roles were now different, where people depended on them differently, and where new expectations awaited them.

And I feel that this is what birth has done for me.

When nothing else intervenes in the process, birth brings a woman all the way down into the darkest, emptiest, and most primal state of being. This is what I felt in those moments when I felt God's presence. With my eyes closed, there was no more outside world. There was just darkness, warmth, steam—all the same conditions that my child was experiencing at the same time. It brought me back to the beginning, back to the Divine.

I suspect that most traditional societies didn't subject women to such elaborate coming-of-age rituals because giving birth served that purpose. In the words of cultural anthropologist, Robbie Davis-Floyd, "The natural rhythmicity, intensification, and emotionality of the labor process is enough all by itself to put the laboring woman in a far more intensely affective state than all but the most grueling male initiation rites can produce" (2003, p. 39). In other words, labor was the trial. Labor broke a woman down. Labor turned everything on its head. Labor wiped the slate clean so a new life—full of new responsibilities—could be built. Labor reconnected her to the Divine.

In fact, this theme of surrender, death, and rebirth is common to the world's major religions. In Christianity, Jesus states, "Whoever wants to be my disciple must deny themselves and take up their cross daily and follow me. For whoever wants to save their life will lose it, but whoever loses their life for me will save it" (Luke 9:23-24). For a Muslim, the word *islam* means "surrender to the will of God." Hinduism also describes the necessity of surrender and the beauty of destruction in order to open a path for new life. Shiva's acts of destruction often led to new forms of existence. In order to create, there is first the need to remove and destroy.

It is this process of surrender to change in all aspects of life that helps a woman transition into the role of mother. All those new roles and responsibilities can more easily move in and occupy the landscape of her life that was once filled with an entirely different set of priorities and goals.

Labor has also helped me understand why someone would be grateful for pain or hardship. Cursing God I could understand, but I could never understand how someone could manage to sing praises to God after surviving a devastating earthquake.

Now I know that this gratitude comes from a sacred terror—an awe from a certainty that God is present. It comes from having encountered a space where the body and mind are pulled away, leaving nothing but spirit. And spirit is what drives people forward through tragedy and hardship.

Without spirit, we are bones and muscles, hormones and chemicals. Without spirit, we are consciousness without purpose, awareness without meaning. But with spirit, we feel that connection to the Divine that is beyond our mind's rational thoughts and beyond our body's senses.

Birth and death can make these spaces where you can feel your spirit. This is not an idea that I was raised to believe. Instead, it comes from what I felt in labor and in those few days after my father died. For me, I felt that there was a thin plane that divides the physical from the spiritual. And life entering and exiting this world punctures its surface. When it does, energy spills freely between the two planes for a time, touching those who are closest.

I'm not saying that everyone experiences this at moments of birth and death. You have to want to go there. You have to let yourself feel all the pain that birth and death bring with them. Feeling that pain peels away those layers of self that preoccupy our thoughts. And so, it allows us to access that truest, purest piece of ourselves. And that is where you find joy. Joy in birth. And joy in death.

Yes, joy even in death. Because after you have experienced the resilience of your own spirit, you can acknowledge it in others. You can believe with confidence that the spirit in others will also remain. That death is not the final chapter. That the person that you love is not extinguished, only transferred.

I know how all of this can sound to some readers. If you don't believe in any aspect of a spiritual world, I respect that. It is not logical. There is no proof for it. And rational people base their decisions on what can be proven.

But human beings are not only rational, logical creatures. We are also emotional creatures, the lords of our own turfs of truth. We are changed by what we experience in life, not by what other people experience. And what I'm describing here is experiential. There's no logic that I can offer that will prove anything. There is only what I have experienced and what I have felt. Yes, I know, feelings and experiences are unreliable, but never forget, they are also quintessentially human. And you are human.

But to those on the fence—uncertain about whether or not there is something after this life—I hope that someday, you find yourself in a situation that helps your spirit soar to the foreground. I hope you are able to experience these same depths of pain and joy. Because it connects you to the Divine. And believing in the Divine allows you to believe that no matter what happens in life, no matter how much pain you suffer, no matter how many loved ones you lose, there is certainty in knowing that you will eventually fall back into the hand of God and stay there forever.

Kept and loved.

You are forever tethered.

You will never, ever be lost among life's turbulent waves.

References

Cassidy, Tina. (2006). *Birth: The surprising history of how we are born*. New York: Grove Press.

Davis-Floyd, Robbie. (2003). *Birth as an American rite of passage* (2nd ed.). Berkeley: University of California Press.

Eliade, Mircea. (1965). *Rites and symbols of initiation: The myths of birth and rebirth* (W. Trask, Trans.). New York: Harper & Row.

Gaskin, Ina May. (2011). *Birth matters: A midwife's manifesta*. New York: Seven Stories Press.

Grantly-Read, Dick. (2005). *Childbirth without fear: The principles and practice of natural childbirth*. London: Pintar & Martin Ltd. (Original work published 1933).

Hodnett, Ellen. (2002). Pain and women's satisfaction with the experience of childbirth: A systematic review. *American Journal of Obstetrics and Gynecology, 186* (5), 160-172.

Kensigner, Elizabeth. (2007). "Negative emotion enhances memory accuracy." *Current Directions in Psychological Science, 16* (4), 213-218.

Moore, Polly. (2008). *The 90-minute baby sleep program: Follow your child's natural sleep rhythms for better nights and naps*. New York: Workman Publishing.

A Note to the Reader

Becoming Mother is an independently published and marketed work. Therefore, I rely on you, dear reader, to reach the larger audience that it deserves.

If you were moved by this book and think it would touch someone else's life, there are a few simple ways that you can show your support and spread the word:

- Write an Amazon review. Even a short one.
- Like the Becoming Mother Facebook page. Invite your friends to like it.
- Lend your copy of the book to a friend.
- Give a copy of the book as a baby shower gift.
- Visit and follow the Becoming Mother blog at https://becomingmotherblog.wordpress.com.

Thank you for your support.

Sharon Tjaden-Glass
I also welcome feedback and fan mail at becomingmotherblog@gmail.com.

Acknowledgements

So much gratitude to so many people—I will do my best.

To my daughter, Felicity. Before you were born, I thought that I would have to put aside my aspirations of writing a book once I became a mother. Now, I realize that it took your birth for me to finally find my voice. Life is funny.

To my husband, Doug. Writing can only happen in the moments when you're *not* doing something else—like paying bills, or doing taxes, or fixing the house, cooking meals for the 5,678th time, or mowing the lawn (again, already?). Because you constantly do these things, I am able to write. And even though I've never earned a dime for it, you still told me to do it. And you *still* saw the value in paying for daycare so I could write the majority of this book over my "summer break." I never had to plead with you to support me. I am beyond lucky.

To my mother, Cecilia Tjaden. Your optimism is your legacy and it will always inspire me to press on.

To my readers: Faith Kelley, Susan Maly, Jean Maly, Tricia Galvez, Suzanne Richardt, Julie Prugh, Cate Schoenharl, and Jeanne Schoenharl. Your input was invaluable for helping work through the big revisions and questions.

To my closest friends, the Monday Night Dinner Crew (current and alumni, near and far): Ryan (Bear) Schultz, Cate Schoenharl, Sam (Toad) Naik, Ben Smith, Sarah Buckley, Jarod and Katy Patton, Josh and Suzy Richardt, David Sigthorsson, Tara Gravenstine, Jason Parker, Laura Humphrey,

Julie Prugh, Katy Durkin, Holly Tjaden, Kyle and Debbie Clarkson, and Ryan and Andrea Helbach. You help me to be me.

To my amazing L&D nurses, Karen Koble and Nancy Tallyn. To my doula, Pamela Putthoff. And to my many nurses in the Mother and Baby Unit. The care that you gave me truly made a difference. Never doubt the power of your compassion on the women under your care. Bless you all.

And to knitting—which taught me that on the way to improving a craft, you have to first make a lot of shit that no one wants. And for all my friends over the years who have read my shit and given me polite feedback (especially you, Jason). Because of you—knitting and friends—I have been able to pull this off.

About the Author

Sharon Tjaden-Glass teaches in the Intensive English Program at the University of Dayton in Ohio. She spent her 20s dreaming of life in other places, but—it turns out—there's no place like home. She has a B.A. in Linguistics and French from Miami University and an M.A. in Teaching English to Speakers of Other Languages from Wright State University. A perfect day for her includes a tough workout, perfectly balanced coffee, an hour of writing while snow falls outside a big window, a long conversation with her Monday Night Dinner friends, storytime with her daughter, a sushi dinner with her husband, and knitting with *The Office* playing in the background.

You can read more of her writing at her blog,
https://becomingmotherblog.wordpress.com.

Made in the USA
San Bernardino, CA
27 December 2017